Issues in Finance and Monetary Policy

Issues in Finance and Monetary Policy

Edited by

John McCombie

and

Carlos Rodríguez González

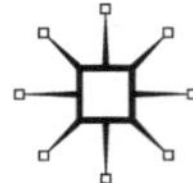

First published 2007 by
PALGRAVE MACMILLAN
Houndmills, Basingstoke, Hampshire RG21 6XS and
175 Fifth Avenue, New York, N.Y. 10010
Companies and representatives throughout the world

PALGRAVE MACMILLAN is the global academic imprint of the Palgrave
Macmillan division of St. Martin's Press, LLC and of Palgrave Macmillan Ltd.
Macmillan® is a registered trademark in the United States, United Kingdom
and other countries. Palgrave is a registered trademark in the European
Union and other countries.

ISBN-13: 978–0–230–00798–7
ISBN-10: 0–230–00798–8

This book is printed on paper suitable for recycling and made from fully
managed and sustained forest sources.

A catalogue record for this book is available from the British Library.

Library of Congress Cataloging-in-Publication Data
International Conference on the "Development in Economic Theory and
    Policy" (2nd: 2005: Bilbao, Spain)
    Issues in finance and monetary policy / John McCombie and Carlos
Rodríguez González.
        p. cm.
    Selected papers from the Second International Conference on the
"Development in Economic Theory and Policy", held in Bilbao, July 7–8, 2005.
    Includes bibliographical references and index.
    ISBN–13: 978–0–230–00798–7 (cloth)
    ISBN–10: 0–230–00798–8 (cloth)
    1. Monetary policy—Congresses. 2. Inflation (Finance)—Congresses.
3. Finance—Congresses. I. McCombie, J. S. L. II. Rodríguez González, Carlos.
III. Title.
HG230.3.I5755 2005
339.5'3—dc22   2006051595

10   9   8   7   6   5   4   3   2   1
16   15   14   13   12   11   10   09   08   07
Printed and bound in Great Britain by
Antony Rowe Ltd, Chippenham and Eastbourne

Contents

List of Tables

List of Figures

Notes on the Contributors

Alvaro Angeriz is a Research Associate with the Centre for Economics and Public Policy, University of Cambridge. He received his PhD from the Universidad Autonoma de Barcelona, his MPhil from the Universidad Autonoma de Barcelona and his BA from the Universidad de la Republica Oriental del Uruguay. His research interests include Applied Econometrics with special focus on macroeconomic issues, such as monetary policy and regional growth, and stochastic and deterministic efficiency assessments, both applied to macroeconomic and to industrial data. Other research includes the determinants of poverty. He has published in such journals as the *Manchester School* and the *Journal of Post Keynesian Economics*, as well as contributing chapters to books.

Philip Arestis is University Director of Research, Cambridge Centre for Economics and Public Policy, Department of Land Economy, University of Cambridge, UK; Adjunct Professor of Economics, University of Utah, US; Senior Scholar, Levy Economics Institute, New York, US; Visiting Professor, University of Leeds, UK; and Visiting Professor, School of Oriental and African Studies (SOAS), University of London, UK. He was a member of the Economics and Econometrics Research Assessment Exercise panel in 1996 and in 2001, and Quality Assessor for the quality assessment exercise in Economics of the Scottish Higher Education Funding Council, the Welsh Funding Council and of the Higher Education Funding Council in England. He was a member of the Council of the Royal Economic Society (RES), and Secretary of the RES Standing Conference of Heads of Department in Economics (CHUDE). He is currently Vice-Chair of the Economic and Social Research Council-funded Macroeconomics, Money and Finance Research Group. He has published as sole author or editor, as well as co-author and co-editor, a number of books, contributed in the form of invited chapters to numerous books, produced research reports for research institutes, and has published widely in academic journals.

Santonu Basu is a Senior Lecturer in Banking and Finance at Queen Mary University London. His most recent works include issues related to financial globalization, the relationship between technological change and employment, and the relationship between economic growth and poverty. Currently he is working on globalization and poverty. He has published widely in these areas in scholarly journals, including *World Development, Australian Economic Papers, Eastern Economic Journal, Journal of Post Keynesian Economics, International Review of Applied Economics* and other journals and books. His works have also been published as a book entitled *Financial Liberalisation and Intervention: A New Analysis of Credit Rationing*, published by Edward Elgar. A prize was awarded to him for his PhD thesis. He has also taught in a number of universities in Australia and the UK.

Emmanuel Carré is a PhD student at the University Montesquieu-IFREDE in Bordeaux. He has Master's degrees in Economics and Sociology. His research interests are in the areas of New Keynesian macroeconomics, monetary policy strategy, inflation targeting regimes, central banking in general, and deliberation inside monetary policy committees. He is the author of papers on these subjects in edited books published in the USA and Mexico.

Georgios Chortareas is a Reader in International Finance at the University of Essex. He holds a BA (University of Thessaloniki), an MPhil in Monetary Economics (University of Glasgow), and a PhD in Economics (University of Connecticut, 1999). Before moving to the University of Essex he worked at the International Economic Analysis Division of the Bank of England. He has been a Post-Doctoral Fellow at Harvard University and had visiting positions at a number of academic and policy institutions including Columbia University, the Federal Reserve Bank of New York, and the European Central Bank. He is also a Visiting Professor at the University of Athens and a member of the Money, Macro, and Finance Research Group Committee.

Paul Davidson is the Editor of the *Journal of Post Keynesian Economics*. He is a Visiting Scholar at the New School for Social Work. He is an emeritus professor at the University of Tennessee where he occupied the Holly Chair of Excellence in Political Economy.

Jesús Gustavo Garza García is a PhD candidate at the Department of Accounting, Finance, and Management at the University of Essex. He has a BA in Economics from ITESM (Institutor Tecnologico y de Estudios Superiores de Monterrey, Mexico) and an MSc in Financial Economics from the University of Essex. He is a recipient of the British Chevening scholarship and the CONACYT (Mexican Government) scholarship. He has worked as an economic analyst at the Bank of Mexico. His main research focus is on banking efficiency and concentration in Latin American countries.

Claudia Girardone is Lecturer in Finance at the University of Essex where she teaches modern banking and introduction to finance. Her main research interests are in the areas of bank performance and efficiency analysis and her recent publications appear in *Journal of Banking and Finance, Journal of Business, Finance and Accounting* and *Applied Economics*. She is also co-author of the book *Introduction to Banking* (Pearson, FT, Prentice-Hall).

Edwin Le Heron is Maître de Conférences in Economics at the Institut d'Etudes Politiques in Bordeaux (France) and a member of the CRECQSS (Centre de Recherche et d'Etudes sur le Canada et le Québec en Sciences Sociales). He is also the president of the ADEK (Association for the Development of Keynesian Studies). ADEK was created by Alain Barrère for the organization of the Keynes Today conference in 1983 (*The Foundations of Keynesian Analysis, Money, Credit and Prices,* and *Keynesian Economic Policies,* edited by Alain Barrère, London: Macmillan, 2 vols, 1990). This association gathers French economists interested in post-Keynesian works. His research interests are monetary policy, post-Keynesian monetary theory, and the history of economic thought (especially French monetary thought in the eighteenth century). His latest published work on monetary policy is: 'The Monetary Policy of the ECB and the Fed: Credibility versus Confidence, a Comparative Approach', in *Financial Developments in National and International Markets,* edited by Philip Arestis, Jesus Ferreiro and Felipe Serrano, Palgrave Macmillan.

Amrit Judge is a Principal Lecturer in Financial Economics at the Middlesex University Business School. His research interests centre on risk management for non-financial corporations, risk management disclosure practices, hedging methods, the use of foreign currency debt, the interest rate exposure of corporate debt, the value effects of corporate hedging and the link between managerial compensation and risk incentives. He has published several articles in international academic journals on the subject of risk management. Currently he teaches risk management and international finance at the postgraduate level. He holds a BA in Business Studies, majoring in Economics and Finance, from Middlesex University, an MSc in Finance from Brunel University and a PhD in Finance from London Guildhall University.

John McCombie is the Director of the Centre for Economic and Public Policy at the University of Cambridge and is Fellow in Economics at

Downing College, Cambridge. He has previously held positions in Economics departments at the University of Hull and the University of Melbourne. His research interests include the study of national and regional growth disparities, economic growth and the balance-of-payments constraint, and criticisms of the aggregate production function and conventional measures of the rate of technical progress. He has published widely in these areas.

Kostas Mouratidis is a Lecturer in Finance at the University of Wales, School of Business and Economics, Swansea, and was research officer at the National Institute of Economic and Social Research (NIESR) in London. He has published in a number of academic journals, produced research reports for research institutes and contributed in the form of an invited chapter to Papers and Proceedings of the third *Eurostat Colloquium on Modern Tools for Business Cycle Analysis*, edited by G.L. Mazzi and G. Savio, European Commission, 2004.

Carlos Rodríguez González is a Lecturer in Economics at the University of the Basque Country and has a PhD from the same University. His research interests are in the area of foreign direct investment and monetary policy. He is the author of several papers and has recently published *The Pattern of Inward FDI Geographical Distribution: Can Developing Countries Base their Development on These Flows?* (Palgrave Macmillan, 2006).

List of Abbreviations

BLC	banking liquidity crisis
CAS	Credit Authorization Scheme
CPI	Consumer Price Index
DEA	Data Envelopment Analysis
ECB	European Central Bank
EIT	Eclectic Inflation Targeting
EMS	European Monetary System
EMU	Economic and Monetary Union
ES	Efficiency–Structure
ESS	scale efficiency
ESX	X-efficiency
FASB	Financial Accounting Standards Board
FDI	foreign direct investment
Fed	The Federal Reserve Bank
FFIT	fully-fledged inflation targeting
GDP	gross domestic product
GDS	gross domestic savings
GNP	gross national product
HPM	high-powered money
HYVP	High Yielding Variety Programme
IDB	Inter-American Development Bank
IDBI	Industrial Development Bank of India
IFC	Industrial Finance Corporation
IFS	International Financial Statistics
IMCU	International Money Clearing Unit
IT	inflation targeting
ITL	Inflation Targeting Lite
LDCs	less developed countries
LHITCs	Longest History Inflation Targeting Countries
MLC	market liquidity crisis
MLE	Maximum Likelihood Estimation
MRS-BVAR	Markov regime-switching-bivariate autoregressive
MS	market share
NBFI	non-banking financial intermediaries
OECD	Organisation for Economic Co-operation and Development
R&D	research and development

RBI	Reserve Bank of India
RMP	relative market power
ROA	return on assets
S&P	Standard & Poor's
SBI	State Bank of India
SC	solvency crisis
SCP	Structure–Conduct–Performance
SFAS	Statements of Financial Accounting Standards
VARs	Vector Autoregressive Models

1
Introduction

John McCombie and Carlos Rodríguez González

> It is not any scarcity of gold and silver, but the difficulty which such people find in borrowing, and which their creditors find in getting payment, that occasions the general complaint of scarcity of money.
>
> (A. Smith, 1776, Book IV.I)

> The theory which I desiderate would deal . . . with an economy in which money plays a part of its own and affects motives and decisions, and is, in short, one of the operative factors in the situation.
>
> (J.M. Keynes, 1973, pp. 408–9)

Money and financial issues have been studied for several centuries and have played a central role in general discussions about the functioning of economies. Nevertheless, there exists among economists, and will probably continue to exist, a fierce debate over monetary relationships. Monetarists placed money as a central determinant of economic activity, at least in the short run, while Keynesians had already rejected the classical neutrality axiom of money in both the short and long run. Today, new Keynesians reject the classical dichotomy that has been revived in, for example, real business cycle theory.

The chapters in this book, which contribute to this debate, are a selection of papers from the Second International Conference on 'Developments in Economic Theory and Policy' held in Bilbao in July 2005. It was organized under the auspices of the Department of Applied Economics V of the University of the Basque Country, Spain, and the Centre for Economic and Public Policy, Department of Land Economy, University of Cambridge, UK. As can be seen from Chapter 2, the contribution of Paul Davidson who presents the foundations of a critique of the neoclassical view, the starting point of the various authors is that money is not neutral. A sound monetary policy and well-functioning financial markets and institutions are crucial to promoting economic efficiency, fast growth, and high employment. Indeed, the chapters of this book try to assess to what extent current developments in monetary policy regimes and financial institutions serve the ultimate goal of producing rapid economic growth.

One of the major recent changes in the monetary policy of many countries has been the adoption of inflation targeting. In the context of financial deregulation and flexible exchange rates, anchors that were used for price stability in the past are now proving ineffective. Many central banks have therefore designed an alternative monetary policy strategy, in which the sole objective is to keep the medium-term rate of inflation low. This is what may be described as the current fashion, but there are also other developments occurring. The Federal Reserve Bank (Fed) is, at least for the moment, following its own path and, since 1999, the European Central Bank (ECB) has been, too. These three ways of conducting monetary policy certainly share many things in common, but there are still substantial differences. Given the different economic performances of economies under these different policies, it is worthwhile critically analysing them.

Chapters 3–6 raise some important questions about this topic. Is there any clear evidence that countries pursing inflation targeting have achieved better results for price stability than those that do not? Are the foundations of this strategy well grounded, or does the 'constrained discretion framework' reveal a weakness rather than a proper synthesis of the rules and discretion approaches? What are the effects of monetary policy if the commercial banks' behaviour is explicitly incorporated into the analysis of the transmission channels? Was the monetary policy of the countries under the European Monetary System (EMS), before adopting the so-called 'two pillar' monetary policy of the ECB, already more oriented towards price than output stability?

Countries have experienced a rapid change in the financial field. The financial liberalization promoted by international and national agencies has induced lenders and borrowers to take advantage of increased opportunities to make profits and access funds. At the end of the day, however, there is no certainty that liberalized financial markets have led to a more efficient allocation of capital and faster growth. Market failures in the form of recurrent currency crises, bankruptcy, tax havens, capital flights and exclusion of the poor from financial resources are all clear indicators of the serious risks that are ignored by the proponents of financial deregulation. These advocates disregard the problems posed by severe uncertainty, information asymmetries, transaction costs and market power, despite their high prevalence in financial markets. The authors of Chapters 7–9 are well aware of these and other market failures when they analyse the hedging and other strategies used by firms to reduce risk and the functioning of banks in emerging economies. Hedging decisions by non-financial firms may lead to the establishment of hedge funds such as Long-Term Capital Management, which collapsed in 1998 with severe consequences and necessitated a bailout coordinated by the Federal Reserve Bank. Financial liberalization in Latin America has made banks more profitable, but this may be due to their increased market power through increased concentration and to the widening of their margins. Government intervention may be required in the initial stages to finance development in poor countries, because private banks are unwilling to bear the risk, as exemplified by events in South Korea and India.

In Chapter 2, Paul Davidson starts with the argument that, under capitalism, governments have an important role to play in order to avoid major economic crises. Investors' desire for liquidity as the preferable way to carry savings into an uncertain (non-ergodic) future could create financial crisis and lead to permanent unemployment. Therefore, the visible hand of the government has to provide liquidity and ensure full-employment demand through, if necessary, budget deficit policies. Despite its ideological commitment to laissez-faire, this is, in fact, what the Federal Reserve did after the 9/11 attacks, when it pumped $45 billion into the banking system to match the liquidity demand generated in the wake of an event that heralded an increasingly uncertain future. In the same vein, an orderly solution to the huge US current account deficit will require the help of the G-7, or better still, the G-24, governments to create a new international financial architecture in line with the author's proposed International Money Clearing Unit plan.

Alvaro Angeriz and Philip Arestis, in Chapter 3, consider that, after more than a decade of inflation targeting (IT), there is enough experience and ample empirical evidence to assess its merits. In their review of the literature, mainly dated after 2000, they grouped studies according to their findings concerning inflation persistence, inflation expectations, sacrifice ratios, monetary policy performance, and several other economic variables, including exchange rates. The empirical evidence for the developed and emerging countries is clearly rather mixed. It is true that IT countries have achieved low inflation rates, but so to have non-IT central banks. In the light of the empirical studies that they review, therefore, the answer to the important question of whether or not a country needs to adopt IT to deflate and maintain price stability is clearly no.

In Chapter 4, Emmanuel Carré very convincingly reveals a major controversy underlying ideas regarding the functioning of the economy that is occurring behind an apparently semantic problem of 'transparency' versus 'openness' in monetary policy. There is an ongoing debate between two schools of thought. On the one hand, there are those who believe in the existence of the natural rate of unemployment economic model (i.e., the New Classical Macroeconomic model) from which they draw simple rules for the conduct of monetary policy. On the other hand, there are those who are well aware, at least in practice, that we are living in a non-ergodic world, where monetary policy evolves in a radically uncertain environment. They therefore argue that decisions at all times must, in fact, be discretional, and depend on the evaluation of the currently changing circumstances.

Meanwhile, the New Monetary Consensus of the new Keynesians (at the risk of over-simplifying) claims that the true position is somewhere in between. They advocate a synthetic strategy for the conduct of monetary policy (IT) for which such seemingly paradoxical terms as 'constrained discretionary framework' have been coined. In these three different contexts, the interplay between the central bank and agents in the implementation of monetary policy implies three different meanings of transparency. For the New Classical Macroeconomics, transparency means simply the publishing of a form of the k per cent monetary growth rule and the announcement of a mandate solely to combat inflation. Transparency is actually less important than reputation, which guarantees credibility and eliminates time-inconsistency problems.

Transparency in inflation targeting is more important, but in a somewhat perverse sense: it is a way of manipulating inflation expectations. In fact, it is the only way to reconcile the anchoring of long-run, low level, inflation expectations with short-run divergences between the current and target inflation rates, as a result of an unexpected economic shock (i.e., it is a policy of constrained discretion). This manipulation of transparency is due to central banks, despite what they say, trying to hide their concern about employment, which would be adversely affected in the short run if they were to neutralize an adverse shock. Carré advocates a Fed-style openness strategy instead of transparency: 'in radical uncertainty, with unpredictable shocks, it is not easy to believe in a "true" model of the economy – it is open to discussion'. The good performance of the Fed in the Greenspan era, with its dual mandate and no explicit inflation target, is seen as the result of extensive communication, shared comprehension of the uncertain model, and confidence (the so-called '3C strategy').

Edwin Le Heron, in Chapter 5, explains the theory behind the effects on the economy of a contractionary monetary policy, once the reaction of commercial banks to such a shock has worked its way through the transmission channels. This is the novelty of his contribution, because bank behaviour is neglected in the standard literature, where banks, despite their active role, are considered simply as the drivers behind the transmission mechanism. His approach is to generalize Keynes's liquidity preference theory to banks. He shows how, at the microlevel, the liquidity preference of banks limits their profitability and increases their solvency risk. At the macrolevel, their liquidity preference influences long-term interest rates through its effect on risk premiums.

Consequently, an increase in short-term interest rates, due to the central bank reducing asset values and increasing liability costs and lenders' risk, provokes an increase in the banks' liquidity preference. This, in turn, leads to a decrease in bank profitability. This may trigger a solvency crisis in the banking system, especially during a speculative bubble. Indeed this transmission channel may become a vicious circle because, when liquidity preference rises, banks try to sell equities, thus pushing asset prices down, further diminishing their solvency. Furthermore, an increase in the central bank interest rate causes the risk premium to rise and leads to higher than normal long-term interest rates.

Chapter 6, by Philip Arestis and Kostas Mouratidis, studies monetary policy credibility with respect to price stability in several countries of the EMS over the period 1979 to 1998. While their use of the Markov Regime-Switching model is similar to a number of other studies, these authors are the first to introduce two new information variables into the analysis: namely, the output gap and inflation variability. The results of this modelling show, for example, that the French monetary authorities were the ones who relied most heavily on bringing down inflation in order to improve France's price competitiveness. The model also indicates that, in the cases of Italy and the Netherlands, the priority was to keep inflation low and stable. In contrast to this, the results show that Finland and Spain, who were already inflation targeters, displayed no significant shifts in inflation. These authors end by noting that EMS countries, in general, adopted more inflation-sensitive monetary policies.

In Chapter 7, Amrit Judge presents a critique of the empirical literature focused on testing the various theories of hedging by non-financial firms. This chapter argues that the lack of a general consensus regarding these theories may be due to several issues. One critical question is how hedging is to be defined, because there are many different risk-reducing methods. A related problem is how hedging is measured. In many studies hedging is simply treated as a binary variable (i.e., either there is a hedge or there is not a hedge) because limited data make it impossible to take account of the determinants of the level of hedging. Another point is the confusion that may arise in studies that use only derivatives in their definition of hedging, because these can be used for speculation as well as hedging. Sample composition also poses problems. Studies tend to concentrate on samples of large firms because they are more inclined towards hedging. There is also a tendency to fail to exclude firms that have an incentive to reduce risks, but lack *ex ante* exposure. This last weakness is due to the fact that some empirical studies include firms hedging other exposures within the non-hedger sample, thus biasing the empirical results. In short, while the literature leaves many issues unresolved, Judge puts forward some clues for solutions, such as the adoption of a more inclusive definition of hedging, and the use of a sample of hedgers that hedge foreign currency only.

In Chapter 8, Georgios Chortareas, Jesus Gustavo Garza and Claudia Girardone assess the implications of financial liberalization on banking concentration and efficiency in Latin America since the late 1980s, in order to explain the higher profits obtained by the banking sector. They discuss the question of how financial liberalization may have propagated or mitigated collusion and/or efficiency using two well-known structural models. The implications of the two possible developments for consumers and the economy as a whole are clear. If the higher profitability is the result of greater concentration in the banking sector, then financial liberalization has benefited banks at the expense of the rest of the economy. The Structure–Conduct–Performance model provides many arguments in support of this, and the empirical evidence includes the wave of acquisitions by foreign banks of local banks. But profitability can also be due to enhanced efficiency from increased liberalization. This would be the 'natural' outcome expected by the mainstream consensus, resulting in a more efficient allocation of resources, lower interest rates, and so on. This is also what the Efficiency–Structure model suggests, in contrast to the previous model: indeed, the same foreign acquisitions argument may be used to explain how managerial innovations in foreign banks (most of them Spanish) have led to increased efficiency.

The volume concludes with Chapter 9, by Santonu Basu, who raises the question of whether or not, in poor countries, government intervention in the banking system will be required to facilitate economic growth and development. Due to the presence of low-profit opportunities and high risks for banks, the important business of financing the development process cannot be led by private banks guided by free market forces. This is exemplified by the case of South Korea and India, which nationalized their major commercial banks in the 1960s. South Korea soon became a success story, while India only started to improve in the 1980s.

This direct intervention was not without problems, however. Regulation concentrated on loan allocation, while overlooking the necessity of effective controls on loan repayments. The South Korean government failed to acknowledge the credit standard issue. This is where, in the face of adverse selection and moral hazard, the bank reduces the risk of default by asking for collateral. The Indian government overlooked the problem of credit risk-adjusted interest rates. These concepts were, at the time, largely unknown, or ignored, by the advocates of financial liberalization. In consequence, the banking systems in both countries were vulnerable to crises. It was no wonder that when the Korean economy slowed down in 1997, it led to a banking crisis while, in India, the whole banking system was put under pressure due to the non-repayment of a small fraction of failed loans. This situation was further magnified by the presence of weak bankruptcy laws. To sum up, Basu argues that government intervention is required, but its associated limitations need to be addressed.

As a final word, we would like to thank the University of the Basque Country, the Basque Government and the Bilbao Bizkaia Kutxa for providing financial support for the conference and to all the participants and contributors.

References

Keynes, J.M. (1973) *The Collected Writings of John Maynard Keynes, Volume XIV, The General Theory and After: Part II Defence and Development*, ed. D. Moggridge (London: Macmillan, Cambridge University Press).
Smith, A. (1776) *An Inquiry into the Nature and Causes of the Wealth of Nations*, ed. W.B. Todd (1967) (Oxford: Clarendon Press). References are to the reprint.

2
Strong Uncertainty and How to Cope with it to Improve Action and Capacity

Paul Davidson

Introduction

The entrepreneurial system that most people call capitalism, though imperfect, is the best system humans have yet devised for promoting economic growth, development and prosperity. In fact, classical economic theory in its nineteenth- and early twentieth-century version and its modern Walras-Arrow-Debreu interpretation that is the foundation of twenty-first century mainstream economic theory can 'demonstrate' that free market capitalism is the most efficient engine possible for propelling our society towards an economic Utopia here on earth. In such a system, a free market coordinates the decisions of self-interested agents without any need for government interference.

After the experience of the Great Depression and the Second World War, however, a myriad of institutional arrangements for regulating product, labour, exchange rate and financial markets were installed. Today's mainstream conventional wisdom tells us that these welfare state institutions are now barriers to economic progress. To improve economic action and growth capacity, we are told, all markets must be liberalized.

Logically consistent classical theory ideologues urge immediate dismantling of these regulatory institutions (the equivalent of the shock therapy recommendations for nations pursuing a transition to capitalism). The common sense of mainstream 'Keynesian' economists breaks into their classical logical consistency when they urge a longer time horizon for complete liberalization. For these economists the only question is: 'How long before complete liberalization?' All mainstream economists theorists agree that in the long run governments should adopt a laissez-faire stance that encourages globalized free trade and unfettered international financial capital mobility. Perhaps for political reasons, these advocates of unhampered capital mobility often remain silent regarding the question of whether governments should encourage free international labour mobility.

When asked what specific market needs most to be liberalized, especially in the more developed nations, the response is typically the domestic labour market. It is my understanding that economic advisers to German politicians believe that Germany's labour market is especially sclerotic. Consequently, they recommend removal of legislation that (1) protects labour unions, collective bargaining, and high minimum wages, (2) provides significant unemployment insurance, (3) restricts working hours per week, (4) encourages 'long' annual vacations for workers, (5) causes exorbitant firing costs, and (6) provides other social safety net protections. The removal of these institutional arrangements will reduce, if not eliminate, the reluctance of workers to accept the free market conditions that lead to classical theory's Utopia.

In our world of experience, the entrepreneurial system is not as perfect as the one classical theory describes primarily because the future cannot be as reliably predicted as classical theory postulates. In our world, where the economic future is uncertain, there are two 'outstanding faults of the economic society in which we live . . . its failure to provide full employment and its arbitrary and inequitable distribution of income and wealth' (Keynes, 1936, p. 372).

Keynes's *General Theory* focused on the unemployment fault as his analysis explained why labour and product market rigidities were not to be blamed for economic maladjustments. Supply-side constraints on prices, wages, exchange rates, and so on are neither necessary nor sufficient conditions to cause persistent unemployment, recessions, depressions and overall poor economic performance. Instead, these economic ills are inevitably tied to the question of liquidity.

Keynes limited his discussion of the inequality fault to a few side comments in the last chapter of *The General Theory*. At the end of this chapter I will spend a few moments providing potential recommendations regarding reducing existing inequalities, while explaining why classical theory assumes that whatever inequalities exist are an inevitable outcome of our progress towards economic Utopia.

What was revolutionary about Keynes's analysis?

On New Year's Day in 1935 Keynes wrote a letter to George Bernard Shaw stating:

> To understand my new state of mind, however, you have to know that I believe myself to be writing a book on economic theory which

will largely revolutionize not I suppose at once but in the course of the next ten years the way the world thinks about economic problems. When my new theory has been duly assimilated and mixed with politics and feelings and passions, I cannot predict what the final upshot will be in its effect on actions and affairs, but there will be a great change and in particular the Ricardian Foundations of Marxism will be knocked away.

I can't expect you or anyone else to believe this at the present stage, but for myself I don't merely hope what I say. In my own mind I am quite sure.

Classical theory attributed unemployment and recessions to built-in labour market institutional rigidities. Keynes (1936, p. 259) demonstrated that this classical argument that rigidities cause unemployment is an *ignoratio elenchi* (i.e., a fallacy in logic of offering a proof irrelevant to the proposition in question). Specifically, in chapter 19 of *The General Theory*, and even more directly in his published 1939 *Economic Journal* response to Dunlop and Tarshis, Keynes argued that unemployment equilibrium could still occur even if the world was one possessing flexible wages and prices. In other words, Keynes's general theory showed that wage and price rigidities are neither necessary or sufficient conditions for demonstrating the existence of involuntary unemployment equilibrium.

Keynes (1936, p. 3) called his analysis a general theory and stated that the axioms underlying

> classical theory are applicable to a special case and not to the general case . . . the characteristics of this special case . . . happen not to be those of the economic society in which we actually live, with the result that its teaching is misleading and disastrous if we attempt to apply it to the facts of experience.

In the preface to the German language edition of *The General Theory* (1936b, p. ix) Keynes noted: 'This is one of the reasons which justify my calling my theory a *general* [emphasis in the original] theory . . . it is based on *fewer restrictive assumptions* ["weniger enge Voraussetzunger stutz"] than the orthodox theory' second (emphasis added). Keynes here is claiming that what makes his analytical system more general than the classical (today's Walrasian–Arrow–Debreu general equilibrium) analysis is that Keynes's theory requires a smaller common axiomatic base (fewer restrictive axioms). In contrast, Debreu has argued that 'a good general theory does not search for the maximum generality but for the right generality'

(Weintraub, 2002, p. 113). Thus Debreu's general equilibrium theory is a special case that imposes additional restrictive axioms to Keynes's axiomatic foundation to get the 'right generality'.[1]

Keynes compared those economists whose theoretical logic was grounded on the classical special case additional restrictive axioms to Euclidean geometers living in a non-Euclidean world,

> who discovering that in experience straight lines apparently parallel often meet, rebuke the lines for not keeping straight – as the only remedy for the unfortunate collisions which are taking place. Yet, in truth, there is no remedy except to throw over the axiom of parallels and to work out a non-Euclidean geometry. Something similar is required today in economics.
>
> (Keynes, 1936, p. 16)

To throw over an axiom is to reject what the faithful believe are 'universal truths'. The Keynesian revolution in economic theory required economists to 'throw over' three restrictive classical axioms from its theoretical foundation.

Keynes's biographer, Lord Skidelsky (1992, p. 512), wrote 'that mainstream economists after the Second World War treated Keynes's theory as a "special case" of the classical theory, applicable to conditions where money wages and interest were "sticky". Thus his theory was robbed of its theoretical bite'.[2]

As explained below, post-war mainstream Keynesians believed the Walrasian classical theory to be the foundation of economic analysis. In the 1960s and early 1970s, classical monetarists led by Milton Friedman (and later by Robert Lucas) were able to emphasize the inconsistencies of the synthesis of mainstream Keynesian macroeconomic policies with its neoclassical (Walrasian) microtheory. As a result, by the 1970s, orthodox policy recommendations had regressed to reiterating the misleading and potentially disastrous prescriptions of classical theory.

Today, 70 years after Keynes wrote of his hopes that his revolutionary analysis would affect economic actions and affairs, we find a majority of economists and political leaders are prisoners of classical theory in their choice of economic policies. This classical foundation is especially obvious in the orthodox justification for outsourcing as merely an aspect of the Ricardian law of comparative advantage. However, in the United States the real income of those without a university degree has actually declined significantly in the last half-dozen years as a result of outsourcing to China and other Asian nations with their almost unlimited supply of unskilled, but easily trained, workers willing to work at a fraction of the costs of comparable labour in the United States. The affected US workers have not been re-employed to work in some other more productive activity where the US supposedly has a comparative advantage. Instead these workers are long-term unemployed, or have accepted part-time, low-wage service industry jobs that can not be outsourced, or have dropped out of the labour force entirely. These workers are unlikely to be re-employed until their wage approaches that paid to Chinese unskilled workers.

Classical theory versus Keynes

A sage once defined a 'classic' as a book that everyone cites but no one reads. In this sense, John Maynard Keynes's book *The General Theory of Employment, Interest and Money* (1936) is truly a classic for mainstream professional economists.

For most students who studied economics in a university in an OECD nation during the last half of the twentieth century, Paul A. Samuelson's neoclassical synthesis of Keynesianism epitomized Keynes's revolution-ary analysis. In a forthcoming paper (Davidson, 2006) I explain that, given the virulent anti-communist political atmosphere (McCarthyism) that existed in the United States in the late 1940s and early 1950s, eco-nomic textbooks that tried to provide a Keynesian *General Theory* analysis were seen as 'politically incorrect' and banished from university campuses. Samuelson, by using clever 'lawyer-like' writings (to use Samuelson's own phrase) in his textbook and by claiming classical microfounda-tions, avoided this textbook witch hunt. Consequently, Samuelson dominated the US economic textbook world with a politically correct classical foundation Keynesianism that is logically incompatible with Keynes's *General Theory*. The result was that Samuelson prevented Keynes's revolutionary theory from being adopted as mainstream macroeconomics.

In a telling interview with Colander and Landreth (1996, pp. 158–9), Samuelson admits that when he read *The General Theory* while a student at Harvard in the 1930s he found its analysis 'unpalatable' and not com-prehensible (Colander and Landreth, 1996, p. 159). Samuelson said:

> The way I finally convinced myself was to just stop worrying about it (about understanding Keynes's analysis). I asked myself: why do I refuse a paradigm that enables me to understand the Roosevelt upturn from 1933 till 1937? . . . I was content to assume that there was enough

rigidity in relative prices and wages to make the Keynesian alternative to Walras operative.

(Colander and Landreth, 1996, pp. 159–60)

In 1986, thirty years after reading *The General Theory*, Samuelson was still claiming that 'we (Keynesians) always assumed that the Keynesian underemployment equilibrium floated on a substructure of administered prices and imperfect competition' (Colander and Landreth, 1996, p. 160). When pushed by Colander and Landreth as to whether this requirement of rigidity was ever formalized in his work, Samuelson's response was 'There was no need to' (Colander and Landreth, 1996, p. 161).

It should not be surprising therefore that, in the academic literature of the 1970s, the Monetarists easily defeated Samuelson's neoclassical synthesis Keynesianism on the grounds of logical inconsistency between its classical microfoundations and its macroeconomic analysis and policy prescriptions. The effect was, in the mid-1970s, to shift the emphasis for developing domestic and international choices of policies from prescriptions founded on Keynes's *General Theory* to the age-old laissez-faire policies promoted by classical theory that had dominated nineteenth- and early twentieth-century thought. Consequently, socially acceptable policies to prevent unemployment, to promote economic development, and even the method to finance government social security systems have regressed, with the result that the 'golden age of economic development' experienced by both OECD nations and less developed countries (LDCs) during the more than quarter-century after the Second World War has disappeared,[3] despite the technological changes in the study of economics.

As a result of the Monetarist victory over Samuelson's neoclassical Keynesianism in the 1970s, economic advisers encouraged policy makers to dance to the Panglossian siren song that 'all is for the best in the best of all possible worlds provided we let well enough alone' and let liberalized markets work.

The classical axioms that Keynes threw out in his revolutionary economic theory equivalent to non-Euclidean geometry general analysis were (1) *the neutrality of money axiom*, (2) *the gross substitution axiom*, and (3) *the axiom of an ergodic economic world.*

In 1933 Keynes explicitly noted that in his analytic framework money matters in both the long and short run (i.e., *money is never neutral*: Keynes, 1933, pp. 408–9). Keynes developed his theory of liquidity preference late in his evolving analysis when he recognized that his theory of involuntary unemployment required specifying 'The Essential Properties of Interest and Money' (1936, ch. 17). These 'essential properties' clearly differentiated his theory from classical theory and ensured that money and all other liquid assets are never neutral. These essential properties (Keynes, 1936, pp. 230–1) are: (1) the elasticity of production associated with all liquid assets including money is zero or negligible, and (2) the elasticity of substitution between liquid assets (including money) and reproducible goods is zero or negligible. The gross substitution axiom is not universally applicable to all demand functions, and therefore, as Arrow and Hahn (1971, p. 361) have demonstrated, in the absence of ubiquitous gross substitution all existence proofs of general equilibrium are jeopardized.

A zero elasticity of production means that money does not grow on trees and consequently workers cannot be hired to harvest money trees when the demand for money (liquidity) increases. Or, as Keynes wrote: 'money . . . cannot be readily reproduced; labour cannot be turned on at will by entrepreneurs to produce money in increasing quantities as its price rises' (Keynes, 1936, p. 230). Thus, when income earners, instead of spending their entire income on the products of industry, save in the form of money and/or other nonproducible liquid assets, effective demand for goods declines.

The zero elasticity of substitution ensures that the portion of income that is not spend on by the products of industry (i.e., savings) will find, in Hahn's (1977, p. 31) terminology, 'resting places' in the demand for nonproducibles. Some 40 years after Keynes, Hahn rediscovered Keynes's point that a stable involuntary unemployment equilibrium could exist *even in a Walrasian system with flexible wages and prices* whenever there are 'resting places for savings in other than reproducible assets' (Hahn, 1977, p. 31).

Hahn rigorously demonstrated what was logically intuitive to Keynes. Hahn (1977, p. 37) showed that the view that with 'flexible money wages there would be no unemployment has no convincing argument to recommend it . . . Even in a pure tatonnement in traditional models convergence to (a general) equilibrium cannot be generally proved' if savings were held in the form of nonproducibles. Hahn (1977, p. 39) argued that 'any non-reproducible asset allows for a choice between employment inducing and non-employment inducing demand'. The existence of a demand for money and other liquid nonreproducible assets (which are *not* gross substitutes for the products of the capital goods producing industries) as a store of 'savings' means that all income earned by households engaging in the production of goods is not, in the short or long run, necessarily spent on the products of industry. Households who want to store that portion of their income that they do not consume (i.e., that they do not spend on the products of industry) in liquid assets are choosing, in Hahn's words 'a non-employment inducing demand' for their savings.

Just as in non-Euclidean geometry lines that are apparently parallel often crash into each other, in the Keynes–Post Keynesian non-Euclidean economic world, an increased demand for 'savings', even if it raises the relative price of nonproducibles, will not spill over into a demand for producible goods and hence when households save a portion of their income they have made a choice for 'non-employment inducing demand'.

Uncertainty and the ergodic axiom

To explain why utility-maximizing individuals would desire to store savings in the form of nonproducible durables requires the rejection of the classical ergodic axiom. Classical theory presumes that all income earners make optimum time preference decisions regarding allocating income between current and future consumption over their lifetimes. This requires each income earner to 'know' exactly what they will want to consume every day in the future and by their resulting market actions today inform entrepreneurs about their future consumption demands.

If one conceives of the economy as a stochastic process, then future outcomes are determined via a probability distribution. Logically speaking, for income earners to make statistically reliable forecasts about future parameters that will affect their future consumption activities, each decision maker should obtain and analyse sample data from the future. Since that is impossible, the assumption that the economy is an ergodic stochastic process permits the analyst to assert that samples drawn from past and current data are equivalent to drawing a sample from the future. In other words, the ergodic axiom implies that the outcome at any future date is the statistical shadow of existing market data.

In contrast, Keynes viewed the economic system as moving through calendar time from an irrevocable past to an uncertain, not statistically predictable, future where income spending decisions are made by people who know that they do not know what the future will bring. This required Keynes to reject the classical ergodic axiom for the latter specifies that all future events are actuarially certain: that is, the future can be accurately known or reliably forecast from the analysis of existing market data. (The ordering axiom plays the same role in classical deterministic economic models.)

Keynes never used the term 'ergodic' since ergodic theory was first developed in 1935 by the Moscow School of Probability and it did not become well known in the West until after the Second World War, and by then Keynes was dead. Nevertheless Keynes's main criticism of Tinbergen's econometric 'method' (Keynes, 1939, p. 308) was that the economic data 'is not homogeneous over a period of time'. This means that economic time series are non-stationary, and non-stationary is a sufficient (but not a necessary condition) for a non-ergodic process. Consequently Keynes, with his emphasis on uncertainty, had (in these comments on Tinbergen) specifically rejected what would later be called the ergodic axiom.

Nevertheless Samuelson (1970, pp. 11–12) has declared that the ergodic axiom must be invoked if economics is to be considered a science. Samuelson indicated that ergodic scientific models will settle 'down to a unique equilibrium position independently of initial conditions'. Consequently, Samuelson notes, invoking the ergodic axiom means that if, in order to reduce income inequalities, 'the state redivided income each morning, by night the rich would be sleeping in their comfortable beds and the poor under the bridges' (Samuelson, 1970, p. 12). If one uses theory based on the ergodic axiom, then Keynes's inequality fault is really not a defect in our economic system; it is a result of the entrepreneurial system's relentless efficient drive to Utopia. Given the ergodic axiom, the unequal distribution of income and wealth cannot be changed by an act of government, any more than the legislature can change the law of gravity.

In an ergodic system (or in a deterministic model based on the ordering axiom), today's income earners can reliably forecast when, and on what, every dollar of savings will be spent at each and every future possible date. Income earned today will be entirely spent either on produced goods for today's consumption or on buying investment goods that will be used to produce specific goods for the (known) future consumption spending pattern of today's savers. There can never be a lack of effective demand for things that industry can produce at full employment. The proportion of income that households save does not affect total (aggregate) demand for producibles; it only affects the composition of demand (and production) between consumption and investment goods. Thus, savings create jobs in the capital goods producing industries just as much as consumption spending creates jobs in the consumer goods producing industries. Invoking the ergodic axiom means that since more capital goods mean more productive capacity, savings are to be preferred over consumption.

When Nobel Prize laureate Samuelson claims that the ergodic assumption is necessary for economists to be hard-headed scientists, it is not surprising that Keynes's revolutionary analysis has been ignored by mainstream economic theory since the Second World War. If we could resurrect

Keynes, or at least his theory, the argument would be that, in an uncertain (non-ergodic) world, it is the desire of income earners to save in the form of nonproducible liquid assets that is the basis of the economic problems of the twenty-first century global economy. In such a world, encouraging the savings propensity will not be desirable if the economy is operating with unemployed workers.

In Keynes's theory, as opposed to the classical theory and the scientific approach of Professor Samuelson, people recognize the future is uncertain. Consequently, people decide how much of current income is to be spent on consumer goods and how much is *not to be spent on consumption goods but is instead saved by purchasing various liquid assets that can be used to transport this store of wealth to an indefinite future time period.*

Keynes devised a two-stage spending decision making process for those who save out of current income (*see* Figure 2.1 overleaf). At the first stage the income-earner decides how much of current income will be spent today on produced goods and how much of current income will *not* be spent on currently produced goods and services (i.e., how much of current income will be saved in the form of nonproducibles). Classical economists call this first-stage saving decision process the *time preference decision* since it supposedly reflects consumers' *preference* for putting off buying some pleasure-yielding consumer goods today to obtain pleasure-yielding producibles at some specific *time* in the future. In the real world, however,

> an act of individual savings – so to speak – is a decision not to have dinner to-day. But it does not necessitate a decision to have a dinner or buy a pair of boots a week hence or a year hence or to consume any specified thing at any specified date. Thus it depresses the business of preparing to-day's dinner without stimulating the business of making ready for some future act of consumption . . . it is a net diminution of such demand.
>
> (Keynes, 1936, p. 210)

Keynes called this first stage decision of the allocation of income between spending and saving the *propensity to consume*. In contrast to the time preference of classical theory, Keynes's propensity to consume implied that income earners are willing to commit some portion of current income to purchase consumer goods today but are uncertain about the future and therefore do not want to commit all their income (claims) on real resource use. Keynes's propensity to consume and save indicates that 'He who hesitates (to consume) is saved to make a decision (regarding consumption) another day!'

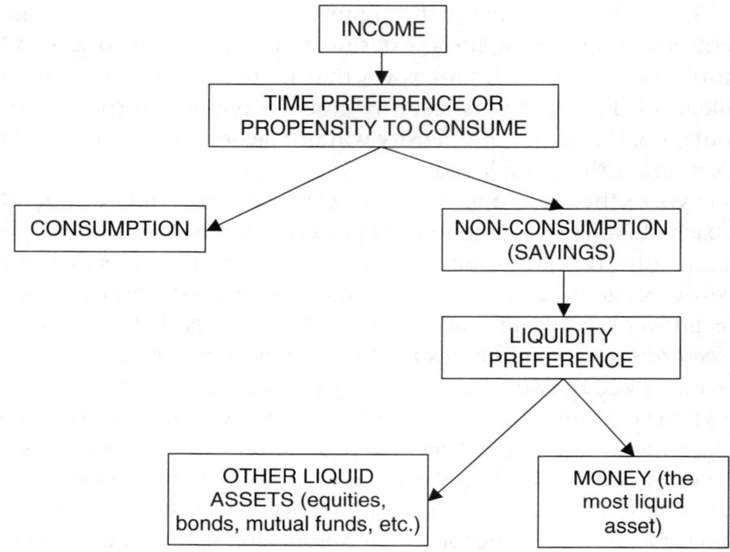

Figure 2.1   Keynesian two-stage spending decision

Savers are required to make a second-stage decision, the *liquidity preference decision,* where each saver must choose among the many liquid assets available which ones to utilize for moving current savings into the indefinite future.[4] To carry forward their saved (unused) spending power of current income, savers have to decide on one or more vehicles (time machines) for transporting this unspent income into the future. If the future is uncertain and cannot be reliably predicted, then savers can never be sure as to the future specific date(s) when they will want to utilize the spending power of these savings. Consequently savers will look for durable time machines that possess a minimum of carrying costs (e.g., maintenance, repair, insurance, and warehousing costs) for the indefinite period that this saving will be held and not spent.

In a monetary economy where 'Money buys goods and goods buy money; but goods do not buy goods' (Clower, 1969, pp. 208–9), if at some unspecified future date a saver decides to use his or her savings to purchase some products of industry, and if the saver has not stored his or her saving in the form of money, he or she will have to sell his or her time machine for money in order to finance this future purchase. Thus, savers will look for time machines that not only have negligible carrying costs, but also incur a minimum of transactions costs of buying and reselling liquid assets that can be easily offset by income flows received while holding the assets plus any capital gains (or net of capital losses). In sum, savers will use as time machines for their savings only things that have small or negligible carrying and transactions costs.

Real assets, such as plant and equipment, consumer durables, and so on, have relatively high carrying and transaction costs, especially the transaction costs of reselling these durables, if these second-hand durables can be sold at all. Real producible durable goods, therefore, are not very useful time machines for savings, especially in a monetary economy with a developed financial system where savers have a plethora of liquid assets to choose from. Liquid assets are preferable time machines for carrying savings into the future in any economy as long as people have trust in their government's monetary system.

A permanent role for government

Since it is the desire for liquidity that can create the major faults of an entrepreneurial system, the permanent role for government is (1) to provide whatever liquidity is necessary to maintain orderly financial markets, and (2) to ensure that the effective demand necessary for full employment is never lacking.

Keynes suggested (1930, p. 220) that bank 'credit is the pavement along which production travels, and the bankers if they knew their duty, would provide the transport facilities to just the extent that is required in order that the productive powers of the community can be employed at their full capacity'.

This 'paving stone' aspect requires government to install a well-understood institutional arrangement which guarantees that financial markets will always operate in a well-organized and orderly fashion that encourages employment hiring and economic growth. As long as individuals abide by the civil law of contracts, governments have the power to maintain orderly domestic financial markets even when an unexpected event creates a tremendous fear of the uncertain future in the minds of the public.

For example, the events in New York on 11 September 2001 created great uncertainty about the future of financial markets in the United States. When the symbols of the great New York financial markets, the World Trade Towers, collapsed, there was the potential for a massive fast exit of US residents and foreigners from US bond and stock markets. Despite its ideological bias for the liberalized laissez faire efficient financial markets of classical theory, the pragmatic side of the Federal Reserve management flooded the financial system with liquidity immediately after the 9/11 terrorist attacks. In the two days following the attack, the Federal Reserve pumped $45 billion into the banking system. Simultaneously, according to the *Wall Street Journal* (18 October 2001, p. 1):

> to ease cash concerns among primary dealers in bonds – which include investment banks that aren't able to borrow money directly from the Fed – the Fed on Thursday [13 September 2001] snapped up all the government securities offered by dealers, $70.2 billion worth. On Friday it poured even more into the system, buying a record $81.25 billion of government securities.

The *Wall Street Journal* also reported that just before the stock market opened the following Monday for the first time since the terrorist attack, investment banker Goldman Sachs, loaded with liquidity due to Fed activities, phoned the chief investment officer of a large mutual fund group to tell him that Goldman was willing to buy any stocks the mutual fund managers wanted to sell.

The post-9/11 activities of the Federal Reserve, flooding the banking and financial system with liquidity, vividly demonstrate that the Monetary Authority can ensure stable, orderly financial markets whenever the public's fast exit propensity threatens financial crisis. Does anyone seriously believe that laissez-faire financial markets that rely on private sector market makers to maintain orderliness could have achieve the results that the Fed did on the days following 9/11?

After the East Asian currency crisis and the Russian bond default, President Clinton called for a 'new financial architecture' to avoid future international financial panics. Classical theorists' response was that all that is required is a faster liberalization of exchange rate markets until exchange rates float freely without any government or central bank interference in the exchange rate market. To permit exchange rates to become objects of speculation without any government institution to promote orderliness and organization is to flirt with potential disaster.

Currently the globalized economic community faces a growing dilemma in the currency markets that may have even more serious repercussions than the terrorist strike on 9/11. Given the huge and growing US current account deficits, a decline in the market value of the dollar sufficient to make a significant reduction (even if it does not eliminate) the US trade deficit can be a weapon of mass destruction. Can we muddle through on the hope that, despite the uncertainty about the future, speculators in our liberalized international financial markets 'know' what is good for the global economy, as the classical theory implies? Or should we wake up our policy makers and insist that they develop contingency plans for a new financial architecture based on Keynes's general theory principles as an absolute necessity to avoid this potentially devastating bursting of the dollar standard?

Orthodox economists are almost unanimous in preaching the virtues of floating, and its logical inevitability; yet many, perhaps most, countries remain attached to some form of fixing. Is this a case of economists being out of touch with reality? Or is it that reality is out of touch with economists?

The post-Bretton Woods world has never been one of pure, generalized floating. There is a kaleidoscope of currency arrangements ranging from 'hard' fixers to 'pure' floaters, and almost anything in between. Conventional wisdom claims floaters are gaining over the currency fixers and currency rate managers and that soft pegs are unsustainable. Are we moving towards a bipolar world where most currencies float freely and a minority, such as the Euroland nations, adopt hard pegs (cf. Fischer, 2001)?

Conventional wisdom assumes that the motives of the 'fixers' always has been predominantly economic. For decades after the Second World War, however, fixers were motivated in large part by geopolitical, rather than purely economic, reasons. The Western European countries accepted the dollar standard in return for military protection against communism. Today, willingness of the Euro countries to float against the dollar can be viewed as an assertion of political independence.[5]

Nevertheless, the growing financial maturity and the reduction of trade barriers in Euroland did *not* lead the European countries to float against each other; instead, it led them towards the most extreme version of hard fixing. The Euro nations have recognized that fixed, but not necessarily undervalued, rates should be preferred both for macroeconomic stability and to facilitate inter-regional trade expansion. If this is true for Euroland, is it not true for the globalized economy of the twenty-first century? But politics make it almost certain that a supranational global central bank is not possible. Elsewhere I (Davidson, 2002) have suggested an alternative arrangement that promotes a stabilizing new international financial architecture that can ensure full employment without workers in the US or Euroland being required to accept wages approaching those such as in China or India.

It should be clear that the most vocal advocates of floating are predominantly Americans, operating under the ideological spell originally cast by

Milton Friedman's classical theory Monetarist approach that is founded on the long-run neutral money axiom[6] where only relative prices are important in determining the composition of output of a fully employed economy. But, as Frank Hahn (1973, p. 14) noted, 'practical men and ill-trained theorists everywhere in the world do not understand what they are claiming . . . when they claim a beneficent and coherent role for the invisible hand' of a market with freely flexible prices and exchange rates.

The desire of nations such as China, India, Japan and other Asian rim countries to maintain a competitive fixity of exchange rates against the dollar reflects the desire of these nations to pursue export-led growth, with the US economy the ultimate primary marketing target for these Asian nations' export industries. Of course this Asian decision to pursue export-led growth permits the consumers in the US to live well beyond their means. At the same time it means that these export oriented nations are pursuing policies that encourage significant savings in their rapidly growing international accounts.

Taking advantage of the world's appetite for dollars, the US has accepted the view that other nations should bear the onus for American's exuberant consumption spending patterns. These other nations have a choice on how they accept this responsibility. They can either (1) revalue their currencies, but to do so would mean they would have to accept lower rates of real growth, or (2) they can accept dollars almost without limit to maintain their real economic growth and movement to prosperity. Given these options, it is not difficult to understand why the imbalance between the Asian creditors and the world's largest international debtor tends to persist despite a declining dollar. Asiatic nations recognize that their rapid export-led economic growth policies success relies on encouraging the United States to 'overspend' on its international account. The Euro nations, on the other hand, perhaps in their desire to demonstrate their geopolitical independence from the US, apparently prefer to impose overall lower real economic growth on their residents.

What generalization regarding economic growth policies can we draw from this current world situation? In essence there exist today two roads to real economic growth. Most of the world relies on export-led growth for achieving significant rates of real economic growth.[7] On the other hand, the road that the US travels (and Euroland apparently desires to follow) requires significant labour productivity growth to generate real output growth. Under the Bush Administration, despite a slight recession, there has been a respectable rate of economic growth, while total employment is still less than the employment levels in January 2001 when President Bush took office. Higher real GDP with fewer workers signifies a strong rate of productivity growth associated with the real economic growth experienced by the US in the twenty-first century.

To make sure that there is never a persistent lack of effective demand, the government must develop institutional arrangements that encourage some decision makers to spend in excess of their current income so that aggregate spending on the products of industry will offset any excess savings propensity at full employment. Years ago, when Hyman Minsky heard me express this idea, he used to say that Davidson never saw a deficit he did not love.

The second important permanent role for governments in our entrepreneurial system is to 'love deficits' which ensure that if income recipients tend to save more out of income, then others are encouraged to increase spending in excess of their income.

In the analysis of a less than fully employed, closed economy – or an open economy where the nation does not have to worry about current account deficits – this love of deficits means a cheap money policy that lowers interest rates until, if possible, the private sector deficit spends itself to full employment. If this cheap money policy does not induce sufficient aggregate effective demand then the federal government should either directly, or with the cooperation of the private sector, deficit spend sufficiently on capital account to provide additional productive capacity and stimulate growth at full employment. Unfortunately, given free trade and the current international payments system, most governments find that any deficit stimulating domestic policy induces additional spending on imports that ultimately results in a current account deficit problem.

At the next Bretton Woods conference, ideally nations will agree on a new financial architecture such as my International Money Clearing Unit (IMCU: Davidson, 2002) plan. Under my IMCU proposal, nations that have persistent and significant unemployed resources can promote domestic spending growth without fearing they will be burdened with unmanageable current account deficits. Each nation can operate as if it was a closed economy (while reaping whatever benefits of trade that exists) where the size of the government deficits (or total government debt) relative to its gross national income is only an accounting problem, and should not act as a barrier towards fully and profitably employing its labour force.

The inequality fault

Finally we should say a word about reducing, if not eliminating, the second major fault of entrepreneurial economies: the arbitrary and inequitable distribution of income and wealth. Since many of the world's poor are unemployed or underemployed, actively pursuing the paving stone and deficit loving (in tandem with a new financial architecture) will propel the world closer to a global full employment position. Full employment will increase significantly the income of the previously unemployed and underemployed, thereby contributing substantially to reducing income inequalities. Moreover a cheap money policy should provide constraints on the income of wealthy rentiers. As we approach full employment, however, we may experience aggressive rent seeking activities on the part of sellers of goods and labour services, leading to a phenomenon that in the mid-twentieth century was labelled wage–price inflation. To avoid inflation at less than full employment because of these rent seeking actions, nations should adopt a socially acceptable form of income policy such as Sidney Weintraub's Tax-based Incomes Policy (TIP).

Finally, even if we approach full employment and avoid inflation via an incomes policy, the resulting distribution of income and wealth may still exhibit levels of inequality that the majority of the citizens of a nation may find socially undesirable. At that point fiscal policy via more progressive income and estate tax rates should be considered for possible reduction in the existing inequalities of income and wealth. The additional revenues obtained from this increase in rate progressivity can be used, for example, to provide free public education up to and through university level for all those having sufficient intelligence to qualify. Provision of such educational opportunities can further enhance the income earning power of the children of lower income classes who are at a disadvantage *vis-à-vis* the children of higher income groups in obtaining a good education.

Conclusion

In the brief time allocated to me, I have not presented a comprehensive programme for solving all the possible economic problems facing a twenty-first century global entrepreneurial economic system. I hope, however, I have provided some enlightenment on how we can mitigate the two major faults of our economic system and thereby transform it into something that more closely approaches the results that the special case classical theory presumes already exists. I look forward to other presenters at this conference addressing these issues.

Notes

1 The onus is therefore on those who add the restrictive axioms to the general theory to justify these additional axioms. Those theorists who invoke only the

general theory axiomatic base are not required, in logic, to prove a general negative, (i.e., they are not required to prove the additional restrictive axioms are unnecessary).

2 Mainstream economists called this sticky interest rate argument the 'liquidity trap' where at some low, but positive, rate of interest the demand to hold money for speculative reasons was assumed to be perfectly elastic (i.e., horizontal). After the Second World War, econometric investigations could find no empirical evidence of a liquidity trap. Had mainstream economists read *The General Theory*, however, they would have known that on p. 202 Keynes specifies the speculative demand for money as a rectangular hyperbola: a mathematical function that never has a perfectly elastic segment. Moreover eyeball empiricism led Keynes (1936, p. 207) to indicate that he knew of no historical example where the liquidity preference function became 'virtually absolute' (i.e., perfectly elastic). In sum, from both an empirical and theoretical view, Keynes denied the existence of a liquidity trap.

3 For almost 25 years after the Second World War, governments actively pursued the types of economic policies that Keynes had advocated in the 1930s and 1940s. The result was that per capita economic growth in the capitalist world proceeded at a rate that had never been reached in the past and has not been matched since. The *average* annual per capita economic growth rate of OECD nations from 1950 to 1973 was almost precisely double the previous *peak* growth rate of the Industrial Revolution period. Productivity growth in OECD countries was more than triple (3.75 times) that of the Industrial Revolution era.

The resulting prosperity of the industrialized world was transmitted to the less developed nations through world trade, aid and direct foreign investment. From 1950 to 1973, average per capita economic growth for all LDCs was 3.3 per cent, almost triple the average growth rate experienced by the industrializing nations during the Industrial Revolution. Aggregate economic growth of the LDCs increased at almost the same rate as that of the developed nations, 5.5 per cent and 5.9 per cent respectively. The higher population growth of the LDCs caused the lower per capita income growth. (See Davidson, 2002, pp. 1–3.)

4 In essence, liquid assets are efficient *time machines* that savers use to store and transport savings to the future. Unlike savers in the classical system, real world savers do not know exactly what they will buy, and what contractual obligations they will incur at any specific future date. As long as in the world of experience money is that thing that discharges all contractual obligations and money contracts are used to organize production and exchange activities, then the possession of money (and liquid assets that have small carrying costs and can be easily resold for money) means that savers possess the ability (1) to demand products whenever they desire in the uncertain future and/or (2) to meet a future contractual commitment that they have not foreseen. Liquid assets are a saver's security blanket, offering protection against the possibility of hard times in the future. As Nobel Price winning economist, Sir John Hicks (1977, p. vii) stated, income recipients know that they 'do not know just what will happen in the future'.

Without sufficient liquidity, today's income earners fear they may face insolvency, or even bankruptcy, at some point in the future. In contradiction to classical theory which claims people maximize their happiness when spending everything they earn, in Dickens's *David Copperfield*, Mr Micawber, recognizing that happiness involves not spending all one's income, said 'Annual income twenty pounds, annual expenditure, nineteen nineteen six, result happiness. Annual income twenty pounds, annual expenditure twenty pounds ought and six, result misery.'

    Mr Micawber's misery result could only come in a world where future expenditures and income were not known with certainty. In a classical world, Mr Micawber's dictum would be declared 'irrational' behaviour.

5 If the Euro was pegged to the dollar, would European support for President Bush's intervention in Iraq be different?

6 An axiom is a doctrine that is accepted as a 'universal truth' for which no proof is required.

7 I have explained why export led growth is such an attractive option in Davidson (1996).

References

Arrow, K. J. and Hahn, F. H. (1971) *General Competitive Analysis* (San Francisco: Holden-Day).

Clower, R. W. (1970) 'Foundations of Monetary Theory', in R. W. Clower (ed.), *Monetary Theory* (Baltimore, MD: Penguin).

Colander, D. C. and Landreth, H. (1996) *The Coming of Keynesianism to America* (Cheltenham: Edward Elgar).

Davidson, P. (1996) 'The General Theory in An Open Economy Context', in *A Second Edition of the General Theory*, Vol. 2, edited by G. C. Harcourt and P. Riach (London: Routledge); reprinted in *Uncertainty, International Money, Employment and Theory* (Vol. 3 of the Collected Writings of Paul Davidson) edited by Louise Davidson (London: Macmillan, and New York: St Martin's Press).

Davidson, P. (2002) *Financial Markets, Money and The Real World* (Cheltenham: Edward Elgar).

Davidson, P. (2006). *Samuelson and the Keynes/Post Keynesian Revolution: The Evidence Showing Who Killed Cock Robin* (forthcoming).

Fischer, Stanley (2001) 'Exchange Rate Regimes: Is the Bipolar View Correct?', *Journal of Economic Perspectives*, 15, 3–24.

Hahn, F. H. (1973) *On the Nature of Equilibrium in Economics* (Cambridge: Cambridge University Press).

Hahn, F. H. (1997) 'Keynesian Economics and General Equilibrium Theory: Reflections on Current Debates', in *The Microeconomic Foundations of Macroeconomics*, edited by G. C. Harcourt (London: Macmillan).

Hicks, J. R. (1977) *Economic Perspectives* (Oxford: Oxford University Press).

Keynes, J. M. (1930) *A Treatise on Money*, Vol. 2 (London: Macmillan).

Keynes, J. M. (1933) 'A Monetary Theory of Production', in *Festschrift für Arthur Spietoff*, reprinted in *The Collected Writings of John Maynard Keynes*, Vol. 13, edited by D. Moggridge (1973) (London: Macmillan). All references are to the reprint.

Keynes, J. M. (1936) *The General Theory of Employment, Interest and Money* (New York: Harcourt, Brace).

Keynes, J. M. (1939) 'Professor Tinbergen's Method', *The Economic Journal*, September, reprinted in *The Collected Works of John Maynard Keynes*, Vol. 14, edited by D. Moggridge (1973) (London: Macmillan). All references are to the reprint.

Samuelson, P. A. (1970) 'Classical and Neoclassical Theory' in R. W. Clower (ed.), *Monetary Theory* (Baltimore, MD: Penguin).

Skidelsky, R. (1992) *John Maynard Keynes: The Economist as Saviour, 1920–1937* (London: Macmillan).

Weintraub, E. R. (2002) *How Economics Became a Mathematical Science* (Durham, NC: Duke University Press).

3
Inflation Targeting: Assessing the Evidence

Alvaro Angeriz and Philip Arestis

Introduction

Inflation targeting (IT) as a policy framework, designed to tame inflation, has been with us since the early 1990s. Recent work makes the point that a significant number of countries adopted this strategy, and the number is growing. For example, Sterne (2002) suggests that 54 countries pursued one form or another of IT by 1998, compared with only six in 1990. A more recent study (IMF, 2005) suggests that 21 countries (8 developed and 13 emerging) are now clear inflation targeters, pursuing a fully-fledged IT strategy (FFIT). Indeed, a number of other countries are seriously considering the adoption of this strategy. Many studies have attempted to examine empirically the degree and extent of the impact of IT on inflation in various countries. We review this literature in what follows and conclude that the available empirical evidence produces mixed results.

In pursuing an IT strategy, countries commit themselves to price stability as the main objective of monetary policy, along with stipulating that medium- to long-term inflation is the nominal anchor where an inflation target is set. There are, of course, varying degrees of commitment to IT amongst countries. In more general terms, one may distinguish between three types of inflation targeting: the FFIT, as suggested above, the 'Inflation Targeting Lite' (ITL) type, and the 'Eclectic Inflation Targeting' (EIT) type.[1] The main distinguishing feature is the degree of clarity and institutional commitment to price stability.[2] Along with this commitment, an explicit inflation target (either point- or range-inflation target) is set; absence of other nominal anchors, policy instrument independence and absence of fiscal dominance, transparency, accountability and credibility of the commitment to IT by the central bank are further requirements (Mishkin and Schmidt-Hebbel, 2001; Carare and Stone, 2003; Stone, 2003; Kuttner, 2005: see also Porter and Yao, 2005). FFIT countries enjoy a medium to high degree of credibility and clarity in pursuing IT, along with a transparent framework that adheres to accountability of the central bank to the set target, and also adhering to the rest of the distinguishing features to which we have just referred. These countries cannot achieve and maintain low inflation without a clear commitment to IT, so that they are forced to sacrifice output stabilization to various degrees. ITL countries enjoy a relatively low credibility. This is a regime where central banks 'announce a broad inflation objective but owing to their relative low credibility they are not able to maintain inflation as the foremost policy objective' (Stone, 2003, p. 8). This is due essentially to their vulnerability to large economic shocks, and to their weak institutional framework and financial instability. EIT countries have a very high degree of credibility, which allows them to achieve and maintain low and stable inflation without full adherence to the rules of IT. These ingredients, combined with their financial stability, enable these countries to pursue the output stabilization objective along with price stability.

In this chapter we focus on those countries that pursue a FFIT strategy, but we refer to the other two categories as necessary in what follows. The FFIT strategy dictates that countries commit themselves to achieving a targeted inflation rate and announce a relevant framework to achieve the set target. This approach is based on the belief that inflation is negatively related to economic growth in the long run, and also that high inflation is associated with high inflation variability, which is harmful to the economy.[3] If authorities are allowed discretion in monetary policy, they produce 'surprise' inflation especially so for electoral benefits, which leads to the (well-known by now) time-inconsistency problem. Such a problem, though, can be avoided if the government delegates to an independent central bank responsibility for monetary policy, based on a principal–agent relationship between the government and the central bank. The government sets the broader goal of monetary policy, while the central bank has complete discretion to use its instrument to achieve the target in view of its goal. The new monetary policy framework thereby gives 'constrained discretion' to the independent central bank to respond to new information, an important dimension of the new framework given information asymmetries and policy lags, while at the same time putting in place rules regarding the conduct of monetary policy.[4]

We proceed by reviewing the existing empirical evidence and by identifying a number of questions that emerge from this inevitably short review. We then examine these questions, and subsequently deal with problems that are more specific to the emerging countries. The final section summarizes and concludes.

Existing empirical evidence in developed countries

In the mid-1990s, Leiderman and Svensson (1995) reviewed the early experience with IT, with, however, rather limited number of observations. Later studies (Bernanke *et al.*, 1999; Clifton, Hyginus and Wong, 2001; Corbo, Landerretche and Schmidt-Hebbel, 2001, 2002; Arestis, Caporale and Cipollini, 2002; Johnson, 2002, 2003; Neumann and von Hagen, 2002; Scott and Stone, 2005) inevitably afforded longer periods and more data. Overall, this evidence supports the contention that IT matters. Those countries which adopted IT managed to reduce inflation to low levels and to curb inflation and interest rate volatility. Anecdotal evidence has also been propounded to make the IT case. Bernanke (2003) suggests that 'central banks that have switched to inflation targeting have generally been pleased with the results they have obtained. The strongest evidence on that score is that, thus far at least, none of the several dozen adopters of inflation targeting has abandoned this approach' (p. 1). However, and interestingly enough, the Reserve Bank of New Zealand, the first central bank to have introduced IT, was worried about the consequences of volatile nominal exchange rates and has set up a new Policy Targets Agreement (see, for example, Bollard, 2002).

This evidence, however, is marred by three weaknesses (see also Neumann and von Hagen, 2002): the first is that the empirical studies reviewed fail to produce *convincing* evidence that IT improves inflation performance and policy credibility, and lowers the sacrifice ratio. After all, the environment of the 1990s was in general terms a stable economic environment, 'a period friendly to price stability' (Neumann and von Hagen, 2002, p. 129), and inflation was on a downward trend in many countries, especially developed countries, prior to the introduction of IT; inflation persistence continued to drop after the introduction of IT (Sikklos, 1999), helped by the increase in the degree of risk aversion to inflation volatility in inflation-targeting countries in the 1990s. So IT may have had little impact over what any sensible strategy could have achieved; indeed, non-IT countries also went through the same experience as IT countries (Cecchetti and Ehrmann, 1999). Furthermore, Honda (2000) finds no evidence that IT had an effect on either inflation or any other variable in Canada, New Zealand and the UK. The second weakness is that, despite the problem of lack of convincing evidence, the proponents argue very strongly that non-adoption of IT puts at high risk the ability of a central bank to provide price stability (for example, Bernanke *et al.*, 1999, 'submit a plea' for the Fed to adopt it; also Alesina *et al.*, 2001, make the bold statement that the European Central Bank could improve its monetary policy by adopting IT; neither study provides any supporting evidence, though). And yet, both the Fed and the European Central Bank remain highly sceptical (Gramlich, 2000, and Duisenberg, 2003, do not actually regard IT as appropriate for the US and the Euro area, respectively). The third weakness refers to the argument that in a number of countries (for example, New Zealand, Canada and the UK) inflation had been 'tamed' well before introducing IT (Ball and Sheridan, 2003).

The studies that deal with the IT empirical evidence ask a number of questions with the most pertinent being the following: first, whether IT improves inflation performance and persistence; a second aspect treated in the literature deals with the improvements in policy credibility and the ability to predict inflation under IT; a third group of studies consider whether the sacrifice ratio (i.e., the cost of lowering inflation) does not increase significantly over the period of IT implementation; a fourth range of issues stems from considering whether Central Banks' behaviour changes under IT regimes. Finally, the effect of the introduction of the IT new regime on the behaviour of other relevant macroeconomic variables (for example, on the exchange rate) is assessed. We pursue this distinction in what follows below, and discuss the evidence under several headings.

Evidence of inflation targeting's impact on levels and persistence of inflation

Studying the first of these issues, Mishkin and Posen (1997) find that IT has proved an effective 'strategy' in the fight against inflation, especially in maintaining the benefits of registering low inflation levels. These authors base their argument on the premise that whenever IT was adopted, the countries experienced inflation rates and interest rates which were lower than the magnitudes simulated with unrestricted Vector Autoregressive models (VARs), while no major effect is apparent on the output. Besides, in the three IT countries considered, New Zealand, Canada and the UK, disinflation had largely been completed when IT was adopted, but inflation did not bounce back as expected with business cycle expansions as it had in the past. The evidence produced by the same study, however, does not enable the authors to support the contention that IT is superior to money supply targeting (for example, the Bundesbank monetary targeting between 1974 and 1998), or to the Fed's monetary policy in the

1980s and 1990s (which pursued neither a monetary nor an inflation targeting policy). Similar results are provided by Debelle (1997), who compares average inflation levels for seven IT countries with G-7 countries excluding non-inflation targeters. This contribution finds a much steeper decline in inflation in the case of the former group, concluding that IT is useful for countries facing lack of anti-inflation credibility. Neumann and von Hagen (2002) interpret similar results as a process of 'convergence', in that on average IT countries converge to the inflation rates of the non-IT countries in the targeting period. Corbo, Landerretche and Schmidt-Hebbel (2002) are able to conclude that IT countries have been able to meet their inflation targets and reduce inflation volatility. Chortareas, Stasavage and Sterne (2002) make the important point that central bank transparency is always important under both IT and non-IT regimes. Indeed, the more detailed the publication of central bank forecasts, the more it is associated with lower inflation rates.

Ball and Sheridan (2003) produce evidence that is not quite supportive of these conclusions. They study the effects of IT on macroeconomic performance in the case of 20 OECD countries, seven of which adopted IT in the 1990s. After controlling for the effect of regression to the mean, they conclude that they are unable to find any evidence that IT improves economic performance as measured by the behaviour of inflation, output and interest rates. As in the previous literature, they find that inflation fell in countries which adopted IT and became more stable; and output growth stabilized during the IT period as compared to the pre-IT period. But the apparent benefit disappears altogether after accounting for the effect of regression to the mean, referred to above. According to these authors, the apparent success of IT countries is merely due to having 'high initial inflation and large decreases, but the decrease for a given initial level looks similar for targeters and non-targeters' (Ball and Sheridan, 2003, p. 16). The same result prevails in the case of inflation variability and inflation persistence. As to whether IT affects output and interest rates, that study concludes in the same vein that IT does not affect output growth or output variability, and neither does it affect interest rates and their variability. In view of this evidence, the authors are suspicious of the results reported in the rest of the literature.[5] Furthermore, the evidence collected by Pétursson (2004) for the 'Longest History IT Countries' (LHITCs), which include New Zealand, Canada, UK, Sweden and Australia, reaches similar conclusions, producing only a marginally significant or non-significant effect of IT adoption on inflation level. According to the author this is due to the fact that IT countries had accomplished a substantial part of the disinflation process before adopting IT. This strategy would have been implemented, therefore, in order to lock-in previous successes in controlling inflation rather than to facilitate disinflation.

IT may also have an impact on the relationship between current inflation and its past history. Using univariate time series, Sikklos (1999) finds that the autoregressive coefficients show a noticeable drop in the strength of the relevant relationship for countries such as New Zealand, Canada, Finland, Sweden and Spain. Similarly, Levin, Natalucci and Piger (2004) find that actual inflation exhibits lower persistence in IT countries, and that the total variance of actual inflation is only slightly higher than the variance for shocks to the autoregressive model, whereas it is twice as big or higher in the case of non-IT countries, thereby exposing a substantial degree of propagation in the latter. They conclude that, as the variance of inflation is roughly the same in both groups, low levels of inflation persistence prevented higher levels of inflation volatility in IT countries. Uhlig (2004) takes issue with the estimation of the autoregressive model by Levin, Natalucci and Piger (2004). He maintains that on the assumption that inflation is the sum of a trend plus noise, expected inflation should be modelled against the trend instead of actual inflation, which is just a noisy signal of this regressor. The result would lead to a downward bias, positively correlated with IT shocks. As IT countries present higher volatility, the bias would be larger for this group of countries. Finally, he recommends the use of a fully specified model, including a signal-extraction-type equation.

Opposite views are expressed by Ball and Sheridan (2003) who, as mentioned earlier, report no significant improvements regarding inflation persistence after the adoption of IT. Further results on inflation persistence are reported in Vega and Winkelried (2005), who find that persistence depends on the measure selected to detrend the series of inflation. When the average across the period is selected they find that IT increases persistence (though the estimates are not significant). Allowing for a varying mean of inflation computed with the Hodrick–Prescott filter, IT does reduce the persistence parameter. It is important to note at this stage that detrending non-stationary series using a fixed average is not clear. The Hodrick–Prescott filter as a detrending algorithm is criticized in the literature for its ad hoc mechanism, which creates spurious cycles (Harvey and Jaeger, 1993).

Evidence of inflation targeting's impact on inflation expectations

The evidence on this front is as unclear as on the aspect as discussed above in the last section. Pétursson (2004) compares the average standard deviation of actual inflation in the five years previous to IT introduction with that corresponding to the following year of IT introduction, and suggests that adoption of IT contributes to reduced fluctuations in inflation. It is also pointed out in the same study that this is also the case for non-IT targeters, and it should not be surprising as both groups of countries present lower inflation levels. Similarly, Debelle (1997) reports a significant decline in the spread of long bond yields in IT countries relative to the US (used as a benchmark). The author considers this change as an indicator of enhanced credibility, but points out that other factors may have also contributed to this apparent success. The evidence of Ball and Sheridan (2003), however, contradicts these results. Controlling for regression to the mean, they find that IT raises the standard deviation of inflation in the countries included in their sample.

Johnson (2002) provides evidence that shows a significant impact on inflation expectations following the adoption of IT regimes in developed countries. Controlling for the business cycle and for the ongoing fall in inflation rates, the author reports a substantial reduction in the private expectations of inflation levels after IT announcements. In line with this evidence, Levin, Natalucci and Piger (2004) find that a one-year ahead expected inflation in response to actual inflation is lower in absolute values for IT countries than for non-IT countries, so that the persistence of inflation among IT countries is found to be lower than among non-IT countries. More mixed, though, is the evidence gathered in the exercise undertaken by Johnson (2003), where actual forecasts undertaken by professional forecasters are compared with predicted forecasts according to a model on how this expectations are built, for five consecutive 12-month periods after the announcement of inflation targets. Predicted forecasts of inflation rates are determined by a number of variables: past inflation rates, current unemployment rates (assumed to capture the state of the domestic business cycle), current world inflation, and current world unemployment that depicts the state of world business cycle. This study isolates the additional effect of the announcement of inflation targets on the level of expected inflation in the case of Australia, Canada, New Zealand, Sweden and the UK (where most of the responses on expected inflation come from professional forecasters). Immediate reduction in expected inflation is registered in New Zealand and Sweden with a smaller effect and slower impact in Australia and Canada; inflation targets do not appear to have a significant impact in the UK.

The possibility of IT anchoring significantly long-run expectations is studied in Levin, Natalucci and Piger (2004). Private sector inflation forecasts of horizons of 5–10 years are uncorrelated with previous records of inflation in IT countries, while this is not the case for the US, Japan and countries from the European Union (EU). Variability of expectations, however, does not decrease according to the evidence produced by Johnson (2002). This author controls for past level and variability of inflation, finding that neither the variability of expected inflation nor the average absolute forecast error present significant additional reductions, beyond the effect through the drop in inflation. By contrast, Corbo, Landerretche and Schmidt-Hebbel (2001) find that IT has reduced inflation uncertainty and inflation forecast errors towards the low level prevalent in non-targeting industrial countries.

A clear success for the IT strategy is recorded in Levin, Natalucci and Piger (2004) regarding the objective of de-linking expectations from realized inflation. Their reported estimations suggest that long-term expectations have been less responsive to recorded patterns of past inflation in IT countries than in non-IT countries. In the latter case, the relevant estimates are insignificant at a 6–10-year horizon. This finding implies that long-term expected inflation rates are related to shifting views of the long-term course of monetary policy (see also Ball and Sheridan, 2003).

Finally, Pétursson (2004) finds that interest rates have fallen significantly more than inflation for all countries and in particular for the LITHCs where controls for business cycles and the general global fall in world interest rates are included. This suggests that more weight is placed on long-run developments in expectations in IT countries, and that IT is interpreted with flexibility, considering also real and financial stability as determinants of interest rates. Increased credibility is not, however, immediate. The 'announcement' effect is shown not to be enough and only when real progress and the will by central banks to accept a temporary contraction became apparent was credibility achieved.

Evidence of inflation targeting's impact on disinflation costs

Bernanke *et al.* (1999) produce an assessment of the real output costs related to disinflation using sacrifice ratios and parameter instability tests. Following the method suggested by Ball (1994), they use a moving average process with nine lags to compute a trend in inflation and assume an ad hoc method to compute the GDP trend.[6] They then compute the sacrifice ratio and find that disinflation does not appear to be less costly than would have been the case had IT not been adopted. They also estimate Phillips curves for the periods before and after IT, rejecting the hypothesis of instability in the parameters estimated for these functions.

Corbo, Landerretche and Schmidt-Hebbel (2001) calculate the sacrifice ratios as the cumulative GDP variation of a trend utilizing the Hodrick–Prescott filter, divided by the corresponding inflation change in any period. Inflation targeting improvements are registered with important decreases in sacrifice ratios in Canada, Australia and the UK, but a relevant deterioration is also reported in New Zealand and Sweden. Corbo, Landerretche and Schmidt-Hebbel are able to conclude that sacrifice ratios have declined in emerging IT countries, with output volatility having fallen in both developed and emerging countries after they had adopted inflation targeting. The fall reached levels similar, if not lower, to those of non-IT developed countries.

Clifton, Hyginus and Wong (2001) estimate Phillips curves that incorporate inflation expectations. They conclude that IT enhanced the credibility of central banks which adopted IT. In IT countries and in the pre-IT periods, inflation expectations were backward looking, but after the IT adoption expectations became both backward- and forward-looking. They also find that the unemployment–inflation trade-off improved in OECD countries after IT. This is not clear, however in the period immediately after its implementation, but it improves over time as monetary policy gains in credibility. According to the authors, this pattern could explain Bernanke *et al.*'s (1999) earlier results.

Evidence of inflation targeting's impact on the conduct of monetary policy

The evidence as to whether IT changed the way in which monetary policy is conducted is analysed in a number of ways and the outcome is mixed. Mishkin (2002) finds that the results of estimating Taylor rules suggest that central banks focus more on the control of inflation after IT adoption, in their attempt to achieve price stability. This result is supported by the VAR evidence, which indicates that the relative importance of inflation shocks as a source of the variance of interest rates rises after IT adoption. Mishkin (2002), in discussing Neumann and von Hagen (2002), however, points out that since both short-term and long-term coefficients on inflation in the Taylor rules estimated relationships are less than 1, the inflation process is highly unstable. The implication here is that when inflation rises the central bank increases the rate of interest by a smaller amount than that required, thereby reducing the real rate of interest. This is of course an inflationary move by the central bank when the opposite is intended, and it is also true for the non-IT countries, such as the US. This is a result that is contrary to Taylor's (1993) findings. In the latter study, the relevant coefficient is greater than 1 in the case of the US in the post-1979 period, when allegedly monetary policy performance improved relative to the pre-1979 period, when more emphasis was placed on controlling inflation.

Mishkin (2002) identifies another interesting problem, which relates directly to the VAR approach. This problem originates from the fact that this approach does not contain any structural model of dynamics, so that the interpretation that inflation shocks contribute to the variance of interest rates does not necessarily imply increased focus on the control of inflation. This is so since if inflation shocks contribute to interest rate variability in an IT era, then inflation expectations would prevent inflation from deviating much from the inflation target; this would imply that the central bank is less focused on inflation, not more! Consequently, it would clearly suggest 'that the VAR evidence in the paper tells us little about the impact of inflation targeting on the conduct of monetary policy' (Mishkin, 2002, p. 150).

Cecchetti and Ehrmann (1999) and Corbo, Landerretche and Schmidt-Hebbel (2001) also assess changes in central bank aversion to inflation, delivering mixed results. Cecchetti and Ehrmann (1999) find that, where an increase in central bank aversion to inflation is apparent, both for IT countries and non-IT countries, it is within the group of IT countries that it has increased the most. Among these cases UK is an exception, not registering significant changes in these magnitudes. Corbo, Landerretche and Schmidt-Hebbel (2001) elaborate on these measures, discovering that inflation aversion increased among the non-industrialized countries which applied IT, but the same cannot be said for the industrialized ones.

A different approach to dealing with the question of whether improved results in inflation are due to the way monetary policy responds is to examine the official short-term interest rates. Following this line, Kahn and Parrish (1998) collect high and stable values for real official short-term interest rates, which are associated with tight monetary policies. In order to account for changes to policy due to incoming information, they estimate policy reaction functions, which regress the interest rate against several explanatory variables. Their results are mixed. On the one hand, they find structural breaks in New Zealand and the UK. The former presents a stronger reaction of official rates to lagged inflation and unemployment, and a weaker reaction to exchange rate. The UK registers a loss in significance for the exchange rate, most likely reflecting the changing role of the exchange rate after the break away from the ERM. These results however, are not clearly attributable to IT. On the other hand,

Canada, Sweden and the US (the latter considered as a benchmark) show no significant changes.

Neumann and von Hagen (2002) also estimate monetary policy reaction functions by estimating Taylor rules, incorporating a 'smoothing' variable for interest rates. Employing monthly data, they find substantial increases in the long-run response to inflation such that, during the post-IT period, there is convergence to the Bundesbank and the Swiss National Bank long-run responses, thereby corroborating the findings of Cecchetti and Ehrmann (1999) and Corbo, Landerretche and Schmidt-Hebbel (2001, 2002). They also find that less weight is put on stabilizing the cycle, with the exception of Sweden, which presented a more activist policy. The contribution of inflation shocks to the variance of interest rates is also computed using unrestricted VARs, confirming previous results. Neumann and von Hagen (2002) also apply an event-study analysis whereby they compare the performance of IT and non-IT central banks under similar exogenous shocks in both cases. They examine the increases in oil prices in the years 1978 and 1998. According to their evidence, actual and expected inflation responses to shocks improved more in IT countries. These gains in credibility allowed IT central banks to apply increases in short-run interest rates, which are similar to their IT counterparts. In comparison with the crisis starting in 1978, this represented a substantial improvement in the management of the 1998 oil price hike. Altogether, the authors conclude that the new IT regime has affected central bank behaviour and credibility more than it has changed inflation outcomes, which improved for both groups.

Corbo, Landerretche and Schmidt-Hebbel (2001) also find that the strength in the reaction of interest rate changes to both inflation and output shocks decreased significantly among IT countries, but these reductions were weaker or non-existent among non-IT industrial countries. Ball and Sheridan (2003) conclude that IT does not affect output growth or output variability, and neither does it affect interest rates and their variability. A related study by Bodkin and Neder (2003) examines IT in the case of Canada for the period 1980–9 and 1990–9 (the IT period). Their results, based on graphical analysis, clearly indicate that inflation over the IT period did fall, but at a significant cost of unemployment and output. This result leads the authors to the conclusion that a great deal of doubt is cast 'on the theoretical notion of the supposed long-run neutrality of money', an important, if not the most important, ingredient of the theoretical IT framework. They also, suggest that the 'deleterious real effects (higher unemployment and . . . lower growth) during the decade under study suggests that some small amount of inflation (say in the range of 3 to 5 per cent) may well be beneficial for a modern economy' (p. 355). Pétursson (2004), however, shows that (unconditional) growth rates are sensibly higher in the year following IT adoption than the 5-year average of records previous to the IT. Output fluctuations are also shown to decline, in line with findings of Corbo, Landerretche and Schmidt-Hebbel (2001), Neumann and von Hagen (2002) and Truman (2003).

Evidence of inflation targeting's impact on macroeconomic variables

Cohen Sabbán, Gonzalez Rozada and Powell (2003) consider the response of exchange rates (both nominal and real) to real and nominal shocks in order to assess IT benefits and sacrifices. They point out that IT regimes developed as a way of moving away from exchange rate targets. Increased flexibility in nominal exchange rates should, therefore, be considered as a benefit, since it would smooth out real shocks, acting as a type of shock absorber for the rest of the economy. In assessing the impact of IT they compare the effect that real shocks have on nominal exchange rates both before and after IT, and hypothesize a smaller impact as credibility is built. IT may, instead, imply a sacrifice if real exchange rates became more volatile with nominal shocks and purchasing power parity deviations being more severe. If IT regimes build up credibility, however, it is expected that nominal shocks would only have small and non-persistent effects on nominal exchange rates after IT, and hence real exchange rates would not be excessively affected. For LITHCs they produce evidence, which overwhelmingly supports a positive evaluation of IT strategy. First, sacrifice ratios expressed as percentage changes in nominal exchange rates due to nominal shocks are negative in most countries except for Australia (where no difference is registered), and in Chile and Brazil, where positive sacrifice ratios are registered. Second, benefit ratios, defined as the increase in the percentage of real exchange rate explained by real shocks, increase in all LITHCs, but not for all cases examined. The benefit ratio is negative in the case of Israel, making the case for IT in general more dubious according to this criterion.

Inflation targeting in emerging countries

Emerging countries have had varied experience in terms of targeting. A number of them over the recent past have been targeting the money supply or the exchange rate, especially the latter. Money supply targeting has been shown to be a rather unreliable means of controlling inflation in view of instabilities in the demand for money.[7] Changes in the exchange rate can be important in the case of emerging countries since such changes can have major effects on inflation. They can also produce acute vulnerability to currency crises since capital inflows can easily turn to capital outflows. A critical factor in this process is that since these countries have much of their debt denominated in foreign currency, depreciation of the domestic currency increases the debt burden of domestic firms. Typically the assets of these countries are denominated in domestic currency, so that depreciation of the domestic currency results in serious decline in net worth of the country in question. The adverse effect on investment and economic activity are evident. This may suggest that central banks of the countries that fall within this category should target their exchange rates. This, of course, would go against one important pillar of IT, namely that of 'absence of other nominal anchor' (Mishkin and Schmidt-Hebbel, 2001). There is also the further difficulty that the impact of changes in the exchange rate on inflation depends on the nature of the exchange rate change: a pure portfolio shock increases inflation, while the effect of a real shock would depend on its nature (i.e., whether it is a demand or supply shock).[8]

There have been further arguments suggesting that control is limited. The level of the exchange rate is ultimately determined by the international demand and supply of the domestic currency *vis-à-vis* that of the 'anchor' currency, such that shifts in sentiment about the domestic currency can trigger abrupt changes in its relative value that cannot be offset easily by central bank actions. Related to this reason is the fact that speculative attacks can easily materialize, which may very well force an unintended parity change not necessarily based on economic fundamentals. Such controls can often be followed by financial and banking crises and debt defaults. Another reason is that monetary autonomy is lost in view of the delegation by the central bank of the country in question to another country, the 'anchor' country, of its monetary policy. Still another reason is that the burden of achieving the proper real exchange rate falls entirely on the level of domestic prices. This can be particularly costly when prices are sticky in which case it is output that must adjust first.

It may very well be that for these reasons that a number of emerging countries have switched to a form or another of inflation targeting as suggested in the introduction. The evidence so far on the experience of these countries with IT, FFIT or ITL has not been as numerous and varied as in the case of the developed countries (Angeriz and Arestis, 2005a). Such evidence as there is suggests that IT is a success story in emerging countries (see, for example, IMF, 2005, and Porter and Yao, 2005; Angeriz and Arestis, 2005b, however, produce different results). It is associated with a statistically significant larger reduction in the level and standard deviation of inflation as compared to other regimes. It also leads to a reduction in the level and volatility of inflation expectations. It is conceded, nonetheless, that such experience 'comes against a backdrop of relatively subdued inflation worldwide', and, indeed, it is still too early to generalize, for it remains to be ascertained how the 'inflation targeting [lite] regime will fare if global inflation rises significantly, although a formalization of the current regime may limit any erosion of the gains already achieved' (Porter and Yao, 2005, p. 18). Our own evidence of IT on emerging countries, though, suggests that non-IT central banks have also been successful in achieving and maintaining consistently low inflation rates (Angeriz and Arestis, 2005b). This evidence clearly implies that an emerging country's central bank does not need to pursue an IT strategy to achieve and maintain low inflation.

A further comment on the experience of IT emerging countries is that whatever 'success' they may have had ought to be set against the background of the 'preconditions' that need to be met before IT adoption. IMF (2005) summarizes these pre-conditions as follows: technical capability of the central bank in implementing IT; an efficient institutional set-up to motivate and support the commitment to low inflation, including institutional independence; a healthy financial system; an economic structure characterized with fully deregulated prices; and absence of fiscal dominance. On current evidence, these preconditions admittedly do not prevail in most, if not all cases (IMF, 2005; but see Jonas and Mishkin, 2005, for a more neutral view on the importance of preconditions). Under such circumstances, the IT framework may be highly unsuitable for these countries. This argument clearly strengthens the finding of this chapter that whatever success we may attach to fighting inflation in the IT emerging countries, it cannot be due to this strategy. Factors other than IT must surely be responsible for the lower rates of inflation achieved by these countries. The opposite argument may also be true. Adoption of the IT strategy by these countries may lead to an improvement of the institutional 'preconditions', but the experience with the emerging IT countries is far too short for an assessment of this hypothesis to be undertaken persuasively. Still, the limited available evidence adduced from emerging countries which have pursued 'inflation targeting lite' implies that 'even in a country with solid institutions, a lack of fiscal dominance, and low external debt, it can take a long time before the central bank has earned sufficient credibility to anchor expectations for low inflation' (Porter and Yao, 2005, p. 18).

Two further problems, which are particularly relevant to Latin America, are worth exploring. These relate to the government-controlled prices and to the high incidence of pass-through from exchange rate fluctuations in domestic prices. The first requires a high degree of co-ordination between the monetary and fiscal authorities on the timing and magnitude of changes in controlled prices. The second requires a great deal of vigilance by the monetary authorities in terms of exchange rate fluctuations; this aspect, though, is viewed as temporary, since as inflation is tamed it is thought that the degree of pass-through is weakened (Mishkin and Savastano, 2001). These aspects, and all the others alluded to in this section – indeed, in the whole chapter – are important issues in the case of emerging countries. The chapter that follows vividly demonstrates this proposition, especially at the empirical level.

Summary and conclusions

We have attempted in this study to gauge empirical evidence for both developed and emerging countries which adopted the new monetary policy strategy that has come to be known as IT. It may very well be the case that IT countries, developed and emerging, have been successful in taming and controlling inflation. But then there is also evidence which clearly suggests that non-IT central banks have also been successful in achieving and maintaining consistently low inflation rates. Our overall conclusion, then, is that the available evidence we have managed to gauge clearly suggests that a central bank does not need to pursue an IT strategy to achieve and maintain low inflation. Indeed, and as Friedman (2004) suggests, acute focus on the IT strategy may very well lead to 'the atrophication of concerns for real outcomes, especially so in an environment of supply-side shocks of the kind we are experiencing at this juncture with increasing energy prices'.[9]

The IT strategy, however, keeps evolving. Two recent developments, which are of paramount importance, are the following: the argument put forward by a number of policy makers (see, for example, King, 2005), which emphasizes the role of price expectations and the ability of central banks to influence them; and the prominent dimension of communication, especially in terms of the inflation forecasts reported by central banks, where 'there has been a fair amount of change, at least for some central banks: the general trend is clearly towards reporting explicit forecasts over increasingly long horizons' (Kuttner, 2005, p. 18). These two areas in particular need to be researched a great deal more, especially under the current economic conditions of serious supply-side shocks that central banks have to tackle in a 'measured', and sensible, way.

Notes

1   Truman (2003), however, does not see much value in this classification scheme, branding it as 'dressed-up self-destruction'. In a recent paper, we have demonstrated that this classification is both sensible and worth undertaking (Angeriz and Arestis, 2006).
2   A widely-cited definition of price stability has been offered by Greenspan (1988): 'By price stability, I mean a situation in which households and businesses in making their saving and investment decisions can safely ignore the possibility of sustained, generalized price increases or decreases.'
3   Further implications of the IT strategy include: a long-run vertical Phillips curve; inflation is a monetary phenomenon in as much as it can only be tackled by monetary policy in the long run; and NAIRU is a supply-side phenomenon determined essentially by market flexibility, especially labour market flexibility.
4   The strategy contains the single objective of price stability for monetary policy, and not output stabilization, to avoid the time-consistency problem and thus the inflationary bias referred to in the text. This is consistent with the monetarist view that in the long run monetary policy can only affect inflation and not real variables.
5   Hyvonen (2004), however, challenges Ball and Sheridan's (2003) conclusions on the premise that mean reversion does not happen by itself. In the absence of a policy framework, such reversion does not occur.
6   A problem with the Ball (1994) approach is that the model relies on the absence of supply shocks, so that all deviations of actual output from potential output are attributed to policy-induced demand contraction (Cechetti, 1994). This could potentially have substantial effects on the results (King and Watson, 1994).
7   Although it is true to say, as in the text, that monetary targeting has been attempted in a number of emerging countries, Latin American countries have not used this strategy in a similar fashion, especially in the recent past. The main reason is the recognition of the serious possibility of instability in the demand for money as suggested in the text, a feature not merely of Latin American countries but also of other emerging and developed countries (Mishkin and Savastano, 2001). As the chapter that follows shows, Brazil has been no exception to this rule.
8   The arguments so far in this section are applicable in the case of asset prices, such as housing and stock prices. Bernanke and Gertler (1999) suggest that IT strategy should not target asset prices directly, but should utilize the information provided by movements in asset prices. In this way the possibility of asset price bubbles is less likely, thereby promoting financial stability. Arestis and Karakitsos (2005) summarize the arguments against such a thesis and propose targeting of net wealth instead.
9   Interestingly enough, the evidence on supply-side shocks is that when central banks are confronted with them they do not over-react to above-target inflation when it is accompanied by slow economic growth (Kuttner, 2005, p. 37).

References

Alesina, A.F., Blanchard, O., Gali, J., Giavazzi, F. and Uhlig, H. (2001) *Defining a Macroeconomic Framework for the Euro Area: Monitoring the European Central Bank 3* (London: Centre for Economic Policy Research).

Angeriz, A. and Arestis, P. (2005a) 'Assessing Inflation Targeting Through Intervention Analysis', *Working Paper* (Cambridge: Centre for Economic and Public Policy, University of Cambridge), http://www.landecon.cam.ac.uk/real_estate_grp/econ_and_public_polic/publications_ccepp.htm.

Angeriz, A. and Arestis, P. (2005b) 'An Empirical Investigation of Inflation Targeting in Emerging Economies', *Working Paper* (Cambridge: Centre for Economic and Public Policy, University of Cambridge), http://www.landecon.cam.ac.uk/real_estate_grp/econ_and_public_polic/publications_ccepp.htm.

Angeriz, A. and Arestis, P. (2006) 'Assessing the Performance of "Inflation Targeting Lite" Countries', *Working Paper* (Cambridge: Centre for Economic and Public Policy, University of Cambridge), http://www.landecon.cam.ac.uk/real_estate_grp/econ_and_public_polic/publications_ccepp.htm.

Arestis, P., Caporale, G.M. and Cipollini, A. (2002) 'Is There a Trade-off Between Inflation and Output Gap?', *The Manchester School of Economic and Social Research*, 70(4), 528–45.

Arestis, P. and Karakitsos, E. (2005) 'On the US Post-"New Economy" Bubble: Should Asset Prices be Controlled?', in P. Arestis, M. Baddeley and J. McCombie (eds), *The 'New' Monetary Policy: Implications and Relevance* (Cheltenham: Edward Elgar).

Ball, L. (1994) 'What Determines the Sacrifice Ratio?', in G. Mankiw (ed.), *Monetary Policy* (Chicago: University of Chicago University Press), 155–82.

Ball, L. and Sheridan, N. (2003) 'Does Inflation Targeting Matter?', *NBER Working Paper Series*, No. 9577 (Cambridge, MA: National Bureau of Economic Research).

Bernanke, B.S. (2003) 'A Perspective on Inflation Targeting', Remarks at the Annual Washington Policy Conference of the National Association of Business Economists, 25 March, Washington, DC.

Bernanke, B.S. and Gertler, M. (1999) 'Monetary Policy and Asset Price Volatility', in *New Challenges for Monetary Policy* (Kansas City: Federal Reserve of Kansas City).

Bernanke, B.S., Laubach, T., Mishkin, F.S. and Posen, A. (1999) *Inflation Targeting: Lessons from the International Experience* (Princeton, NJ: Princeton University Press).

Bodkin, R.G. and Neder, A.E. (2003) 'Monetary Policy Targeting in Argentina and Canada in the 1990s: A Comparison, Some Contrasts, and a Tentative Evaluation', *Eastern Economic Journal*, 29(3), 339–58.

Bollard, A. (2002) 'The Evolution of Monetary Policy in New Zealand', A Speech to the Rotary Club of Wellington, *Federal Reserve Bank of New Zealand*. Available on: http://www.rbnz.govt.nz/speeches/0127615.html.

Carare, A. and Stone, M.R. (2003) 'Inflation Targeting Regimes', *IMF Working Paper 03/9* (Washington, DC: International Monetary Fund).

Cechetti, S. (1994) 'Comment', in G. Mankiw (ed.), *Monetary Policy* (Chicago: University of Chicago University Press), 188–93.

Cecchetti, S.G. and Ehrmann, M. (1999) 'Does Inflation Targeting Increase Output Volatility? An International Comparison of Policymakers' Preferences and Outcomes', *NBER Working Paper*, No. 7426 (Cambridge, MA: National Bureau of Economic Research).

Chortareas, G., Stasavage, D. and Sterne, G. (2002) 'Does it Pay to be Transparent? International Evidence from Central Bank Forecasts', *Federal Reserve Bank of St Louis Review*, 84(4), 99–117.

Clifton, E.V., Hyginus, L. and Wong, C.-H. (2001) 'Inflation Targeting and the Unemployment–Inflation Trade-Off', *IMF Working Paper 01/166* (Washington, DC: International Monetary Fund).

Cohen Sabbán, V., Gonzalez Rozada, M. and Powell, A. (2003) 'A New Test for the Success of Inflation Targeting', mimeo.

Corbo,V., Landerretche, M.O. and Schmidt-Hebbel, K. (2001) 'Assessing Inflation Targeting After a Decade of World Experience', mimeo (Santiago: Central Bank of Chile).

Corbo,V., Landerretche, M.O. and Schmidt-Hebbel, K. (2002) 'Does Inflation Targeting Make A Difference?', in N. Loayza and R. Saito (eds), *Inflation Targeting: Design, Performance, Challenges* (Santiago, Chile: Central Bank of Chile).

Debelle, G. (1997) 'Inflation Targeting in Practice', *Working Papers Series*, No. 97/35 (Washington, DC: International Monetary Fund).

Duisenberg, W. (2003) 'Introductory Statement, and Questions and Answers', *ECB Press Conference*, 8 May, Frankfurt, Germany.

Friedman, B.M. (2004) 'Commentary' on 'Is Inflation Targeting Best-Practice Monetary Policy?' (J. Faust and D.W. Henderson), *Federal Reserve Bank of St Louis Review*, 86(4), 145–9.

Gramlich, E.M. (2000) 'Inflation Targeting', Remarks to the *Charlotte Economics Club*, 13 January, Charlotte, North Carolina.

Greenspan, A. (1988) 'Statement before the Subcommittee on Domestic Monetary Policy', *Committee on Banking, Finance and Urban Affairs*, US House of Representatives, Washington, DC, 28 July.

Harvey, A. and Jaeger, A. (1993) 'Detrending, Stylized Facts and the Business Cycle', *Journal of Applied Econometrics*, 8(2), 231–47.

Honda, Y. (2000) 'Some Tests on the Effects of Inflation Targeting in New Zealand, Canada and the UK', *Economics Letters*, 66(1), 1–6.

Hyvonen, M. (2004) 'Inflation Convergence Across Countries', *Discussion Paper N. 2004-04*, Federal Reserve Bank of Australia.

IMF (2005) 'Does Inflation Targeting Work in Emerging Markets?', *IMF World Economic Outlook*, September 2005-09-16 (Washington, DC: International Monetary Fund).

Johnson, D.R. (2002) 'The Effect of Inflation Targeting on the Behaviour of Expected Inflation: Evidence from an 11 Country Panel', *Journal of Monetary Economics*, 49(4), 1,521–38.

Johnson, D.R. (2003) 'The Effect of Inflation Targets on the Level of Expected Inflation in Five Countries', *Review of Economics and Statistics*, 85(4), 1,076–81.

Jonas, J. and Mishkin, F.S. (2005) 'Inflation Targeting in Transition Countries: Experience and Prospects', in B.S. Bernanke and M. Woodford (eds), *The Inflation Targeting Debate*, Studies in Business Cycles, No. 32, Part III (Chicago: University of Chicago Press).

Kahn, G. and Parrish, K. (1998) 'Conducting Monetary Policy With Inflation Targets', mimeo, Federal Reserve Bank of Kansas City, www.kc.frb.org.

King, M. (2005) 'Monetary Policy: Practice Ahead of Theory', Mais Lecture, Cass Business School, City University, London.

King, R.G. and Watson, M.W. (1994) 'The Post-War U.S. Phillips Curve: A Revisionist Econometric History', *Working Paper Series*, Macroeconomic Issues 94–14 (Chicago: Federal Reserve Bank of Chicago).

Kuttner, K.N. (2005) 'A Snapshot of Inflation Targeting in its Adolescence', *RBA Annual Conference Volume*, Reserve Bank of Australia. Available on: http://www.rba.gov.au/PublicationsAndResearch/Conferences/2004/Kuttner.pdf.

Leiderman, L. and Svensson, L.E.O. (eds) (1995) *Inflation Targets* (London: Centre for Economic Policy Research).

Levin, A., Natalucci, F. and Piger, J. (2004) 'The Macroeconomic Effects of Inflation Targeting', *Federal Reserve Bank of St Louis Review*, 86(4), 51–80.

Mishkin, F.S. (2002) 'Does Inflation Targeting Matter? Commentary', *Federal Reserve Bank of St Louis Review*, 84(4), 149–53.

Mishkin, F.S. and Posen, A.S. (1997) 'Inflation Targeting Lessons from Four Countries', *Federal Reserve Bank of New York Economic Policy Review*, 3(1), 9–117.

Mishkin, F.S. and Savastano, M.A. (2001) 'Monetary Policy Strategies for Latin America', *Journal of Monetary Economics*, 66(3), 415–44.

Mishkin, F.S. and Schmidt-Hebbel, K. (2001) 'One Decade of Inflation Targeting in the World: What do We Know and What do We Need to Know?', *Working Paper*, No. 101, Central Bank of Chile, July.

Neumann, M.J.M. and von Hagen, J. (2002) 'Does Inflation Targeting Matter?', *Federal Reserve Bank of St Louis Review*, 84(4), 127–48.

Pétursson, T. (2004) 'The Effects of Inflation Targeting on Macroeconomic Performance', mimeo, Central Bank of Iceland: Reykjavik.

Porter, N. and Yao, J.Y. (2005) ' "Inflation Targeting Lite" in Small Open Economies: The Case of Mauritius', *IMF Working Paper 05/172* (Washington, DC: International Monetary Fund).

Scott, R. and Stone, M. (2005) 'On Target: The International Experience with Achieving Inflation Targets', *IMF Working Paper 05/163* (Washington, DC: International Monetary Fund).

Sikklos, P.L. (1999) 'Inflation-Target Design: Changing Inflation Performance and Persistence in Industrial Countries', *Federal Reserve Bank of St Louis Review*, 81(1), 47–58.

Sterne, G. (2002) 'Inflation Targets in a Global Context', in N. Loayza and N. Soto (eds), *Inflation Targeting: Design, Performance, Challenges* (Santiago, Chile: Central Bank of Chile).

Stone, M.R. (2003) 'Inflation Targeting Lite', *IMF Working Paper 03/12* (Washington, DC: International Monetary Fund).

Taylor, J.B. (1993) 'Discretion Versus Policy Rules in Practice', *Carnegie-Rochester Conference Series on Public Policy*, 39, 199–214.

Truman, E.M. (2003) *Inflation Targeting in the World Economy* (Washington, DC: Institute for International Economics).

Uhlig, H. (2004) Comment on *'The Macroeconomic Effects of Inflation Targeting'*, by A. Levin, F. Natalucci and J. Piger, written for 'Inflation Targeting: Prospects and Problems', 28th Annual Economic Policy Conference, Federal Reserve Bank of St Louis, October 2003.

Vega, M. and Winkelried, D. (2005) 'Inflation Targeting, a successful story?', *Working Paper*, http://econwpa.wustl.edu/eps/mac/papers/0502/0502026.pdf.

4
Transparency versus Openness in Monetary Policy

*Emmanuel Carré**

> No-one would dare say that they were against transparency . . . it would be like saying you were against motherhood or apple pie.
>
> Joseph Stiglitz[1]

The revolution of central banking from a position of secrecy to one of transparency has been widely observed (Goodfriend, 1986). This trend is considered as being desirable by proponents of what may be termed the 'credibility strategy' (see, for example, Kydland and Prescott, 1977; Svensson, 1997). In the credibility strategy, transparency is seen as the most efficient solution to the major problem facing the effective implementation of monetary policy, namely, time inconsistency (Geraats, 2001). As a key feature of inflation, transparency in inflation targeting has come to be seen as increasingly important with the implementation of this monetary policy regime.

Nevertheless, there is a debate over transparency. First, a problem arises because its precise meaning remains elusive; different authors have different interpretations of the concept. There is no consensus on the exact meaning of transparency, as illustrated by the debate between Buiter (1999) and Issing (1999); instead, there is a widespread confusion between transparency, communication, information, and disclosure. Second, it is now commonly accepted that there are limits to transparency: it is impossible to be perfectly transparent (Bernanke, 2004; Mishkin, 2004). Third, several authors, starting with the seminal article of Morris and Shin (2002), have pointed out the disadvantages of transparency. Finally, a branch of the literature concerned with the 'confidence strategy' shows that transparency

---

* My grateful thanks go to Joann Bianchini, Tony Webb and Michael Hughes for helping me with the translation.

is not crucial for monetary policy; more important is the notion of 'governance'. Basically, this approach advocates what may be termed the 3C strategy (i.e., communication, common understanding and confidence), which will be discussed in greater detail below.

The US Federal Reserve Bank, for example, is committed to the confidence strategy: 'openness is more than just useful in shaping better economic performance. Openness is an obligation of a central bank in a free and democratic society' (Greenspan, 2001, p. 3).

The main contribution of this chapter is to propose an alternative to the transparency approach with a general theory of 'openness' which is based on two complementary pillars. The first is the *economics of openness* and shows how this enhances monetary policy efficiency. Openness clarifies the main concern of the confidence strategy: the effect of the expectations transmission channel from the short-term official rate to the long-run market-based rate. The second is the *politics of openness*, which analyses how openness can build monetary policy legitimacy in a democratic society. It shows that legitimacy requires a form of governance whereby the central bank is accountable to elected representatives for its legislative dual mandate. Openness is the way in which the central bank attempts to convince the public that its strategy is consistent with its democratic mission.

Transparency in the credibility strategy

According to the credibility literature, the 'inflation bias' of monetary policy results from the use of inappropriate policy: 'they pursued the wrong goals according to the wrong theory' (M. Friedman, 2004, p. 1). Policy makers are inclined to secrecy to generate surprise inflation because only the unexpected component of policy is supposed to be effective. With secrecy, the goal is 'avoiding accountability on the one hand and achieving public prestige on the other' (M. Friedman, 1990). Transparency provides a solution to this problem. It means: 'do the right thing, and reveal everything'. Transparency is the 'absence of asymmetric information between monetary policy makers and other economic agents' (Geraats, 2002a, p. 1).

Transparency as a continuation of the credibility strategy

The macro- and microeconomic background of the credibility strategy is reconciliation between Monetarism and the New Classical School. Transparency is necessary because of the danger of time-inconsistent policies. Monetarists affirm that the long-run Phillips curve is vertical. The rational expectations school, following Kydland and Prescott (1977), consolidates the Monetarist argument. Time-inconsistency is regarded by Barro and Gordon (1983) as a game of deception between the central bank and the agents. The government, with its shortsightedness and electoral concerns, follows the 'wrong' model in an attempt to reduce employment: namely, it assumes that there is a trade-off between unemployment and inflation. As central banks have complete control over inflation, they must also assume complete responsibility for it. Surprise inflation only offers short-term benefits, because in the long-run, with the NAIRU, it simply increases the inflation rate without reducing unemployment and this results in the inflation bias noted above. The 'right' policy is the Monetarist policy. This is centred around the k per cent rule. An appropriate definition of the money supply (M1, M2 or M3) must be controlled so that it increases no faster than the money target rate of k per cent a year. There has been a plethora of solutions to the inflation bias: improving institutional arrangements, enhancing reputation (Barro and Gordon, 1983), a conservative central banker (Rogoff, 1985), and a contract between the central bank and the government (Walsh, 1995). The last is a state-contingent contract between the central bank and the government and is supposed to be an incentive mechanism that reduces central bank's temptation to inflate. Transparency is the latest solution to the inflation bias and the credibility strategy to solve the inflation bias is:

> *Announcement* (rule), *Commitment* (binding agreement), *Enforcement* (penalties and rewards)

Transparency in practice: a commitment to the 'true' natural rate of unemployment model

Transparency and the credibility problem

The credibility strategy is based on the hypothesis that the central bank does not tell the truth because it has an incentive to inflate the economy. There is a credibility problem that means any announcement by the central bank as to its intentions has treated with scepticism.

In the conventional wisdom, credibility means saying what you do and doing what you say. But in the credibility strategy you do not become credible by telling the truth, because it does not reduce the incentive to inflate. Credibility here does not mean telling the truth: it is rather a matter of drawing implications from the truth (the Friedman/Lucas synthesis).

Credibility implies sustaining a reputation for revealing, through one's actions, a commitment to the long-run macroeconomic equilibrium theory. Inspired by Backus and Driffill (1985), the basic article on transparency of Faust and Svensson (2000a) shows how transparency can solve the credibility problem because it is incentive-compatible. Basically, transparency makes deceptive announcements so costly in terms of reputation that the incentive to deceive disappears. The problem is that this reputational solution is now considered obsolete in the literature.

Knowledge transparency and goal transparency

In the credibility strategy, policy making must be rule-based. Transparency consists in publishing a form of the k per cent rule: 'Transparency about monetary policy in a *stylised* model world simply involves revealing the central bank's optimal policy rule' (Winkler, 2002, p. 410). This rule-based approach is consequently model-dependent. Transparency means the central bank tying its hands to the 'true' model of the economy through a policy commitment (i.e., through a rule or a target). Transparency shows the public that the central bank is following the correct model. It is not a question of communication in simply verbal terms.

It is now acknowledged that the growth of the money supply in the form of M3 is no longer a consistent intermediate target. All that remains is the fundamental hypothesis that there exists a 'true' model of the economy. Central bank transparency consists in publishing its 'true' model and the corresponding inflation forecasts. 'Knowledge transparency' consists in verifying the adoption of the 'true' model.

The central bank has to concentrate on inflation. It does so not only because it can totally control inflation, but also because inflation is the unique variable that it is supposed to influence in the long run. In line with Backus and Driffill (1985), transparency consists of central bank 'type' revelations. The 'true' type derives from the 'true' model. Transparency requires announcing that there is a unique mandate with inflation as the 'true' type. The main objective is to reduce inflation and, beyond that, ultimately to ensure zero inflation. If a democratic authority gives the central bank a mandate consisting of multiple goals, transparency means providing a definitive prioritization of these objectives, with the priority given to inflation. It has also been argued, however, that with one instrument, only one goal is possible.

Transparency and independence

Independence was the major plank of the credibility strategy in the 1980s. Rogoff's (1985) 'conservative' central banker was supposed to provide the theoretical foundation for this independence. Transparency is complementary to independence: 'the old legacy of independence-through-secrecy and the new paradigm of central bank independence-cum-transparency' (Geraats, 2002b, p. 15). The underlying rationale is that transparency is an 'incentive-compatible mechanism' that prevents the government from exerting pressure on the central bank. The public disclosure of the rule or a monetary target makes any government manipulation observable, and thus costly. The combination of these two properties should permit the promotion of central bank independence.

In the credibility strategy, transparency is considered to be an improvement *vis-à-vis* the alternative of mystique, secrecy and constructive ambiguity. However, a closer analysis reveals that it is not quite as simple as this. Secrecy, in fact, was a strategy for a dependent central bank to gain independence. When the central bank's targets are implicit and its decisions are not published in real time, the government has some difficulty in making the central bank accountable. In this respect, transparency is similar to secrecy. (Transparency and secrecy are therefore similar in their common objective of independence.)

Ambiguities in the case for transparency

The credibility strategy is ambiguous because it continues to recommend full transparency, while acknowledging that central banks could benefit from a degree of ambiguity (Geraats, 2005). Transparency cannot be consistently relevant because the underlying model used is itself not consistent. The 'correct' model often fails due to the presence of uncertainty. Therefore the credibility strategy is obliged to admit that there can be limits to transparency:

> transparency is not equivalent to complete certainty or perfect information. For instance, in the case of monetary policy, the central bank and the private sector could both face uncertainty about the structure of the economy; but as long as both have the same information and are aware of it, transparency prevails.
>
> (Geraats, 2002a, p. 2)

In short, there is no longer a focus on complete transparency, but on a more limited concept of the maximum possible transparency. The general scheme for transparency in the credibility strategy is:

> *Natural rate of unemployment model – Unique mandate – Rule-based policy – Rational expectations – Transparency– Commitment – Reputation – Expectations anchorage – Credibility*

There are several drawbacks to transparency. First, it appears that by 'transparency', the credibility literature analyses the preferences, incentives, announcements and publications of the central bank, but is less able to judge the economic effects of transparency, because of problems with the underlying model.

Second, the credibility problem is not necessarily solved by greater transparency. The basic assumption of the credibility strategy is that a central bank with low credibility needs maximum transparency, while one with high credibility does not need much at all. Why, then, has there been an increasing amount of literature on transparency if ambiguity is the optimal policy for a high credibility central bank? Moreover, the credibility framework does not explain how to attain credibility. This literature can explain the result (credibility), but not how credibility is formed, because transparency alone does not produce credibility.

Third, it is difficult to understand why transparency is sometimes regarded as an all-or-nothing state (central banks are either transparent or they are not) and sometimes as matter of degree (how transparent are they?). The conclusion is straightforward: transparency is not necessarily a requisite for achieving credibility. 'Is transparency necessary for credibility? Logically, the answer is no. A central bank that consistently delivers low and stable inflation will have credibility even if it does not publicly acknowledge that it is its goal' (Thornton, 2002, p. 11). The disjunction between credibility and transparency is easy to understand: in the credibility strategy, credibility comes from reputation, rather than transparency. It is more a question of commitment than a question of communication of the aims and intentions of the central bank.

Transparency in the inflation targeting regime

According to both central bankers and academics, the credibility strategy is an outdated attempt to construct credibility (Blinder, 2000). The new consensus is inflation targeting. In this transition from monetary to inflation targeting in the 1990s, transparency has become a key component.

In inflation targeting, there is no 'true' model or rule and, consequently, there can be no possible commitment to them. But the macroeconomic consensus remains: according to New Keynesians and the New Neoclassical Synthesis, price stability is the best strategy to obtain sustainable long-term growth.

Transparency is a means of helping to maintain the commitment to price stability, whereas in the credibility strategy the commitment was to zero inflation. Transparency alleviates the credibility problem, not because of reputation, but because of the imperfect knowledge of agents. In the credibility strategy, communication was unnecessary because agents supposedly possessed a perfect knowledge of the economy. Their expectations were formed by the 'true' model. In IT, with imperfect knowledge, the model is partly given by the central bank, so that the latter can influence the agents' expectations via its announcements and its communications. Hence, a defining characteristic of a transparent central bank could be the situation of having all agents knowing that the central bank is credibly committed to price stability.

Nevertheless, transparency is but a reformulation of the credibility strategy and IT is simply an 'old lady in new clothes'. IT pretends to be concerned only with inflation, but the policy will also impact on output: there is a severe lack of clarity. Transparency, understood here to be the matching of deeds to words, is not respected: in other words, 'Say what you do, without doing what you say.'

The macroeconomic background for transparency in inflation targeting

The credibility framework once again

In IT, as in the credibility strategy, transparency is seen as a solution to the time-inconsistency problem (Mishkin, 2000, p. 1). Monetary policy is systematic, forecast-based or 'rule-like'.[2] It is not based on a strict rule, but a 'state contingent' rule or contract.The medium-term horizon of monetary policy is not really concerned with the consequence of shocks, trade-offs or lags. It is rather a product of the New Consensus in macroeconomics. Such a 'divine coincidence' (Blanchard, 2003) assumes that, in the long run, stabilizing inflation is equivalent to having output at its potential level. Price stability and maximum sustainable growth are not conflicting objectives.

Transparency is not about unveiling the 'truth', but the commitment to the consensus: namely, the importance of price stability. It is a new version of the credibility strategy, and defines price stability by a particular inflation target which is seen as superior to the earlier aim of zero inflation as the optimal outcome. There is no obligation to achieve a unique objective, but the prioritization of the various goals remains imperative for clarity. The failure to give price stability top priority will result in a lack of transparency.

Transparency and the expectations transmission channel

The main transmission channel of IT is inflation expectations. It is a channel, and not a mechanism, because of uncertainty. The central bank does not perfectly control inflation, but it can anchor inflation expectations that in turn determine inflation. Transparency is thus aimed at 'shaping' or 'fostering' the public's expectations. Inflation forecasts are the major components of this transparency which aims at perfect predictability. With transparency, all agents have the New Neoclassical Synthesis in mind when they form their expectations by what is known as the 'common-knowledge' assumption.

Unlike the credibility literature, the IT approach investigates the economic effects of transparency:

1 It helps the central bank to achieve its objective at lower costs and thus lowers the sacrifice ratio. Transparency also helps to obtain the same economic result with a lower interest rate.
2 It gives the central bank more flexibility to respond to shocks in the short term, because transparency anchors inflation expectations in the medium term.
3 Transparency reduces financial market volatility by reducing the central bank's private information. It increases the accuracy of agents' forecasts by facilitating the inference process from the central bank's actions. By reducing uncertainty in the markets, it improves social welfare.

Transparency and responsibility as twin notions

The central bank is responsible for its performance solely in terms of controlling inflation. In the extreme case of the Reserve Bank of New Zealand, the Governor can be fired if he does not meet the inflation target. The target is a quantification of what constitutes price stability (i.e., a specified numerical rate of inflation). The announcement of the inflation target is the key element of transparency. The central bank's performance can be judged in terms of it meeting this objective and from this it is possible to observe its commitment to price stability (Walsh, 2002).

In IT, it is generally asserted that transparency is not an independence enhancement, but the corollary of independence. In a check and balance approach, transparency counterbalances independence, yet the relationship between independence and transparency is unclear. The inflation target is determined by democratic authorities, so that the independence of the central bank lies only in its choice of the strategy and instrument setting to achieve the target. The central bank has instrument independence, not goal independence. However, the public disclosure of the inflation target makes the central bank the sole body that is responsible for achieving this. Thus there is a duality.

On the one hand, transparency is different from that in the credibility strategy. There is no political independence, as the target is defined by the government and in this way the autonomy of the central bank is limited to the choice of instrument in achieving this. Transparency is a consequence of the emphasis placed on democratic accountability. On the other hand, IT promoters provide a second argument which is close to that found in the credibility strategy, because it is based on the political independence of the central bank. They consider that the transparency given by the explicit inflation target provides an element of independence of the central bank, as it would reveal any attempt by the government to create 'surprise inflation' by making any such move obvious. For the government, the transparency of the target is an incentive to keep to its announced policy. With transparency, the target announcement becomes credible, because it is publicly disclosed.

Transparency in practice: a policy framework for the commitment to price stability

IT is based on two pillars: (1) the policy framework; and (2) a communications strategy. Together the two pillars provide a strategy of 'constrained discretion'. In the famous rule versus discretion debate, IT provides a revolutionary third approach. It suggests that there is not a dichotomy, but rather a dialectic. Transparency contributes to the synthesis of 'rules' and 'discretion'. It is supposed to offer, at the same time, a commitment to the inflation target (the constraint) and the ability to deviate from this target (the discretion), giving constrained discretion. In IT language, transparency improves the incentive to pursue price stability, while providing the flexibility to respond to shocks.

By abandoning secrecy for transparency, central banks that adopt IT now 'talk' (the second pillar). 'Talk' comprises various forms of communication to the public, such as inflation reports and inflation forecasts. It differs from the credibility strategy in that the latter is averse to this type of communication.

In IT, communication is strategic insofar as it aims to manipulate inflation expectations in order to maintain price stability. Transparency intends to show agents that any deviation from the inflation target is not synonymous with an inflationary bias. Any such deviations do not result from the incentive on the part of the central bank to inflate the economy, but as a response to unexpected shocks.

In short, transparency acts as an enforcement mechanism that makes the commitment to controlling inflation credible. Transparency may be viewed as the credibility strategy revisited in the following manner:

Announcement (inflation target) – Commitment (to price stability) – Enforcement (transparency)

Transparency and uncertainty

Central bankers practising IT claim that uncertainty is crucial. Flexibility is required in order to respond to unforeseen contingencies. Flexibility means that the inflation target has to be achieved not in the short term, but only in the medium-term. In the short run, there are deviations of observed inflation from the inflation target. These deviations are gradually reduced in order to take into account the sacrifice ratio produced by the Taylor trade-off (Taylor, 1996) between the variance of output and inflation. It radically differs from the credibility strategy which recommends the instantaneous reaction of policy to the occurrence of deviations to maintain credibility. This is because disinflation is a 'free lunch' with rational expectations.

The enigma of transparency is how it reduces uncertainty. Is it a result of the credibility and commitment to the price stability that it generates? Or does it anchor expectations through explanations of the deviations that occur from shocks? This is the crucial question for the communications strategy. Should transparency be about the commitment to the inflation target, or about the inflation target itself? Put differently, in the case of large deviations of the inflation rate from its target, should the commitment to an announced target that is no longer credible be kept, or should the target be changed?

If IT follows the credibility strategy, the answer is the transparency of the commitment is what is important; that is to say, attempting to maintain the announced target, even if it is unachievable. In practice, central banks prefer to change the target. In some parts of the world there are even procedures to change the inflation target, especially in Brazil; and Mishkin (2004) approves of this. The surprising result is that the advocates of IT consider that credibility is sometimes produced by such changes, and not by sticking to the target. Shocks may have to take priority over price stability; the priority is no longer placed on price stability, which is time-varying.

Inflation targeting: limited transparency

The existence of symmetric information between the central bank and the agents is a basic assumption of the credibility strategy. It contrasts with

IT supporters who recognize that this is unfeasible, mainly due to the effect of pervasive uncertainty. In IT, transparency is intrinsically limited.

The folk wisdom: 'do what you do, but do not talk about growth or unemployment'

In IT, transparency means exhibiting a commitment to price stability. Multiple goals remain the 'dirty little secret' (Mishkin, 2004). Faust and Henderson (2004, pp. 23–4) point out that IT pursues the traditional selective communication of central banking: 'they do what they do, but only talk about inflation'. Blinder (2002, p. 32) asserts that: 'In truth, however, the concerns about employment are typically unstated and often hidden – a clear violation of transparency.'

That there is a unique mandate for price stability is a fallacy. The notions of 'flexible' or 'judgemental' inflation targeting clearly indicate that there is a hierarchical or even a dual mandate. There are multiple goals such as targeting inflation, output, unemployment. This lack of transparency on the output goal is not understandable in light of flexible IT which places an emphasis on a short-run Taylor trade-off and the related gradual path of return to the inflation target. IT has found a solution to this problem. It is necessary to abandon the discussion on short-run trade-offs and multiple goals by focusing on the medium term and its unique goal of controlling inflation.

This discord between theory and practice is a source of opacity: 'in particular that inflation targeting usefully enhances the transparency of monetary policy are not just unproved, but false. To the contrary, as actually practised, inflation targeting is a framework not for communicating the central bank goals but for obscuring them' (B.M. Friedman, 2004, p. 2).

Inflation targeting's transparency problem: can there be too much of a good thing?

The chief problem of IT lies in discussing the limits to transparency. Transparency about what and how much? What is the equilibrium degree of transparency (Faust and Svensson, 2000b)? This problem emerges from the contradiction between transparency and uncertainty. Transparency cannot be achieved via three-year inflation forecasts, such as the Reserve Bank of New Zealand provides, due to the existence of unpredictable shocks. It is not feasible to seek transparency by publishing the true model of the central bank, as it does not exist. It is unrealistic to be transparent with respect to a targeting rule that requires an extensive use of judgement. The Bank of England is the most provocative about the limits to transparency: 'There is surely information relevant for policy-making that is simply incapable of being put in the public domain' (Vickers, 1998, p. 370).

Expectations: management and manipulation

The lack of transparency on the goal for the level of output in IT can be attributed to the strategy for the management of expectations. The latter comes from the New Keynesian consensus underlying IT. The new Phillips curve indicates that the lower the future inflation is expected to be, the lower inflation actually is and thus the higher will be the actual output, relative to its potential level. IT has an incentive to make agents believe that inflation will be low in the future.

Transparency attempts to separate inflation expectations from observed inflation. Put differently, inflation expectations should be shaped by the central bank's tactics to accommodate the shock, and not by the current level of inflation produced by the shock (Van Der Cruijsen and Demertzis, 2005, p. 15).

Due to uncertainty, shocks and deviations, transparency is not a static, but a dynamic, anchorage. It is not an 'expectations anchorage', but a means of 'expectations management' (Woodford, 2004, p. 3). Transparency helps to 'educate' the public (Bernanke *et al.*, 1999) about the shocks and the return path to the inflation target. But, in the most recent analysis, this type of management is a new solution to an old question: namely, the search for a nominal anchor for expectations.

One of the most important elements of transparency is the publication of forecasts. These explain the tactics required to return to the target within a given optimal time horizon. Yet, inflation forecasts are not sufficient to affect expectations if they do not involve the revelation of the underlying model of the economy from which they are produced: 'the forecast simply is not enough' (Posen, 2002, p. 120). IT cannot be transparent in this way, for it claims that there is no 'true' model of the economy and because policymaking requires judgment to be used in the forecasts. The transparency task is even more complicated if IT reveals its multiple goals.

The management of expectations achieved through transparency rests on a *reductio ad absurdum* of policy making. Central bank transparency could be viewed as manipulation, and not just as expectations management:

> When the central bank in fact has multiple goals but quantifies only one – indeed, when it refuses to talk explicitly about any of the other except in terms of how they bear on the achievement of that one, as is normally the case under inflation targeting – one is entitled to suspect

that the motivation is not just to manage the public's expectations but to manipulate them.

(B.M. Friedman, 2004, p. 8)

In IT, a hysteresis problem appears in so far as IT remains model-based. In this respect, IT still has one foot inside the credibility camp. On microeconomic grounds, IT vacillates between rational expectations and adaptive learning. On macroeconomic grounds, the natural rate of unemployment and long-run neutrality of money remain key assumptions of the underlying theory.

Transparency is ambiguous because there are contradictions in the macroeconomic framework of IT. It insists that there is no 'true' model of the economy, while it is committed to the New Neo-Classical Synthesis and its price stability. This kind of transparency eludes the debate as discussion is concerned with conformity to the consensus and expectations theory, but not about the consensus itself.

The conclusion is clear: with transparency, the policy framework hides the macroeconomic foundations. The institutional design of transparency produces an institutional commitment to price stability that masks the theoretical commitment.

The confidence paradigm: openness rather than transparency

The turning point in monetary policy towards the emphasis on confidence took place in the 1990s (McCallum, 1995, 1997). It marked a break with the credibility literature. Time inconsistency and credibility problems are no longer considered to be relevant issues. What matters is confidence. Here, the basic assumption is not central bank deception, but trust. The relationship between the central bank and the heterogeneous agents is not a game of deception, but of confidence. In common language, central banks *'say what they do and do what they say'*.

In the *confidence approach* to monetary policy, uncertainty is the defining characteristic of the policy environment; so that the central bank cannot be fully transparent due to unpredictable shocks. The question of the optimal degree of transparency has no relevance for two reasons. First, it is not a question of the degree, or the extent the central bank can be transparent; it is simply transparent or it is not. Second, due to the macroeconomic foundations (the existence of radical uncertainty, and no true model) central banks cannot be transparent.

The confidence paradigm talks about openness rather than transparency. Openness is broadly promoted by central banks, with the Fed taking a leading role. The confidence school investigates both the economic and democratic dimensions of openness, but we will first discuss the confidence regime.

Openness and the 3C Strategy

In the *credibility strategy*, there is assumed to be a single true economic model of the economy, with an exogenous theory of money.

In marked contrast, in the *confidence strategy*, money is endogenous. Openness means that monetary policy is also endogenous, i.e., it is produced by an interaction between the central bank and the agents. Co-ordination on monetary policy is not given but it is constructed. Based on a communication strategy, openness is the will to build a consensus on monetary policy through a common understanding between the central bank and the agents: 'A clear understanding of the policy process builds confidence' (Bell, 2005, p. 5). It is the 3C strategy: *Communication – Common understanding – Confidence.*

Openness and communication

In the *credibility strategy*, with transparency and common knowledge, there is a limited need for communication through explanation. Put simply, action is the best way to achieve reputation. The issue of communication, that is to say, the relationship between the agents and the central bank is neglected. It is clear in the game-theoretic approach to common knowledge and the famous prisoners' dilemma; agents do not talk.

In the *confidence strategy*, however, communication matters. It plays a role in the construction of a common understanding. The central bank has to be open to discussion to convince agents. The monetary policy is the production of an interactional learning process between the central bank and the agents, based on language (Winkler, 2002, p. 423),

Openness is part of the solution to the signal extraction and co-ordination problems. Communication becomes a critical issue because heterogeneous agents can have different interpretations of the central bank's actions that lead to *multiple equilibria*. Communication allows for the elimination of this equilibrium selection problem by allowing an interactional learning process.

Openness is related to communication that conveys explanations, not the revelation of the 'truth'. Openness and clarity in the motivations of central banking decisions are revolutionary ideas in central banking. This explanatory imperative is embedded in a communications framework, which is not rule-based.

In IT, transparency is presented as a process of inferring the central bank's intentions, whereas openness means that the central bank itself provides explanations, leading to a process of understanding. Communication should contain relevant information, i.e., making the central bank understandable to the general public. There are three characteristics of comprehensive explanations: (i) extensive explanations ('explaining more for greater understanding');[3] (ii) clear explanations; and (iii) forward-looking explanations, that is, should provide a representation of the future.

Openness: the construction of a common understanding

In the *credibility strategy*, transparency works because agents cannot agree to disagree. They interpret the same information the same way because they have rational expectations and form their expectations with the same economic model in mind. Transparency is efficient due to the efficient market hypothesis and enhances the efficiency of the economy since it restores the perfect information environment that was destroyed by the central bank's private information.

Common knowledge is synonymous with complete information. In game theory, agents do not 'talk' as they are supposed to know enough for co-ordination. They both know the 'true' model of the economy and can also anticipate the central bank's actions (rational expectations). In this stylized model of transparency characterized by *quasi* certainty, the co-ordination of the central bank's decisions is automatic as agents are homogeneous. Transparency is a public disclosure that increases the co-ordination power of common knowledge. The combination of common knowledge and transparency leads to a state which approaches a situation of perfect information. There is no need for common understanding because agents know all they that they need to know for their expectations formation.

In contrast, the *confidence strategy* considers that monetary policy is embedded in a radically uncertain environment. The formation of private expectations according to central bank signals is not automatic. The signal extraction comes from understanding (interpretation), not from knowledge (induction). To form their expectations, agents do not need to know, they need to understand. Agents can know without understanding monetary policy decisions. If they do not understand, it is unlikely that agents would form their expectations upon monetary policy. Transparency or common knowledge does not require the central bank to be clear. Transparency is the opposite of secrecy, not of ambiguity.

The expectations formation is not a unilateral process stemming from the central bank or a derivation from a unique model of the economy. It

is rather a mutual scheme that implies that agents are capable of interpretation. Common understanding is a mutual and shared comprehension
of the economic environment explaining the central bank's actions. It is
defined as 'how much the strategy is interpreted and understood in the
same way by the central bank and the public' (Winkler, 2002, p. 413).

When common understanding has been reached, agents can interpret
the central bank's decisions. They can understand and validate (or not)
short-term tactical deviations from the medium-term strategy. Common
understanding makes the public a partner in monetary policy making.

The economics of openness

Why a central bank cannot be, and should not be, transparent

Central banks should not be transparent since total transparency can lead
to a counterproductive reflexivity between the central bank and the financial markets. Unlike the credibility strategy that insists on the independence of the central bank from political authority, openness highlights
the importance of independence from financial markets: 'this, of course,
is not to say that a central bank will never surprise the market. As I mentioned earlier, the most important task of a central bank is to get monetary policy right. At times, getting policy right will involve taking action
unexpected by the market – for example, in its timing and magnitude'
(Ferguson, 2001, p. 5). In the confidence strategy, 'surprise' does not mean
deception. Surprise is used to signal a shock, loud and clear, as well as
structural or unforeseen changes in the strategy. Surprise is also intended
to quickly transmit information to the markets.

Openness and the question of confidence

A crucial issue is the connection between the official short-term rate and
the market-based long-run rate of interest. It is the latter that regulates the
economy, making the central bank a statue with feet of clay as it is ineffective without the agents' support. The central bank is not a high-powered
institution that totally controls inflation, expectations, and the economy
in general. It has to work with the agents, as it cannot work against them.

What matters is to convince players that the central bank's actions are
relevant, so that market participants accept and co-ordinate themselves
according to monetary policy decisions:

> If the monetary policy can be more open about what it is doing and
> why and about how it perceives the economic outlook, then market
> participants can improve their expectations of future short rates,

bringing the interest rates and financial prices that matter most for the economy closer into alignment with the intentions of the central bank.

(Ferguson, 2002, p.2)

In the credibility strategy and IT, transparency is an attempt to anchor inflation expectations in order to neutralize the expectations transmission channel. In marked contrast, the confidence strategy is inefficient if the channel does not work. Communication with agents is aimed at operating on the linkage between the official interest rate and the market interest rate and beyond to shape the whole yield curve. Openness is related to the expectations theory of the term structure. Openness exploits the expectations channel in favour of flexible inflation expectations. Indeed, it is widely admitted that long maturities of the term structure, i.e., long-run rates, are largely determined by inflation expectations. Movements in the long-run rate imply that inflation expectations are flexible, not anchored. Openness is aimed at creating an 'expectations accelerator': the public's expectations strengthen the policy transmission channel and shorten policy transmission lags.

Openness, uncertainty and efficiency

With radical uncertainty and unpredictable shocks, it is not easy to believe in the existence of a 'true' model of the economy. Similarly, the goals of the central bank are open to discussion. There is a dual mandate, not a unique or a hierarchical mandate. Depending on the state of the economy, the central bank weighs up the risks and prioritizes the prominent objectives. Monetary policy is goal symmetric, there is *a priori* no priority amongst final objectives.

Regarding the definition of price stability, no number is placed on the target rate of inflation as it is time-varying. In accordance with Greenspan, the confidence strategy develops an expectational and psychological theory of price stability. In order to limit the sacrifice ratio and facilitate the understanding of the central bank's actions, a gradualist approach is required. As with IT, there is a medium-term strategy, with a short-term tactic to accommodate shocks. Such flexibility and discretion make a rule-based or rule-like monetary policy non-feasible. It does not generate a credibility problem if agents understand and validate the central bank's strategy and tactics. This means that while in IT the sacrifice ratio is reduced by the transparency of the medium-term commitment to the inflation target, in the confidence strategy it is reduced by a common understanding between the central bank and the agents about the goals and strategy of monetary policy.

The politics of openness

The politics and economics of openness are not conflicting but complementary. Politics is an integral part of economics. It insists on the regulation imperative in a democratic society: statutes of delegation make it mandatory to regulate the economy in accordance with the democratic mandate. This is the meaning of 'policy' in monetary policy. It is not considered democratic to hide the real objectives of monetary policy from the public (cf. the situation in IT), in the name of a particular economic model. The dual mandate is intimately related to democratic principles. The choice of objectives is a basic principle of democracy that is not available with a unique or a hierarchical mandate.

Openness and legitimacy

In the *credibility strategy*, central banking is a technical affair. Central bankers are the experts that obtain their legitimacy from their understanding of the true economic (natural rate of unemployment) model.

The *confidence strategy* proposes a different approach. Openness, however, has to be perceived as a general characteristic of democracy. Openness makes the actions of the central bank consistent with democracy. The politics of openness is the quest for the construction of legitimacy. In a representative democracy, legitimacy comes from elections. Since central bankers are not officially elected, they obtain their legitimacy through subservience to elected representatives, and also by explanations to the public. Openness is a way to convince the public, through a deliberative process, that the central bank is consistent with its democratic mandate. A central bank practising openness in a democratic society might be called 'communicational'.[4]

Openness and governance

Most central banks use the concept of 'governance', not 'independence'. This fact sheds light on the political turning-point in monetary policy at the end of the 1990s. After the collapse of the natural rate of unemployment model, monetary policy legitimacy now comes from a democratic authority. Full independence is now rejected. There is no isolation from political pressure, but instead there are relationships with elected representatives. In governance, there is no separation of power, but a delegation of power to the monetary institution. It is not a de-politicization, but a re-politicization of the monetary policy.

Openness embodies the idea that the central bank must now be open to discussion with elected representatives. Openness is a reminder that central bank is first and foremost a democratic institution that belongs to the public. The central bank has a role to play in society. It is an institution that regulates social conflicts regarding the distribution of wealth. This political task implies that the central bank cannot be free of all democratic control. Governance aims at organizing the democratic embeddedness of the central bank with accountability procedures.

Openness and effective democratic accountability

Contrary to transparency, openness does not mean that the achievement of the inflation target can necessarily be verified. Openness 'is to open the central bank to public scrutiny in relation to the exercise of a delegated power' (Archer, 2005, p. 2). The political subservience of the central bank is the result of effective democratic accountability. It implies two elements. First, that the central bank is accountable to elected representatives for its mandate; and, second, that the central bank has to take into account the claims of elected representatives. Accountability is effective if the central bank remains subservient to the elected representatives from which it receives its mandate. Elected representatives can change the mandate, and punish the central bank. The Fed is a 'creature of the Congress' (Meyer, 2000, p. 6), and not a creature of economic theory.

Openness to accountability is an obligation for the monetary authority: 'It cannot be acceptable in a democratic society that a group of unelected individuals are vested with important responsibilities, without being open to full public scrutiny and accountability' (Greenspan, 1996, p.4). Accountability cannot be achieved through the transparency of a rule or inflation target. It is based on explanations of how the strategy is consistent with the legislative mandate:

> Central bank openness allows the public and its elected representatives to make informed judgments and constructive criticisms about policies made by its central bank and to assess economic outcomes relative to the specified long-run objectives.
>
> (Ferguson, 2002, p.2).

Conclusion

The three monetary policy strategies (the credibility strategy, IT and the confidence strategy) all agree on the idea that transparency increases the central bank's level of effectiveness. But a problem arises because the strategies disagree about what is the correct policy action. This disagreement is important because it leads to radically different viewpoints on transparency (see Table 4.1). Resulting from this disagreement is the distinction between transparency (credibility strategy and IT) and openness (confidence strategy).

The credibility strategy. This is based on the assumption that the 'correct' policy action is based on the 'true' model of the economy (the Friedman/Lucas synthesis). Transparency is the revelation of the true model. Avoiding time inconsistency requires transparency, i.e., the explicit rejection of the traditional Phillips curve: there is no trade-off between inflation and unemployment. There is no co-ordination problem among agents as they have common (perfect) knowledge. This implies that they all know the correct model of the economy. Transparency is associated with a rule-based policy – in other words, a rule that derives from the model. Transparency also consists of the announcements and publications of the central bank. We cannot talk about openness because the 'correct' action is not open to discussion. That is why there is no communication between the central bank and the agents. The credibility strategy's approach to transparency is best conveyed by the expression *'do the right thing, and all will be clear'*.

Inflation targeting. There is no 'true' model of the economy due to the presence of uncertainty. The central bank has to provide the rationale for its policy framework and its decisions. Transparency is aimed at showing that the central bank is pursuing the 'correct' policy. Communication becomes a critical issue. The communication problem arises for a number of reasons. First, as there is no natural 'correct' action, there is a need to show the relevance of the central bank's actions. Second, due to uncertainty, there are unforeseen contingencies that generate short-run tactical shifts in the medium-term strategy. These changes ought to be justified in order to keep inflation expectations anchored. Since shocks generate deviations from the inflation target, transparency intends to show that these are not due to time-inconsistency, but to a tactic to keep to the inflation target in the medium term. Third, the absence of a 'correct' model and the presence of uncertainty make it impossible to propose a rule-based monetary policy and *a fortiori* rule-based transparency.

The management of expectations is achieved by a communications strategy. There is no longer common knowledge, but rather adaptive learning. Nevertheless, because it is partly based on the outdated credibility literature, IT has an unclear theory of transparency. The question is how to be transparent when there is no 'correct' action. When there is uncertainty, how can you reveal a 'correct' model that does not exist? This paradox emerges because IT contains parts of the Friedman/Lucas

Table 4.1 Transparency in the different monetary policy regimes

Credibility strategy	Confidence strategy	
	'Soft' confidence strategy. **Inflation targeting regime:**	**'Hard' confidence strategy.** **Confidence strategy:**
Transparency problematic	*Transparency problematic*	*Openness problematic*
1. Disclosure: 'do the right thing, and all will be clear'.	1. Publicity: 'Do what you do, but talk only about inflation'.	1. Openness: 'say what you do and do what you say'.
2. Credibility enhancement.	2. Nominal anchor.	2. Democratic legitimacy, economic efficiency.
3. Institutionalization of a stability culture.	3. Institutionalization of a common definition of price stability.	3. Institutionalization of prosperity and democratic cultures.
4. Commitment to the natural rate of unemployment model.	4. Reduction of the imperfect knowledge of the economy.	4. Arbitration of social conflicts.
5. Unique mandate for price stability.	5. Clear prioritization of the objectives of the hierarchical mandate: primacy to price stability.	5. No prioritization of the objectives of the dual mandate.
6. To solve the problem of asymmetric information between the central bank and the agents.	6. Understood as an attempt to build a common knowledge of the announced target as a nominal anchor.	6. Understood as an attempt to build a common understanding between the central bank and agents about the strategy and objectives.
7. Transparency as a solution to time inconsistency problem.	7. Solution to signal extraction and intentions inference problems; and to the credibility/flexibility dilemma.	7. Solution to the co-ordination problem.
8. Solution to the credibility problem.	8. Recommendation of the forward-looking aggregate supply curve.	8. Solution to the problem of the statute with the feet of clay.
Transparency analysis	*Transparency analysis*	*Openness analysis*
1. Connection of both central bank and agents on the natural 'true' definition of price stability.	1. De-connection between inflation expectations and measured inflation.	1. Acceptation and co-ordination of agents on central bank strategy, tactic and objectives.

(Continued)

Table 4.1   (Continued)

Credibility strategy	Confidence strategy	
	'Soft' confidence strategy. Inflation targeting regime:	**'Hard' confidence strategy. Confidence strategy:**
2. Pre-commitment technology to price stability as a unique mandate. 3. Enforcement mechanism of zero inflation. 4. Public disclosure of private information and of monetary control errors. 5. Revelation of the central bank's preferences and type.	2. Policy framework to pursue primarily price stability defined by the inflation target. 3. Enforcement mechanism of the. announced inflation target. 4. Communications strategy that gives the rationale for deviations from the inflation target. 5. Exposition of the short term tactic to return to the medium term strategy.	2. Deliberative process to construct a consensus. 3. Obligation to be consistent with the democratic mission. 4. Explanation of how the strategy is consistent with the mandate. 5. Discussion about the more prominent risk in the economy, and the implied policy priority.
Transparency policy 1. Optimal transparency: Full or maximum transparency. 2. Transparency as an independence enhancement and a substitute for accountability. 3. A yardstick for scrutinizing the credibility of the announcement. 4. An incentive compatible mechanism 5. Conformity to the 'true' model. 6. Permits monetary policy free lunch.	*Transparency policy* 1. Limits to transparency, optimal degree of transparency, equilibrium degree. 2. Transparency as a *qui pro quo* for independence. 3. As a benchmark for monitoring central bank performances. 4. As a focal point and a nominal anchor. 5. Predictability. 6. Reduces the sacrifice ratio, allows for more flexibility to respond to shocks.	*Openness policy* 1. Limits to openness: uncertainty, understanding and independence towards markets. 2. Openness as a way to be accountable. 3. As procedures to make monetary policy consistent with its legislative mandate. 4. As a focal point, a co-ordination standard, a consensus. 5. Clarity and understandable. 6. Discussing trade-offs in order to gain more flexibility to respond to shocks.

synthesis (i.e., rational expectations). It is no longer rule-based, but remains model-dependent within the New Keynesian or New Neo-Classical Synthesis. It holds that price stability must be the unique goal. Transparency then becomes a commitment to the new consensus. It is an 'old lady in new clothes'.

This position leads to an ambiguous case for transparency in monetary policy. IT promotes both ambiguity and transparency and is contradictory because its theoretical definition of the 'correct' action is only concerned with targeting inflation, while in practice the central banks action also focuses on growth or unemployment. It pretends there is unique mandate, while it has hierarchical or even a dual mandate. In IT, transparency is identified as *'say what you do, but don't do what you say'*.

The confidence strategy is based on the idea that there is no natural 'correct' action and it is open to discussion; that is why we talk about openness. Monetary policy becomes a 'deliberative process' (Ferguson, 2002, p. 4) that consists in an interactional learning process between the central bank and the agents. The general scheme of confidence is the 3C strategy: Communication-Common understanding-Confidence. Openness is not a goal, *per se*. It is aimed at enhancing action. The confidence paradigm places priority on action. Communication cannot be a substitute for action. To sum up, 'actions speak louder than words', but 'actions and words likely speak louder than actions alone' (Thornton, 2002, pp. 11–12).

Communication remains a crucial issue because the central bank cannot control inflation totally. 'Words' do matter after all. The central bank is not a high-powered institution (as in the credibility strategy), but a statue with feet of clay. It needs the support of the public to be effective. Communication is a difficult task because agents are assumed to be no longer characterized by rational expectations but are capable of making different interpretations. Openness is aimed at avoiding the misinterpretation of the central bank's signals. Communication does not reveal all the information because agents do not need to know everything; rather they need to understand. Furthermore, openness strives to build a common understanding between the central bank and the agents, and not common (perfect) knowledge.

Openness suits central banking practice better than transparency, which seems to be an inappropriate application. Central banks are not literally transparent because they cannot be. Full transparency could be counterproductive. The Fed is a prototype of this evolution of central banks towards more openness. Before, 'Fedspeak' corresponded to the enigmatic and esoteric art of the Fed. This 'mystique' culture of central banking disappears in the confidence paradigm. Nowadays, 'Fedspeak'

(Bernanke, 2004) means clear and extensive communication of the Fed's actions.

As a consequence, if there is a revolution in central banking thinking. It is not moving from secrecy to transparency, but rather from absent or cryptic explanations to clear and extensive explanations. It is a revolution from mystique to openness.

Notes

1   Quoted in *The Financial Times*, 5 October 1998.
2   'Behaviour is that in selecting interest rate (or other instrument) settings month by month, the central bank is systematic in its responses to prevailing conditions and also forward-looking enough to abstain from attempts to exploit existing inflationary expectations' (McCallum, 1996, p. 107)
3   Ricoeur (1985, p. 37)
4   It is related the communicational theory of Habermas (1987).

References

Aglietta, M. (2005) *Macroéconomie Financière* (Paris: La Découverte).

Archer, D. (2005) 'Central Bank Communication and the Publication of Interest Rate Projections', mimeo.

Backus, D. and Driffill, J. (1985) 'Inflation and Reputation', *American Economic Review*, 75(3), 530–8.

Barro, R. and Gordon, D. (1983) 'Rules, Discretion and Reputation in a Model of Monetary Policy', *Journal of Monetary Economics*, 12, 101–21.

Bell, M. (2005) 'Communicating Monetary Policy', Speech, 17 May.

Bernanke, B. (2004) 'Fedspeak', *Remarks*, San Diego, 3 January.

Bernanke, B., Laubach, T., Mishkin, F., and Posen, A. (1999) *Inflation Targeting: Lessons from the International Experience* (Princeton: Princeton University Press).

Blanchard, O. (2003) 'Comments on "Inflation Targeting in Transition Economies; Experience and Prospects" by J. Jonas and F. Mishkin', mimeo, April.

Blinder, A. (1999) *Central Banking in Theory and Practice* (Cambridge, MA: MIT Press).

Blinder, A. (2000) 'Central Bank Credibility: Why Do We Care? How Do We Build It?', *American Economic Review*, 90(5), 1421–31.

Blinder, A., Goodhart, C., Hildebrandt, P., Lipton, D. and Wyplosz, C. (2001) 'How Do Central Banks Talk?', *Geneva Reports on the World Economy*, no.3, (London: Centre for Economic Policy Research).

Buiter, W. (1999) 'Alice in Euroland', *Journal of Common Market Studies*, 37(2), 181–210.

Carré, E. (2005) 'Central Bank Communication', Paper presented at the 9th Workshop 'Macroeconomics and Macroeconomic Policies – Alternatives to the Orthodoxy', Berlin, 28–29 October.

Carré, E. and Le Heron, E. (2004) 'Credibility, Confidence and Inflation', in M. Mantey and N. Levy (eds), *Crédito y Salarios: Nuevos Enfoques de Politica Monetaria para Mercados Imperfectos* (Mexico: UNAM Publications), 191–223.

Carré, E. and Le Heron, E. (2006) 'Credibility Versus Confidence in Monetary Policy', in Forstater, M. and R. Wray (eds), *Money, Financial Instability and Stabilisation Policy* (Aldershot: Edward Elgar).

Carré, E. and Le Heron, E. (2006) 'The Monetary Policy of the ECB and the Fed: Credibility versus Confidence, a Comparative Approach', in P. Arestis, J. Ferreiro and F. Serrano (eds), *Financial Developments in National and International Markets* (Basingstoke: Palgrave Macmillan), 77–102.

Faust, J. and Henderson, D. (2004) 'Is Inflation Targeting Best-Practised Monetary Policy?', 28th annual economic policy conference 'Inflation Targeting: Prospects and Problems', FRB of St Louis, 16 October.

Faust, J. and Svensson, L. (2000a) 'Transparency and Credibility: Monetary Policy with Unobservable Goals', *International Economic Review*, 42(2), 369–97.

Faust, J. and Svensson, L. (2000b) 'The Equilibrium Degree of Transparency and Control in Monetary Policy', mimeo, December.

Ferguson, R. (2001), 'Transparency in Central Banking: Rationale and Recent Developments', Remarks, 9 September.

Ferguson, R. (2002) 'Why Central Banks should Talk', Remarks, 8 January.

Friedman, B.M. (2004) 'Why the Federal Reserve should not Adopt Inflation Targeting', mimeo, January.

Friedman, M. (1990), quoted in Fischer, S. (1990), 'Rules Versus Discretion in Monetary Policy', in B. Friedman and Hahn, F. (eds), *Handbook of Monetary Economics* (Amsterdam: North Holland/Elsevier).

Friedman, M. (2004) Interview in *The International Economy*, Winter.

Geraats, P. (2002a) 'Central Bank Transparency', mimeo, March.

Geraats, P. (2002b) 'Transparency of Monetary Policy: Does the Institutional Framework Matter?', mimeo, July.

Geraats, P. (2005) 'The Mystique of Central Bank Speak', mimeo, April.

Goodfriend, M. (1986) 'Monetary Mystique: Secrecy and Central Banking', *Journal of Monetary Economics*, 17(1), 63–92.

Greenspan, A. (1996) 'The Challenge of Central Banking in a Democratic Society', Remarks, 5 December.

Greenspan, A. (2001) 'Transparency in Monetary Policy', Remarks, 11 October.

Habermas, J. (1987) *Théorie de l'Agir Communicationnel*, vol.2 (Paris: Fayard).

Issing, O. (1999) 'The Eurosystem: Transparent and Accountable or Willem in Euroland', *Journal of Common Market Studies*, 37(3), 503–20.

Kohn, D. and Sack, P. (2003) 'Central Bank Talk: Does it Matter and Why?', mimeo, May 23.

Kydland, F. and Prescott, E. (1977) 'Rules rather than Discretion: The Inconsistency of Optimal Plans', *Journal of Political Economy*, 85(3), 473–91.

McCallum, B. (1995) 'Two Fallacies Concerning Central Bank Independence', *American Economic Review*, 85(2), 207–11.

McCallum, B. (1996), 'Commentary', Jackson Hole conference 'Achieving Price Stability', 105–14.

McCallum, B. (1997), 'Critical Issues Concerning Central Bank Independence', *Journal of Monetary Economics*, 39(1), 99–112.

Metha, J., Starmer, C. and Sugden, R. (1994) 'The Nature of Salience: An Experimental Investigation of Pure Co-ordination Games', *American Economic Review*, 84(2), 658–73.

Meyer, L. (2000) 'The Politics of Monetary Policy: Balancing Independence and Accountability', Remarks, October 24.

Mishkin, F. (2000) 'From Monetary Targeting to Inflation Targeting: Lessons from the Industrialised Countries', mimeo, January.

Mishkin, F. (2004) 'Can Central Bank Transparency Go Too Far?', Reserve Bank of Australia, August.

Morris, S. and Shin, H. (2002) 'Social Value of Public Information', *American Economic Review*, 92(5), 1521–34.

Posen, A. (2002) 'Commentary', *FRB St Louis Review*, 84(4), 119–26.

Ricoeur, P. (1985) *Philosophie et Sociologie. Histoire d'une Rencontre* (Centre des Mouvements Sociaux, Paris: EHESS).

Rogoff, K. (1985) 'The Optimal Degree of Commitment to an Intermediate Monetary Target', *Quarterly Journal of Economics*, 100(4), 1169–90.

Svensson, L. (1997) 'Optimal Inflation Targets, Conservative Central Banks and Linear Inflation Contracts', *American Economic Review*, 87(1), 98–114.

Taylor, J.B. (1996) 'How Should Monetary Policy Respond to Shocks While Maintaining Long-Run Price Stability – Conceptual Issues', in Jackson Hole Symposium, FRB Kansas City, 181–95.

Thornton, D. (2002) 'Monetary Policy Transparency: Transparent About What?', Bank of England, May.

Van Der Cruijsen, C. and Demertzis, M. (2005) 'The Impact of Central Bank Transparency on Inflation Expectations', *DNB Working Paper*, no. 31.

Vickers, J. (1998) 'Inflation Targeting in Practice: the UK Experience', *Bank of England Quarterly Review*, 38(4), 368–75.

Walsh, C. (1995) 'Optimal Contracts for Central Bankers', *American Economic Review*, 85(1), 150–67.

Walsh, C. (2002), 'Accountability, Transparency and Inflation Targeting', mimeo, March.

Winkler, B. (2002) 'Which Kind of Transparency? On the Need for Effective Communication in Monetary Policy-Making', mimeo.

Woodford, M. (2004) 'Inflation Targeting and Policy Rule', 28th annual economic policy conference 'Inflation Targeting: Prospects and Problems', FRB of St Louis, 16 October.

5
The Dynamic Analysis of Monetary Policy Shock on Banking Behaviour

Edwin Le Heron[*]

Introduction

In Keynes's *General Theory*, the 'monetary authorities' are considered to act as a deus ex machina: they should resolve all the problems regarding the creation and control of money. The banking system and financial institutions are analysed solely in terms of central bank activities.[1] The supply of money is fixed exogenously by the central bank. An endogenous theory of the demand for money co-exists with an endogenous theory of the interest rate (liquidity preference).[2]

Most Post Keynesians prefer to think of an endogenous money supply, determined by the demand for funds in the banking sector. They then use an exogenous theory of the interest rate: a short-term rate fixed by the monetary policy of the central bank. This 'horizontalist'[3] approach was developed by Moore (1979) and Kaldor (1985). 'Horizontalism' views banks as intermediaries between the central bank, which fixes the price of money, and borrowers, who adjust their demand according to industrial, commercial and financial needs. However, in this case there is no place for Keynes's theory of liquidity preference and for his 'finance motive' (Keynes, 1937).

For other Post Keynesians (Kregel, 1984; Le Heron, 1984, 1986, 2002; Wray, 1989, 1992), private banks can impose a monetary constraint independently of the central bank, in that they are producers of money within a framework of fundamental (non-probabilistic) uncertainty. By their own anticipation of effective demand, commercial banks can influence growth and employment. While the money supply cannot be higher

[*] I would like to thank Roy Rotheim and John McCombie for helping me with the translation.

than the demand for it, it can be lower and thus restrain demand. Under the influence of the central bank and the effective demand of entrepreneurs, the money supply and the interest rate are endogenous; they are largely determined by banking behaviour. These considerations require that the liquidity preference of banks should be integrated[4] into the Post Keynesian framework.

In my previous work, I have tried to make Keynes's approach (endogenous money and theory of liquidity preference) compatible with an endogenous theory of the money supply. For that purpose, the principle of liquidity preference is generalized to encompass a competitive banking framework. It is important to understand the reason for monetary rationing: that is to say, a 'desired scarcity' of finance.[5] The behaviour of private banks determines the supply of money and, to a certain extent, the long-term interest rate. This application of liquidity preference to commercial banks allows us to preserve the main part of the Post Keynesian theory of money: namely, that the demand for money is endogenous[6] and the short-term interest rate is exogenously determined.

From an examination of the theory of bank liquidity preference, the following phenomena become apparent:

1   There can be an insufficient supply of money: that is to say, a supply that is lower than that which is demanded by firms. Banks can worsen unemployment by rationing the financing of demand and, hence, by slowing down growth.
2   Endogenous long-term interest rates are determined not only by monetary policy (by exogenous short-term interest rates and anticipated inflation), but also by the behaviour of private banks in periods of uncertainty, so the liquidity preference of banks influences long-term interest rates.
3   In a global economy with strong financial markets, well-structured accounting practices of banks often become essential.
4   Banking and financial instability often explain economic cycles and their crises (Minsky, 1975).

The purpose of this chapter is to analyse the consequences of a monetary policy shock on the behaviour of banks and so on the level of money supply.

The channels of transmission of monetary policy originate in changes in the short-term interest rate. Usually, the focus is on the links between monetary policy and firms or households. Banks are considered merely as the 'drive belt' of these fluctuations in interest rates and are assumed to have a neutral effect on the process.

Nevertheless, banks, which may be regarded as entrepreneurs in the money production process, are also subjected to monetary shocks. Their reactions modify the quantity and the structure of financing, as well as having a significant effect on the determination of long-term interest rates. Banking behaviour can amplify a recession or affect the growth of the economy. A monetary policy shock can also induce solvency and liquidity crises in the banking system and these crises can spread throughout the whole economy. On the one hand, there is uncertainty; yet, on the other hand, the financial structures of banks play a prominent part in our understanding of the consequences of a particular monetary policy.

In an attempt to understand how banking behaviour can lead to the deterioration in the global economic situation, this chapter tries to clarify the dynamic process between monetary policy and the banks. Even if, as in the Post Keynesian approach, the anticipations of entrepreneurs remain the most fundamental element in the economic process, the generalization of liquidity preference to include that of the banks – and so the effect of their anticipations – can provide a further explanation of the causes of involuntary unemployment. Monetary policies, then, can be a release mechanism for the difficulties faced by banks in light of monetary shocks. With fundamental uncertainty, the 'artless optimism' of standard Keynesian policies becomes untenable.

First, we generalize liquidity preference to include the commercial banks in order to determine their role in the financing of the economy. Second, we examine the transmission channels of a contractionary monetary policy on banking behaviour to understand the dynamic process that occurs between the monetary policy of the central bank and the reactions of the commercial banks.

Liquidity preference generalized to private banks

All production must be financed. However, current production is financed by the working capital of entrepreneurs (from retained earnings) and by funds contracted from the banks and rolled over at the current rate of interest. These two factors constitute a shock absorber to possible monetary rationing by banks. These credits and short-term securities 'disappear' within the period of production. We therefore do not need to take them into account in analysing banking behaviour, unless, of course, banks choose either to cut off the funds or renegotiate the terms on which they are loaned.

Furthermore, for simplicity's sake, we consider that households have a constant liquidity preference. We are essentially limiting our study to the effects that monetary policy might have on new financing for investment, growth of production, and financial strategies of entrepreneurs.[7]

Let us proceed to examine the supply of finance by banks (O_F), that is to say, the new flow of money, as opposed to the existing stock of money, Mo. Also, there is a stock of money demand, M_D, equal to the transaction, precautionary and speculative motives, whereas the finance demand for money (D_F) represents the new flow of finance required by firms and the government (the finance motive). Assuming a closed economy, this flow demand for money can be satisfied by banks, either by the stock markets or by credit. At the end of the period, net financing demand, D_F, can be constrained by the net money supply from the banks, O_F (new finance less the loans paid off). O_F determines the amount of monetary creation in the period.

Bank liquidity preference operates on three levels:

1 The first level is at the microeconomic level of the commercial banks.
2 The second level is at the macroeconomic level of banks and includes the relation between the banks and the central bank.
3 The third level is at the level of the central banks [8] in open economies.

The liquidity preference of private banks tries to reduce both risks of microeconomic crisis: that is, a banking liquidity crisis (BLC) and a solvency crisis (SC).

We should not, however, confuse a banking liquidity crisis and a market liquidity crisis, which is a macroeconomic crisis. A market liquidity crisis (MLC) occurs when market makers are no longer prepared to buy securities. Security prices fall, depriving capital assets of liquidity. As Davidson (1972) summarizes so well, liquidity is defined as the ability to invert a decision at any time and at the lowest possible cost. Moreover, the ability to liquidate financial assets without serious capital losses is also reduced. The increase of market assets in bank balance sheets makes the banking system more exposed to this crisis. Unlike a BLC, an MLC involves banks only indirectly.

A banking liquidity crisis occurs when there is a mismatch between banks' liquid monetary liabilities (i.e., demand deposits) and their illiquid assets. Any massive liquidation of deposits may lead to bankruptcy of a bank through a shortage of high-powered money. This potential for bankruptcy may occur either because assets are not 'mobilized' quickly enough, or because this mobilization of assets comes at a very high cost and does not generate the necessary reserves to offset the withdrawals. This problem is referred to as the so-called 'banking transformation'.

Finally, a solvency crisis occurs when there is insufficient profitability of banks. An imbalance of assets and liabilities can lead to bankruptcy.

Naturally, there may be significant interactions between these three kinds of crises. Liquidity crises can induce a solvency crisis if the necessary mobilization of assets is made at the wrong time, and involves a loss of capital value and increased transaction costs. This means that bank profitability cannot be guaranteed. Added to this, management errors that lower bank profitability can provoke fear and a flight to higher quality institutions by account holders, triggering a further liquidity crisis. As such, it is clear that the impact of a monetary policy shock on asset prices can be significant, provoking a severe market liquidity crisis. Consequently, the fall in asset values can produce a solvency crisis in the banking sector. The loss of confidence and the consideration of the liquidity preference on the part of banks can contribute to an explanation of a subsequent crisis in the production sector.

First level: banking microeconomics

What, then, are the links between a liquidity crisis and a solvency crisis? By protecting itself against the risk of lack of liquidity, we will see that the liquidity preference of banks leads them to increase their solvency risk. Here, a reduction of solvency risk is ensured by a reduction of their high-risk long-term financing, which has detrimental effects on the financing of the economy.

Lender's risk and financial choices

In deciding whether or not to make a loan, banks examine firms' production and financial expectations and also their financial structure. This investigation is made according to their confidence in the state of long-term expectations of yields on capital assets, influencing what Keynes referred to as 'animal spirits' (Keynes, 1973, p. 162).

Banks know that there is a lender's risk (*lr*), when they underwrite finance[9] and create money. It includes three fundamental risks: default risk, liquidity risk, and market risk. To avoid liquidity and solvency crises, banks want to manage their uncertainty by choosing the kind of financing according to an arbitrage between yield and risk. They look for the method that will give them the easiest possibility of reversing their decisions at the smallest cost, and this imposes a particular balance sheet structure on the banks. The liquidity preference theory is generalized to the banks as follows.

First, the risk of default (r_d) corresponds to the bank's perception regarding the borrower's likelihood of failure to repay the claim. It concerns the bank assets and can involve a crisis of solvency. To limit the possibility of default risk, banks can require that borrowers provide the following: a maximum ratio of debt to capital stock; a quick return on investment; and/or collateral to limit the possibility of moral hazard. If banks' animal spirits about the prospective yields on capital assets of borrowers are unfavourable, they are more likely to favour low-risk borrowers and short-term financing. They will prefer short-term credit and short-term securities (*STS*) to long-term loans (*L*), bonds (*O*), and equities (*E*). (*STS* are the Treasury bills, *B*, issued by the government and the commercial paper, *CP*, issued by firms.)

Next there is the risk of liquidity (r_l). Liquidity entails the ability to reverse a decision at any moment at the smallest possible cost. It is dangerous to confuse 'reversibility' (the capacity to invert a decision at any moment) and 'liquidity' (at the smallest cost). Often, a misunderstanding about the nature of liquidity in financial markets comes from a confusion of these two variables. Liquidity risk corresponds not only to the irreversibility of some decisions, but also to the occasional high cost of the reversibility (the depreciation of stocks and the high costs of transaction). This risk is the foundation of liquidity crises and, to reduce it, banks make their liabilities less liquid (by the issue of securities and also by developing the illiquid saving) and their assets more liquid. To avoid a BLC, market assets assume greater importance in the structure of bank balance sheets. This may be summarized as follows:

Assets:	[Bonds (*O*), short-term securities (*STS*), Treasury bills (*B*), commercial paper (*CP*) > Short-term credit > Equities (*E*) > Long-term loan (*L*)]
Liabilities:	[Banks securities > Non-current liabilities > Money (*Mo*)]

Finally, the market risk (r_m) corresponds to unanticipated changes in the various financial markets (the stock exchange, money market, and foreign exchange market). Market risk can be split into other risks, which are described below.

Fluctuations in capital asset prices modify their value and explain capital risk (r_K), which is very high for market assets, in particular, equities and fixed-yield bonds. For the fixed-yield bonds (*OF*), capital risk, r_K, is inversely proportional to interest rates. We should make a distinction between market assets, for which financial news is sought by the issuer, and loans, for which the information should be looked for by the lender. For banks, loans correspond to a specific activity (in Williamson's sense). Information collected by banks brings an added value to these claims.

From then on, loans provide a good yield and stability of their valuation on the assets side. Banks prefer loans and bonds at variable rates (*OV*) to *OF* and equities.

Uncertainty also concerns the yield of capital assets. Risk of income (r_y) mainly concerns the highly uncertain dividends of shares and the variable rates bonds and loans, which combine to give the risk rate. Equities carry a particularly high risk of income loss and banks thus require high premiums from firms, and will only provider finance when high profits are projected. As for bonds (*OV*) and loans at variable rates, the income risk is low as, on the one hand, they are on both the assets and liabilities sides of the balance sheet and, on the other hand, banks are able to manage it.

Monetary policy involves a money market risk (r_{MP}) when fluctuations in the money interest rates (i_{cb}) occur. The cost of changes in high-powered money (HPM) changes on the asset side. Liability costs change also, because yields are linked sometimes to the short-term interest rate. Market risks thereby involve both solvency and liquidity crises.

Lender's risk (*lr*) is the sum of these three risks: namely, $lr = r_d + r_l + r_m$ (with $r_m = r_k + r_y + r_{MP}$).

By examining the various risks, we can establish a hierarchy of financing as well as the following management of assets and liabilities. In the case of liquidity risks, it is better to develop bonds and STS on the assets side, and certificates of deposits (*CD*), securities and stable saving (*SS*) on the liabilities side. However the opposite is true with regard to the solvency risk. So the choice of a financial-market economy, rather than an overdraft economy, can seem effective in avoiding liquidity crises, yet may at the same time create a more serious solvency risk. A financial-market economy increases asset valuation volatility and raises liability costs, since banks and firms compete to get household savings. Here, a solvency crisis could easily involve a liquidity crisis (even if a guarantee of deposits limits this danger). As such, the preference for short-term financing, which works against both kinds of crisis, is one expression of a strong liquidity preference of banks.

Banking behaviour and balance sheet structure

The natural global constraint is that the yield on assets exceeds the costs of the liabilities. The asset side generates income from long-term interest rates (i_{LT}), while the liability side reflects the costs of short-term interest rates (i_{ST}). So, when the yield curve of the various interest rates takes its normal shape,[10] the spread ($i_{LT} - i_{ST} > 0$) should determine the mark-up of banks. Banks buy equities only with a very expected high-risk premium ($i_E^a - i_L > 0$). Given that loans are some specific assets of banks, there is a standard yield curve and the market risks are perceived to be higher globally than the risk of liquidity. In this instance, the hierarchy of the yields should be as follows:

$$i_{Assets} > i_{Liabilities}$$

Assets: $i_E > i_{OF} > i_{OV} > i_L > i_{CB}$ Liabilities: $i_{SS} > i_{CD} > i_{Mo} = i_{CB}$

The supply of bank financing depends on non-financial agents' demands (both are flows). On the other hand, the distribution of financing flows between securities and loans should take into account the desired structure of the balance sheet, and therefore the stocks. Liquidity preference of banks (LP_B) involves a portfolio arbitrage considered to be optimal between loans, securities and long-term saving to avoid liquidity and solvency crises while allowing the highest possible banking net profits.

Banks try to maximize their net income. To make a profit, they finance the economy and agree to become less liquid. By making the almost irreversible decisions of financing, they are subject to lender's risk and so to solvency and liquidity crises. They can hope for large profits only by lowering their LP_B. We need to take into account the risk from monetary policy.[11]

Economic activity also depends on the animal spirits of banks. The scarcity of finance can only be the consequence of a deliberate choice. 'Desired scarcity' of financing is the sign of banks' liquidity preference. From an optimal structure of their balance sheet (Table 5.1),[12] the banks' net income obtained by monetary financing will be the following:

$$P_B = i_{b-1} \cdot B_{-1} + i_{CP-1} \cdot CP_{-1} + i_{OF-1} \cdot OF_{-1} + i_{OV-1} \cdot OV_{-1}$$
$$+ i_{L-1} \cdot L_{-1} + P_{de} - i_{Mo-1} \cdot Mo_{-1} - i_{CB-1} \cdot REF_{-1}$$

where the associated risks are:

$$
\begin{array}{ll}
i_{b-1} \cdot B_{-1} & (r_d + r_M) \\
i_{CP-1} \cdot CP_{-1} & (r_d + r_M) \\
i_{OF-1} \cdot OF_{-1} & (r_d + r_Y + r_M) \\
i_{OV-1} \cdot OV_{-1} & (r_d + r_Y + r_M) \\
i_{L-1} \cdot L_{-1} & (r_d + r_l) \\
P_{de} & (r_d + r_l + r_m + r_M) \\
i_{Mo-1} \cdot Mo_{-1} & (r_l + r_{MP}) \\
i_{CB-1} \cdot REF_{-1} & (r_{MP})
\end{array}
$$

Table 5.1   Simplified structure of banks' balance sheet

Assets	Yield	Risk	Liabilities	Yield	Risk
Long-term credit (L)	i_L	$r_d + r_l$	Money (Mo)	i_{Mo}	$r_l + r_{MP}$
Medium-term credit (L_{MT})	i_{LMT}	$r_d + r_l$			
Short-term credit (L_{ST})	i_{LST}	r_d			
Equities (E)	$i_E\ (P_{de})$	$r_d + r_l + r_m + r_{MP}$	Certificates of deposits and banking securities (market rates)	i_{CB}	r_{MP}
Bonds (OV, OF)	i_{OF}, i_{OV}	$r_d + r_m + r_{MP}$			
STS (B, CP)	i_B, i_{CP}	$r_d + r_{MP}$			
High powered money (HPM)	i_{CB}	r_{MP}	Illiquid liabilities or stable saving (administered rates)	i_{SS}	r_{MP}

Second level: monetary policy and banking macroeconomics

Banking interest rate

Monetary authorities determine rates on the money markets (exogenous rate, i_{CB}[13]). In 1936, Keynes asserted that this rate is usually determined by convention.[14] While central banks fix the short-term rates, private banks' liquidity preference determines the banking base rate (i_l) (the short-term, medium-term and long-term interest rates). The long-term interest rates (i_L) are of especial significance for growth and financing (credit). The link between short-term and long-term interest rates is complex. The macroeconomic banking interest rates (i_l) are the production costs of money of the commercial banks plus a risk premium. The first element corresponds to functioning costs (wages, investment, fixed assets); payment costs for monetary liabilities (subjected to the firms' competition for households savings) and the cost of high-powered money determined by the central bank (i_{CB}); to a margin χ corresponding to the standard profits of banks. The production costs of money are equal to i_{CB} plus a relatively constant mark-up (χ).

Risk premiums are not constant because they are a function of the banks' liquidity preference. It covers lender's risk (lr). Five types of expectations strongly influence risk premiums:

(a) anticipations about productivity growth, economic evolution (growth, employment) and the budget: we can summarize these by the expected national product (Y^a);

(b) expected inflation (π^a);

(c) the level of future short-term rates of interest ('theory of anticipation'[15]) (i_{CB}^a);

(d) financial markets' evolution and capital assets' prices (p_e^a);

(e) foreign long-term rates (present i_{fLT} and future i_{fLT}^a).

Long-term interest rates are given by:

$$i_L = i_{CB} + lr + \chi$$
$$\text{with } lr = H^o(Y^a, \pi^a, i_{CB}^a, p_e^a, i_{fLT}, i_{fLT}^a)$$

The values of i_{CB} and χ are sufficient to explain the short-term interest rates (i_B or i_{CP}). Lender's risk (lr) is the primary variable that explains long-term interest rates (i_L, i_{OF}, i_{OV}). lr can be negative and reduces the mark-up, χ. Once determined, these rates will be applied to all credit, after an allowance for microeconomic risk[16] resulting from the credit-worthiness of borrowers has been incorporated into these current rates. This marginal lender's risk corresponds to all classes of risk. Rating agencies give a valuation of these. Banks can demand a greater degree of collateral rather than increasing the interest rate. Thus long-term interest rates include the average lender's risk and not the marginal lender's risk. (This is shown by the dotted line in Figure 5.1. The marginal lender's risk explains the banks' decision, not the price i_L.) At a certain level of risk, the banks will reduce the amount they are willing to finance, limiting this first through pricing (via increasing the lending rates, i_L, or a greater

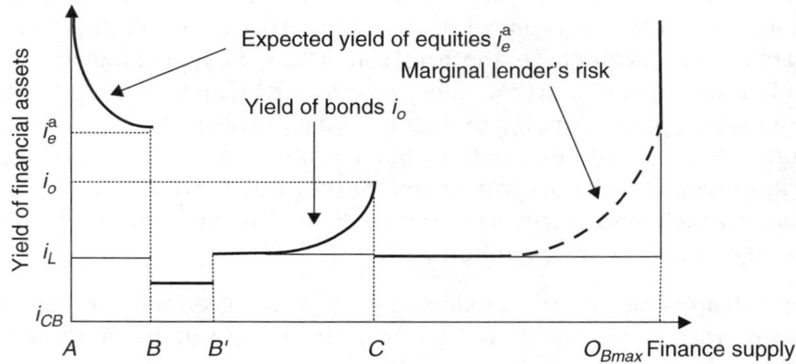

Figure 5.1   Banking finance supply

degree of collateral) and then by quantity rationing (with a maximum level of financing given by O_{Bmax}).

The supply of finance is first horizontal, then ascending and finally becomes vertical when the marginal lender's risk becomes too high. Of course, the supply of money is predetermined by the demand for money. There is not a money market with two independent curves (supply and demand). The supply of money cannot be higher than the demand for money.

Figure 5.1 considers the various types of the supply of finance. Commercial banks can finance firms by buying equities (AB), bonds ($B'C$) or by granting loans (CO_{Bmax}). (BB') represents the amount of government bonds bought by the banks. Financing by equities, bonds and loans is simultaneous; there is not a single hierarchy. The higher risk premium is on the equities. Thus the expected yield on equities (i_e^a) must be higher than the interest rate of bonds (i_o) and loans (i_L). Loans and bonds as a source of finance may seem very close; yet, since bonds and short-term securities are market assets, they are not bound by just one rate but integrate a risk premium into the yield. The rating agencies play an important part in the assessment of the financial risks; a bank can refuse a loan but agree to finance the same firm by a purchase of bonds. The higher the lender's risk, the more banks prefer a bond (which are often better paid and more liquid) to a loan. From government bonds (i_{cb}) to 'junk bonds', the range of interest rates can be very wide. The curve increases up to the level where the marginal risk seems too high in regards to the yield. Banks only finance projects they consider profitable, but confidence in their judgement is variable and can justify various strategies.

The curve of banking financing

In Figure 5.1, the thick line represents the curve of banking financing. Government bonds are considered to have no possibility of default and no liquidity risk ($r_d = 0$, $r_l = 0$). Banks will give limitless credit to government at the current rate, i_{CB}. We have to add the amount of government securities, B, bought by banks (BB') to that bought from firms (namely, B'C) to obtain banking finance by bonds, commercial papers and Treasury bills:

$$BC = BB' + B'C$$

Firms' financing is fundamental in a monetary economy of production. Firms begin by being self-financed then turn to external finance (equities, bonds and loans). Equities and bonds correspond to a securities supply

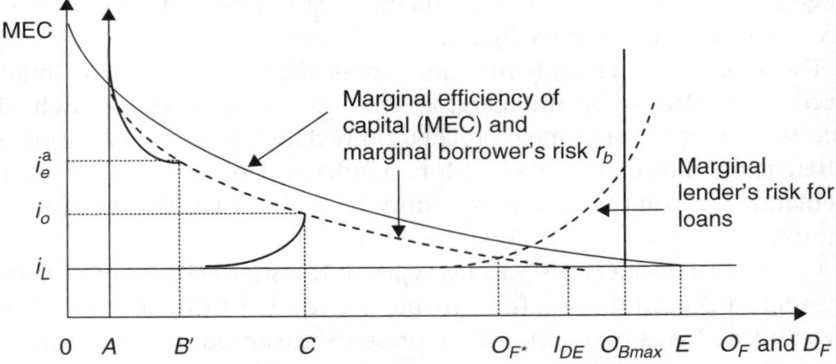

Figure 5.2   Finance of firms by commercial banks

by firms. Banks may agree to buy them on the financial market according to their criteria of yield, risk and structure of balance. Banks finance the amount (AB) and $(B'C)$ in Figure 5.1 because firms' financial risk is already incorporated, whereas financing by loan may be the object of much deliberation. Banks estimate the level of effective demand, as do firms. After the study of the expected production, the anticipated return on capital and the marginal lender's risk, bankers will refuse to finance more than the amount (CO_{Bmax}). Of course, this maximum O_{Bmax} only makes sense given the total demand of firms (Figure 5.2).

However, we should also integrate the firm's borrowing risk. Firms begin by being self-financed (OA) then turn to external finance (i.e., from the banks). The marginal borrower's risk (dotted line) begins with the external finance and reduces the marginal efficiency of capital that is measured without the financial risk.

Figure 5.2 extends Figure 5.1 to incorporate the demand for finance by firms as well as the supply finance of firms by the commercial banks. The various components of the supply of finance are given by:

OA	$=$	Self-financing of firms. Borrower's risk begins after OA
AO_{F^*}	$=$	Firms' financing by banks (creation of money)
AB'	$=$	Banking finance by purchase of equities E
$B'C$	$=$	Banking finance by purchase of bonds O and commercial papers CP
AC	$=$	Banking finance on financial markets: $E + O + CP$
CO_{F^*}	$=$	Banking finance by loans L

00_{F*}	$= I =$	Total finance (internal and external finance) of firms taking into account the financial risks of the firms and the banks
I	$=$	Effective investment
$0I_{DE}$	$=$	Total firms' demand of finance taking into account financial risks
I_{DE}	$=$	Desired investment
AO_{Bmax}	$=$	Maximal banks' supply of finance with marginal lender's risk
$0E$	$=$	Level of the 'standard' investment theory. Without financial risks, the marginal efficiency of capital is equal to the interest rate: $MEC = i_{CB}$
$O_{F*}I_{DE}$	$= I\text{-}I_{DE} =$	Finance constraint by commercial banks

Effective loan supplies are made when marginal borrower's risk is equal to the finance supply of banks. If the marginal borrower's risk cuts the supply in the horizontal part, the financial constraint comes only from firms (the 'horizontalist' case: I_{DE}). If it cuts the supply in its increasing (marginal lender's risk higher than average lender's risk) or vertical part, the financial constraint comes also from the banks (O_{F*}).

A finance constraint issued from banks is shown in Figure 5.2 where $O_{F*} < I_{DE}$: that is to say, the total financing of firms taking into account firms' and the banks' financial risks is less than the total financing of firms taking into account of only firms' financial risk. All the demand for finance of the firms is not satisfied by the commercial banks at the normal conditions, i_L. Banks impose harsher conditions (e.g., more collateral, a shorter loan term, a risk premium). However, a dynamic analysis is now a necessity, as the banking sector acts on the basis of a given convention. Change in banks' liquidity preference and therefore in lender's risk could originate from two factors (from within and outside the banking sector):

(a) a change in the banks' prevailing convention (e.g., banks' revised expectations of firms' performance and of the economic situation);
(b) an exogenous reason, such as a monetary policy shock.

The state of confidence of banks summarizes these factors.

Dynamic analysis of monetary policy shock on banking behaviour

We often give too much importance to the central bank, and yet it cannot directly prevent monetary creation, while private banks are able to impose rationing on effective demand financing. The central bank directly influences competitive banks and indirectly influences the economy by fixing interest rates in the money market (i_{CB}). A 'shock of monetary policy' is understood as 'a change of intervention rates':[17] it modifies the demand for money, the production costs of money and the expectations of inflation. Money is credit-driven and demand-determined. Central banks influence the state of confidence of entrepreneurs, households and banks. Channels of monetary policy transmission become complicated and uncertain. This uncertainty about the transmission mechanism makes the monetary authorities very cautious in their interest rate changes (Goodhart, 1989). The channels of transmission to banks proceed directly through: interest rates i_{CB} and i_L; assets price p_e; the exchange rate;[18] the structure and value of the banks' balance sheets; their off-balance sheet commitments and their expected inflation (π^a). In particular the banks analyse the effect on non-financial agents.

We examine the consequences of a monetary policy shock on banking behaviour and try to understand the dynamic process. We analyse an increase in the interest rate.

Thus, monetary policy has an effect on economies[19] through the demand for money, the expectations of all economic agents and the banks' behaviour (money supply). The impact on the demand for money through the money channel, the assets price channel and the balance sheet channel (of firms, households and government) is very well known, so we analyse only the consequences on banks' behaviour.[20]

The monetary authorities need to make decisions in a situation of uncertainty about the demand for money, about the link between the short-term and long-term interest rates, about the risk and the type of liquidity crises,[21] and about the channels of monetary policy transmission.

A monetary policy shock modifies the valuation of assets, liabilities costs and lender's risk: that is to say, the banks' liquidity preference (LP_B). Solvency, banking-liquidity and market-liquidity crises could occur and afterwards, the monetary policy shock (a rise in i_{CB}) could correspond with a rise of banks' liquidity preference. Interest rate policy has three kinds of consequence:

(a) the modification of bank profitability, analysed as a flow effect;
(b) the modification of capital assets' valuation (size and structure of banks' balance sheet may change, and this would be analysed as a stock effect);
(c) the possible release of off-balance sheet commitments.

Bank profitability

Bank profitability may deteriorate with an increase in the short-term interest rate. First, high-powered money is more expensive. Second, liability costs are determined mainly by short-term interest rates and the spread between short-term and long-term interest rates could diminish. The structure of the bank balance sheet (the ratio between fixed and variable rates, loans and equities) is important. Third, the maturity of assets and liabilities partly explains risk sensitivity.

The first impact is on high-powered money costs. When i_{CB} rises, banks pay more to satisfy their needs for high-powered money (M_{HP}). Zero-reserve requirements policies, such as in Canada, could strengthen the banks' dependency on the central bank. Banks must include these costs in i_L to stabilize their profitability and i_L also rises.

Interest rates on the liabilities side are determined mainly by money markets, either directly or through administered rates, and thus liability costs are strongly connected to i_{CB}. There are two features that explain a lower bank profitability. The first one is the ratio of variable rate of liabilities to assets (R_{IND}); banks acknowledge a monetary policy risk r_{MP} when this ratio is unbalanced.

R_{IND} = Percentage of indexing on liabilities (liabilities with variable
   interest rate divided by total of liabilities) / Percentage of
   indexing on assets (assets with variable interest rate divided
   by total of assets)

R_{IND} = (Mo + CD/Mo + CD + SS)/
   (B + CP + OV + LV + M_{HP}/B + CP + O + L + $e.p_e$ + M_{HP})

If $R_{IND} < 1$, banks' profitability deteriorates when the money market rate falls. This is the French case with 25 per cent on the assets side and 17 per cent on the liabilities side. If $R_{IND} > 1$, banks' profitability deteriorates when there is an increase in the rate. This is shown schematically in equation (5.1):

$$i_{CB}\uparrow \Rightarrow \text{If } R_{IND} > 1 \Rightarrow \Delta \text{ [Liabilities' cost]} > \Delta \text{ [Assets' yield]}$$
$$\Rightarrow \text{Banks' profitability} \downarrow \tag{5.1}$$

The second one is that the liquidity of the liabilities side, in comparison with that of assets, can also involve a monetary policy risk, r_{MP}. Long-term commitments are always higher on assets than on liabilities, as liability costs are connected to short-term interest rates (i_{CB} and i_{LST}) and assets to long-term rates i_L. The spread ($i_{LLT} - i_{LST}$) partly justifies banks' income. An increase in i_{CB} will cause the banks' profitability to deteriorate in the short term, because i_{CB} increases faster than i_{LLT}. An inverse curve of interest rates ($i_{LLT} < i_{LST}$) is bad news for the banks' mark-up. The link between the short-term and long-term rates explains the impact of monetary policy shock on banks' profitability. Therefore, the lender's risk premium (lr) is fundamental. The banks' state of confidence explains banks' expectations about national product (Y^a); expected inflation (π^a); expected short-term interest rates (i^a_{CB}); expected capital assets' prices (P^a_e) and expected foreign long-term rates (i^a_{fLT}).

As a general rule, the stronger confidence in monetary policy is, the narrower the spread between the short and the long-term interest rate is. Indeed a bank's greater confidence in monetary policy explains lower expected inflation (π^a), lower expected short-term interest rates (i^a_{CB}) and therefore higher expected national product (Y^a) and expected capital assets' prices (P^a_e). Lender's risk premium, lr, decreases with this higher bank's confidence, as shown in the following:

$$i_L = i_{CB} + lr + \chi \Rightarrow \Delta\, i_{LLT} < \Delta\, i_{LST}$$
$$\text{with } lr \downarrow = H^\circ\{\, Y^a \uparrow,\, \pi^{\,a} \downarrow,\, i_{CB}{}^a \downarrow,\, P_e{}^a,\, i_{fLT},\, i^a_{fLT}\}$$

We can summarize the effect of a higher short-term interest rate on bank's profitability as:

$$i_{CB} \uparrow \Rightarrow i_{LST} \uparrow \Rightarrow \text{If there is confidence in monetary policy, } \pi^a \text{ and}$$
$$i_{LLT} \text{ are stable} \Rightarrow \text{Spread } (i_{LLT} - i_{LST}) \downarrow \Rightarrow \text{Banks' profitability} \downarrow$$

$$\tag{5.2}$$

Lastly, the maturity of fixed rate bonds (OF) must be taken into account. The shorter the maturity of fixed rate securities, the higher the exposure to a falling interest rate, i_{CB}. The longer this maturity is, the higher the exposure to rising interest rate, i_{CB}.

In contrast to market securities, loans and current liabilities are not revalued when their yield changes. In the case of loans, variable rate bonds and current liabilities, the monetary policy risk impacts on the banks' income (a flow) and not the balance sheet valuation (a stock). Fees must also be taken into account. For French banks, fees account for 25 per cent of banks' net income, but 40 per cent in the United States. Even if monetary policy has an effect on banks' profitability, we should not over-state its importance.

Value of banks' assets

To escape the risk resulting from an increase in interest rates and a banking-liquidity crisis, banks hold more and more equities in portfolio. Income coming from equities is largely unaffected by interest rates, and market assets are supposed to be liquid since they can actually be sold at any time. During the 1990s, the proportion of market assets in the banks' balance sheet increased rapidly, particularly with global assets. Nevertheless, a monetary policy shock modifies the valuation of market assets, namely, equities, fixed-rate bonds, Treasury bills, and so on. The value of these assets is mainly marked to market in banks' balance sheets, the valuation of which is thus under the influence of financial markets.

To take this further, at the macroeconomic level financial market liquidity is often exaggerated, particularly as regards equities. Certainly, their liquidity allows banks to shorten their decision horizons, but the hope of financial markets liquidity is based on the confusion between reversibility and liquidity. When markets are bullish or when there is a speculative bubble, reversibility and liquidity keep pace thanks to capital earnings. On the other hand, as soon as many banks want to obtain this liquidity, the market becomes bearish (the bubble deflates) and this provokes equities depreciation. The hope of high liquidity in the financial markets suddenly fades and this can trigger crises of both liquidity and solvency.

The values of fixed-rate bonds and equities deteriorate with an increase in the short-term interest rate, i_{CB}. The impact of a monetary policy shock on asset prices may provoke a market-liquidity crisis. Then, the fall in asset values could produce a solvency crisis in the banking sector. The loss of confidence and the generalization of liquidity preference can explain a crisis in the production sector (e.g., the recent experience of Japan). Thus to escape banking-liquidity crises and inverse interest curves, banks have developed market assets portfolios and now encounter even more dangerous market-liquidity and systemic crises.

With a more restrictive central bank policy, an increase in i_{CB} accentuates that of i_L. This increase propagates in the curve of the bonds i_O (i_L being the minimum yield of bonds without risk and i_{CB} that of the commercial papers, certificates of deposits and Treasury bills). An increase in 'assets-without-risk' yield enforces that of equities, i_e. As, *ceteris paribus*, dividends are constant, the increase of i_e will be obtained by the decline of the price of equities. With the increase of i_O, the price of the old fixed-rate bonds P_{OF-1} falls. This chain of events may be summarized as:

$$i_{CB} \uparrow \Rightarrow i_B, i_{CP} \uparrow \Rightarrow i_L \uparrow \Rightarrow i_O \uparrow \Rightarrow \text{Assets price } P_{OF-1} \downarrow, P_e \downarrow$$
$$\Rightarrow i_e \uparrow \text{ (a flow)}$$

However, in the short term, the decline of equities price generates a loss in the value of capital ($\Delta e.p_e \downarrow$) and accentuates depreciation. In the short term, the yield of equities (i_e) could fall. We can then observe a cumulative process destabilizing the financial market, especially if the value of dividends is small in the expected income (i_e^a). From then on, an increase of i_{CB} in a speculative market[22] could provoke destabilization and a crisis of liquidity in the financial markets. It could also possibly provoke a crisis of solvency of the banking system by the rapid deflation of its assets (equities and fixed rate bonds), and a decline in its collateral value. Lenders' risks suddenly rise and the banks' financing constraint becomes high. So, even a contractionary monetary policy applied to a speculative market can have catastrophic consequences. Conversely, a decline in i_{CB} explains an increase in the prices of existing fixed-rate bonds and of the equities, though during a market-liquidity crisis this interest-rate policy is ineffective. The central bank is obliged to change from being the lender-of-last-resort to the market-maker-of-last-resort.

In a Post Keynesian world, rationality is essentially autoreferential. Financial instability is a fundamental Post Keynesian hypothesis (Minsky, 1975). Three vicious circles arising from a monetary policy shock on the financial market can explain a market-liquidity crisis. These involve a decrease in banks' assets value, a flight to quality and the self-fulfilling notifications from the rating agencies. The various cumulative processes are shown below in equations (5.3–5):

$i_{CB} \uparrow \Rightarrow P_{OF-1} \downarrow, P_e \downarrow \Rightarrow$ Valuation of banks' assets $\downarrow$, equities appreciation $\downarrow$

$\Uparrow$ $\Downarrow$

Equities $\Leftarrow$ Banks' liquidity $\Leftarrow$ risk of solvency $\Leftarrow$ Lender's
purchases $\downarrow$ preference $LP_B \downarrow$ crisis $\uparrow$ risk $lr \uparrow$

$$(5.3)$$

$i_{CB} \uparrow \Rightarrow P_e \downarrow \Rightarrow$ Valuation of firms' assets $\downarrow$, equities appreciation $\downarrow$

$\Uparrow$ $\Downarrow$

Equities $\Leftarrow$ Flight $\Leftarrow$ Lender's $\Leftarrow$ Indebtedness ratios
purchases $\downarrow$ to quality   risk $lr \uparrow$ of firms $\uparrow$ (5.4)

$i_{CB} \uparrow \Rightarrow P_e\downarrow, P_{OF-1} \downarrow \Rightarrow$ Valuation of banks' and $\Rightarrow$ Notations $\downarrow$ from
                        firms' assets $\downarrow$ rating agencies

$\Uparrow$ $\Downarrow$

Equities $\Leftarrow$ $i_L \uparrow$ and banks' financing $\Leftarrow$ Lender's and
purchases $\downarrow$ constraint $\uparrow$ borrower's risk $\uparrow$

$$(5.5)$$

Off-balance sheet channel

A monetary policy shock could have two off-balance sheet effects: a collateral effect and off-balance sheet release of commitments. First, increases in central bank interest rates decrease equities' prices and existing fixed-rate bond prices and the value of securities lodged as collateral decreases, raising lender's risk levels and increasing banks' liquidity preference. Lack of confidence encourages banks to seek high quality borrowers; and institutional investors withdraw from risky markets. Moreover, if the purchases of equities held as security were financed by means of variable-rate loans, borrowers would experience a double-negative effect. When i_{CB} increases, financing costs also increase, whereas the value of guarantees falls. A vicious circle could result thus:

$$i_{CB} \uparrow \Rightarrow P_{OF-1} \downarrow, P_e \downarrow \Rightarrow \text{'Collateral' valuation} \downarrow \Rightarrow \text{Lender's risk } lr \uparrow$$

$$\Uparrow \qquad\qquad\qquad\qquad\qquad\qquad\qquad \Downarrow$$

$$\text{Equities purchases} \downarrow \Leftarrow \text{'Flight to quality'} \Leftarrow \text{Banks' liquidity}$$
$$\text{preference } LP_B \uparrow \qquad (5.6)$$

Second, a monetary policy shock can release off-balance sheet commitments: hidden options, guarantee of forward repurchase price when takeover bids or mergers are paid for with new securities, and so on.

The expectations channel

There is uncertainty about the link between short-term and long-term interest rates. For instance, if private banks are confident that a monetary policy can lower short-term interest rates (no anticipated inflation π^a, a higher growth so weaker risk premium, lr, and future short-term rates held at a low level), long-term rates (i_L)will decrease as well. Otherwise, if they do not expect that this will happen (an expectation of higher future inflation will lead to expected short-term rates going up again and therefore will increase the bank's liquidity preference), long-term rates will rise. There are thus many different scenarios.

Consequences of monetary policy shock on banks' financing

These four vicious circles given by equations (5.3–6) above show that a monetary policy shock ($i_{CB}\uparrow$) during a speculative bubble may be very dangerous. An increase in banks' interest rates and in the level of finance rationing makes the firms' and households' financing difficult: institutional investors withdraw from risky markets.

Figure 5.3 corresponds to the horizontalist case: the commercial banks are completely accommodating and the supply of finance follows the demand. As a consequence of the monetary policy shock, interest rates increase. The only channel of transmission passes through the demand. In Figure 5.4, there is a strong increase of banks' liquidity preference (LP_B), but

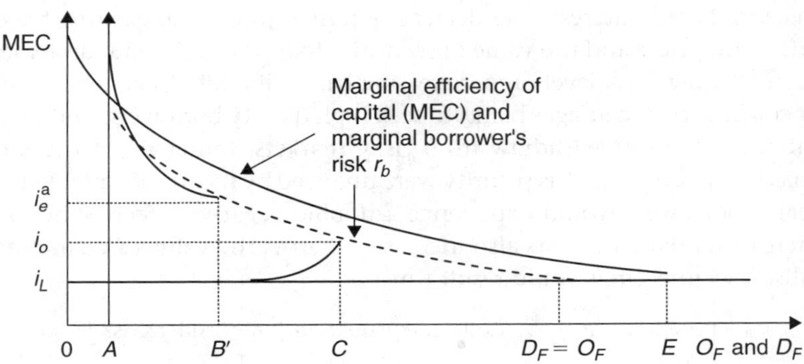

Figure 5.3   Firms' finance without banking constraint ('horizontalist' case) $[D_F \Rightarrow O_F]$

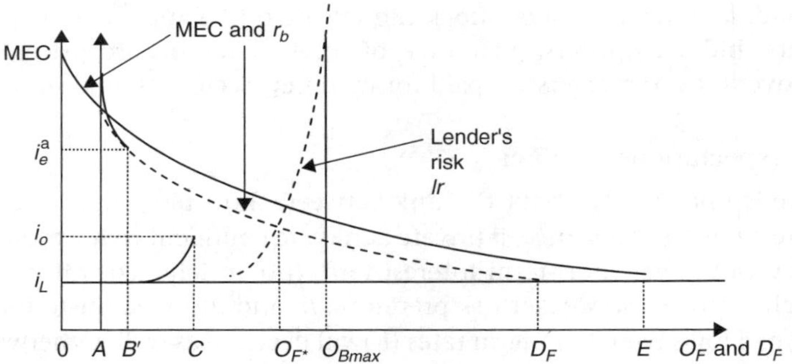

Figure 5.4   Firms' finance with a high banking monetary constraint $[O_{F*} \ll D_F]$

the state of confidence of firms does not change. The lender's risk increases markedly. In Figure 5.5, both firms' (LP_F) and banks' liquidity preference (LP_B) worsen. The marginal efficiency of capital and the firms' self-finance falls. The marginal borrower's and lender's risks increase. The demand for money of firms falls just like the finance supply by banks.

With the strong increase of banks' liquidity preference (LP_B), we get the following effects shown in Figure 5.4 and Figure 5.5:

(a) a rise in the long-run interest rate i_L following the increase in i_{CB} and in lr;

(b) a growing risk premium demanded for equities: that is, $\Delta\,(i_e^a - i_L) > 0$;

(c) a falling rate of yield accepted for bonds, because this rate corresponds to a risk level and there is a 'flight to quality': $\Delta(i_O - i_L) < 0$;

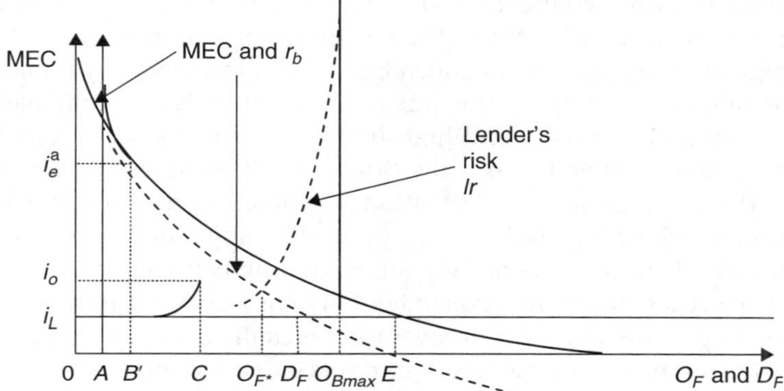

Figure 5.5   Firms' finance with a higher firms' and banks' liquidity preference $[O_{F^*} < D_F]$

(d) a growing marginal lender's risk *lr*, so O_{BMAX} moves towards the left and a credit crunch can occur;

(e) financial rationing is stronger in Figure 5.4 than in Figure 5.5. If the state of confidence falls more in the firms than in the commercial banks, financial rationing can disappear.

Financial rationing appears, explained by an increase in banks' liquidity preference. Following a monetary policy shock, the transition from Figure 5.3 to Figure 5.4 is obviously exceptional. This is because a change in banks' liquidity preference is hardly possible without a change in effective demand (Δmec < 0) and in firms' borrowing risk ($\Delta\ r_b$ < 0). If we take into account the effects on firms of a monetary policy shock (Le Heron, 1986), the state of financing would be closer to Figure 5.5 as the vicious circles are reinforced. After the market-liquidity crisis has started, even the firm's self-financing (*OA*) will be reduced. Banking behaviour is not neutral but, after a few years of finance rationing, the indebtedness ratios will decrease justifying a falling lender's risk. The crisis will stop.

Conclusion

All the measures aimed at ensuring safety and liquidity for bank financing go against both the 'animal spirits' of entrepreneurs and against growth. The most adventurous entrepreneurs can even be completely excluded from financing. This 'desired scarcity', the result of the banks' liquidity preference, can restrict the level of production and employment. Growth requires not only confident entrepreneurs, but also confident banks, whilst a crisis can arise out of the pessimism of only one sector. That strengthens the possibility of underemployment in a monetary economy of production. To simplify, the quieter the situation is (accommodating monetary policy, growth and high profits, weak debts, weak liquidity preference of firms and banks), the closer we will get to the horizontalist case. However, the more the situation is 'animated', the more banking behaviour will have an influence on production and economic situation.

In 1802, Thornton was already differentiating between liquidity and solvency crises. Today, however, a liquidity crisis does not result from a run of depositors seeking to recover their metallic currency, and a solvency crisis is no longer due to simple errors in management. Risk and its evaluation are extremely unstable and usually self-fulfilling. Banking conventions can rapidly change.

By modifying the valuation of financial assets, a monetary policy shock can change a healthy banking system into one with an unbalanced structure of banks' balance. A lender's risk considered normal exposure suddenly becomes considered unbearable. The important increase of the financial markets in the structure of banks' balance sheets, off-balance sheet commitments and self-fulfilling rationality risk all greatly modify the nature of banking risk. A banking-liquidity crisis becomes a market-liquidity crisis and can produce a 'systemic' crisis. The action of central banks is not so much that of lender-of-last-resort, but much more that of market-maker-of-last-resort, stabilizing the price of assets. Moreover, it is often the government, rather than central bank, which makes massive purchases of risky assets in order to maintain liquidity in the market.

It is possible to make Keynes's approach of liquidity preference theory compatible with an endogenous theory of money in a Post Keynesian framework. By taking into account the behaviour of the private banks, the importance of the central bank and of monetary policy is reduced. On the other hand, its responsibility within framework of 'systemic' crises becomes of prime importance. We are far from the 'artless' optimism of standard Keynesian monetary policy. First, fundamental uncertainty makes the understanding of the impact of monetary policy very complex. Second, banks have a great autonomy, particularly in determining long-term interest rates. The banks' state of confidence (their convention) is an essential factor in the understanding of a monetary economy of production.

In a forthcoming paper (Le Heron and Mouakil, 2007), we build a Post-Keynesian stock-flow consistent macroeconomic growth model to model the dynamic of a monetary policy shock.

Notes

1 Keynes analyses bank behaviour and the banking sector at length in the *Treatise on Money*. This detail, as in other instances, was pushed to the background in the *General Theory*. In fact, one of the agendas of Post-Keynesian writers has been to elaborate on financial structures, including bank behaviour, within the framework established by Keynes.

2 For Roy Rotheim, Keynes was well aware of the nature and importance of an endogenous money stock. In fact, he uses this idea as the basis for his criticism in the 1920s of the causal mechanism between changes in the money stock and changes in the rate of inflation.

3 Arestis (1992, pp. 201–3) summarized a 'horizontalist' Post-Keynesian consensus on money, credit and finance. He supports six propositions (another rather close definition is proposed by Lavoie, 1992):

1 *'The money is credit-driven and demand-determined.'* Nothing requires the balance of supply and demand for money.

2a *'The commercial banks are rarely constrained in terms of their reserves.'* We are in a system of 'divisor' of credit. *'The endogenous character of the money supply implies that there can never be an excess supply of money.'*

2b *'Money supply is endogenous at the rate of interest fixed by the monetary authorities . . . The supply of finance is not normally expected to be a constraint: the emphasis on the 'finance motive' has been greatly exaggerated.'*

3 Recent financial innovations show that *'banks are now more able to accommodate changes in the demand for loans with less-frequent use of the central bank penal facilities for reserves'* and that *'bank lending constitutes the driving force of the money stock'.*

4 If *'it is recognized that money is credit-driven and demand-determined, the prevailing exchange rate regime is of no consequence at all in terms of money supply determination.'* This perspective is in sharp contrast with the orthodox view (such as the Mundell–Fleming model).

5 *'Whilst the money supply is not under the control of the monetary authorities, interest rates are controlled by the central bank. This occurs through discount rate adjustments or through the rate of intervention on the open market by central bank.'*

Commercial banks are important because they supply purchasing power to entrepreneurs and determine financial innovations. Horizontalist Post Keynesians consider that the money supply is endogenous because it is infinitely elastic (horizontal supply curve).

4 These authors refute point 2b of the Post-Keynesian consensus proposed by Arestis, although they accept the main parts of the other propositions. There is, in fact, no fundamental opposition between these two approaches. Moore (1988) accepts monetary rationing, but it is included into the demand curve for money. Wolfson (1996) distinguishes 'notional' demand which corresponds to the industry's needs, and effective demand, which is satisfied. These two authors include an analysis of money supply in the demand function. Proposition 4 will not be discussed in this chapter.

5 See Parguez (1986).

6 The demand for money (including the finance motive) predetermines the money supply, so the money supply cannot be greater than the demand for money as the functions of money supply and demand are not independent.

7 In this we follow the approach of Paul Davidson (1972). But with the previous hypothesis, there is no radical opposition to those that take into account the financing of total production (Parguez, 1982). Again, for simplicity's sake, we will not study the financing of households by banks, which might be a significant factor in a more general model, especially where we might include the impact that monetary policy might have on durable consumption, particularly on the purchase of new and existing structures. But study of this would modify neither the reasoning nor the results. A net banking finance of households relaxes the monetary constraints on firms and, *ceteris paribus*, increases their self-financing.

8 At the third level, it is necessary to examine the relations between the central banks, the existence of many currencies, commercial and financial exchanges and the organization of the international monetary system. This chapter does not examine this level.

9 We will take into account the loans L (short, medium and long-term) and the stock certificates: STS (for short-term securities) as Treasury bills B, commercial papers CP and certificates of deposits CD, bonds (fixed-rate OF and variable-rate OV) and equities E. To simplify, we will sometimes group together these various assets, notably STS and bonds O.

10 The yield curve on interest rates is considered to be of normal shape when $i_{LT} > i_{ST}$. This curve is inverted when $i_{ST} > i_{LT}$.

11 The risk is not as in Knight's sense because it is not probabilistic risk. Even though a 'Tobin's theory of portfolio' approach is often attractive (1958), in particular for analysis of bank balance sheet (Dymski, 1988), the Post-Keynesian framework of non-probabilistic uncertainty does not allow it to be easily applied. The lender's risk is developed by Minsky (1975). We will not take into account off-balance sheet commitments, which nevertheless represent about six times today the amount of balances in France and which may involve a high market risk (see the Barings bankruptcy).

12 In this chapter, we will not develop the modelling of this arbitrage.

13 We could consider the central bank monetary policy as weakly endogenous because the product and the level of the prices are in its response function (Wray, 1992).

14 To understand this convention, we should examine central banks' response function.

15 According to this theory (Artus, 1997), the long-term rate of interest is a function of all the future short-term rates.

16 Michel Kalecki, who had developed this approach of the growing risk in 1937, had in fact returned above in 1971 with arguments close to those which would be later developed by Stiglitz and Weiss (1981). The danger of adverse selection, developed by Stiglitz and Weiss, shows that the integration of increasing risk in the rates can increase exposure to risk rather than limiting it.

17 Of course, monetary policies can be something else: prudential rules, exchange rate control, credit rationing. But in the understanding of dynamic processes, fluctuations in short-term interest rates play a leading part. Open market

policies and required reserves aim to modify the banks' need of high-powered money (central bank money: M_{HP}) to make interest rate policies more efficient. In this chapter, we will not explore the possibility of endogenous behaviour in monetary policy.

18 We will not analyse this channel because banks easily neutralize its effect.

19 Monetary policy is generally more efficient in slowing down monetary growth than accelerating it. As Kaldor (1985) says, 'it is easier to stop a thirsty donkey drinking than to force a donkey that is not thirsty to drink'. The recent failure of the Japanese zero-rate monetary policy is a good illustration.

20 The money view examines the direct effect of a fluctuation in the short-term interest rate on entrepreneurs and households. The effect on the banking behaviour is indirect, with the change in the demand for money D_M. After a decrease in i_{CB}, most channels will lead to an increase in the national product Y. Exceptions come from the income effect, from capital balances with fixed exchange rate and, in the long term, from the orthodox real-cash effect. Without denying the relevance of these usual channels, our approach develops along two different lines. First, we will take the endogenous money framework. This Post-Keynesian framework often constitutes a radical criticism of the above channels. Second, we will concentrate on the effect of a monetary policy on the private banks.

21 The history of monetary and financial crisis in the last 30 years unquestionably shows that we are in a system of credit divisor. The divisor of credit was notably developed in 1962 by J. Le Bourva (Baslé and Lavoie, 1996). Monetary authorities cannot accept a big liquidity crisis because they risk a collapse of the whole financial system. In particular, they avoid putting the most important banks in danger (the principle of 'too big to fail'). At the same time, a liquidity crisis is now more often a 'market liquidity crisis' than the usual 'banking liquidity crisis'. Acting as the lender-of-last-resort, a central bank could easily resolve a banking liquidity crisis, but, for a central bank, it is indeed difficult to distinguish between a banking liquidity crisis (the responsibility of the central bank as the lender-of-last-resort) and a solvency crisis (the microeconomic responsibility of the private bank). Furthermore, a market liquidity crisis needs more a 'market-maker-of-last-resort' than a lender-of-last-resort. However, in this case, 'moral hazard' can be very high.

22 Here 'speculative market' is when the expected appreciation (or depreciation) of assets price is the main part of i_e^a. On the contrary, an 'entrepreneur' market' is when expected dividends explain the expected yield of equities.

References

Arestis, P. (1992) *The Post-Keynesian Approach to Economics* (Aldershot: Edward Elgar).

Artus, P. (1997) 'La réaction des taux d'intérêt et de la structure des taux d'intérêt aux chocs inflationnistes et à la crédibilité', Caisse de Dépôts et Consignations, Working Paper No. 1997-02/FI.

Baslé, M. and Lavoie, M. (1996) 'La pensée monétaire de Jacques Le Bourva, analyse et historique', *Revue d'Economie Politique*, vol. 106, no. 2, Mars–Avril 1996, 269–91.

Davidson, P. (1972) *Money and the Real World* (London: Macmillan).

Davidson, P. (1989) 'Introduction: Three Views on the Endogenous Money Supply', *Journal of Post Keynesian Economics*, vol. 12, 201–2.

Dymski, G. (1988) 'A Keynesian Theory of Bank Behavior', *Journal of Post Keynesian Economics*, vol. 4–10, 499–526.

Goodhart, C. (1989) 'Has Moore become too Horizontal?', *Journal of Post Keynesian Economics*, vol. 1–12, 29–34.

Kaldor, N. (1985) *Le fléau du monétarisme* (Paris: Economica).

Kalecki, M. (1937) 'The Principle of Increasing Risk', *Economica*, IV (13), 440–7.

Keynes, J. M. (1937) 'Ex-Ante Theory of the Rate of Interest', *Economic Journal*.

Keynes, J. M. (1971) *The General Theory. The Collected writings of J.M. Keynes, vols V–VI* (London: Macmillan; originally published 1930).

Keynes, J. M. (1973) *The Treatise on Money. The Collected writings of J.M. Keynes, vol. VII* (London: Macmillan; originally published 1936).

Kregel, J. (1984) 'Constraints on the Expansion of Output and Employment: Real or Monetary?', *Journal of Post Keynesian Economics*, (Winter), 7(2), 132–52.

Lavoie, M. (1992) *Foundations of Post-Keynesian Economic Analysis* (Aldershot: Edward Elgar).

Le Bourva, J. (1962) 'Création de la monnaie et multiplicateur du crédit', *Revue Economique*, 13–1.

Le Heron, E. (1984) *Neutralité et contraintes monétaires,* PhD, Paris I Panthéon-Sorbonne.

Le Heron, E. (1986) 'Généralisation de la préférence pour la liquidité et financement de l'investissement', *Economies et Sociétés, Monnaie et Production*, no. 6–7, 67–93.

Le Heron, E. (2002) 'La préférence pour la liquidité des banques: une analyse post keynésienne du comportement bancaire', *Cahiers Lillois d'Economie et de Sociologie*, no. 38, 97–131.

Le Heron, E. and Mouakil, T. (2007) 'A Post Keynesian Stock-Flow Consistent Model for the Dynamic Analysis of Monetary Policy Shock on Banking Behaviour', *Metroeconomica*, forthcoming.

Minsky, H. (1975) *John Maynard Keynes* (New York: Columbia University Press).

Moore, B. (1979) 'Monetary Factors', in *A Guide to Post-Keynesian Economics*, edited by A. Eichner (Armonk, NY: Sharpe).

Moore, B. (1988) *Horizontalists and Verticalists: The Macroeconomics of Credit Money* (Cambridge: Cambridge University Press).

Parguez, A. (1982) 'La monnaie dans le circuit: le voile déchiré', in *La monnaie dans le circuit, Economie Appliquée*, 3.

Parguez, A. (1986) 'Hamlet et Shylock ou la rareté désirée' and 'Au cœur du circuit ou quelques réponses aux énigmes du circuit', *Economies et Sociétés, Monnaie et Production*, no. 3, 3–22.

Stiglitz, J. and Weiss, A. (1981) 'Credit Rationing in Markets with Imperfect Information', *American Economic Review*, vol. 3–71, 393–410.

Thornton, H. (1802) *An Enquiry into the Nature and Effects of the Paper Credit of Great Britain* (Hatchard); edited by Hayek (1939) (London: Allen & Unwin).

Tobin, J. (1958) 'Liquidity Preference as Behavior toward Risk', *Review of Economic Studies*, 25, pp. 65–86.

Wolfson, M. (1996) 'A Post-Keynesian Theory of Credit Rationing', *Journal of Post Keynesian Economics*, 18(3), 443–70.

Wray, R. (1989) 'A Keynesian Theory of Banking: A Comment on Dymski', *Journal of Post Keynesian Economics*, vol. 1–12, 152–6.

Wray, R. (1992) 'Commercial banks, the Central Bank and Endogenous Money', *Journal of Post Keynesian Economics*, vol. 3–14, 297–310.

6
Credibility of Interest Rate Policies in Eight European Monetary System Countries: An Application of the Markov Regime-Switching of a Bivariate Autoregressive Model

Philip Arestis and Kostas Mouratidis

Introduction

This chapter utilizes the Markov regime-switching modelling framework to study the credibility of monetary policy, with respect to the objective of price stability, in some member countries of the EMS throughout its life (i.e., 1979–98). Eight countries are examined for this purpose: Austria, Belgium, Finland, France, Italy, the Netherlands, Portugal and Spain. In addition, Germany is used as a benchmark case.[1] A number of other studies have investigated the issue of credibility during the EMS period (see for example, Dahlquist and Gray, 2000; Arestis and Mouratidis, 2004a). One of the main conclusions of this body of literature is that monetary policy may go through different stages of credibility through time, in such a way that it is perceived to be credible in some circumstances and may lack credibility on other occasions. It is, thus, appropriate to use the Markov regime-switching modelling framework to study this phenomenon. Moreover, some of these studies allow the probability of switching between regimes to be a function of macroeconomic variables (see Engels and Hakkio, 1996; Gray, 1996; Dahlquist and Gray, 2000; Sarantis and Piard, 2000). In particular, most of these studies attempt to explain the currency crises of 1992 and 1993 using as information variables in the transition probabilities a number of alternatives: the exchange rate within a band (i.e., a target zone model framework), real exchange rates, budget deficits, interest rate differentials, and other variables. None of these studies includes in the transition probability the two main variables that determine the loss function of monetary authorities, namely domestic output-gap variability and inflation variability (the exception is Arestis and Mouratidis, 2004a).[2]

A major innovation in this chapter is accounting for these two variables in two bivariate vector autoregressive Markov regime-switching models (MRS-BVAR). The main focus is to evaluate the preferences of the monetary authorities of the eight EMS member countries referred to above, relating to the stabilization of output-gap variability and of the stabilization of inflation variability. In particular, we use two MRS-BVAR models where the first is based on the relationship between the interest rate differential (i.e., between each country's interest rate and that of Germany's) and the inflation variability; and the second is based on the relationship between the same interest rate differential and the output-gap variability. In this way we identify different regimes based on the behaviour of a large number of parameters, as explained below in the sub-section 'General observations'.

We begin, in the section that follows, with the theoretical and empirical underpinnings of credibility in the EMS. The empirical methodology adopted is explored in the subsequent section, with the empirical findings reported and discussed in the penultimate section. The final section summarizes and concludes.

Theoretical underpinnings

In recent years, most explanations of positive average inflation rates have been based on the time-inconsistency problem. If the public expects a low inflation rate then the central bank faces the temptation to inflate. However, the public correctly anticipates this incentive and adjusts its inflationary expectation to a higher level. This implies a positive average rate of inflation that has no effect on output since it is completely anticipated. There is, thus, an inflation bias. The solution to the inflation bias is achieved in the form of lost reputation in a repeated game version of the basic Barro and Gordon (1983a, 1983b) model: that is, giving in to the temptation to inflate in the current period negatively affects the central banks' reputation, making it harder to achieve low inflation in the future. This leads the public to expect higher inflation in the future, which is the punishment of the central bank by the public, since higher future inflation lowers the central bank's reputation. However, the evolution of the public's beliefs over time is based on observed outcomes of inflation, and the central bank can affect these beliefs by its action. Consequently, a central bank that prefers to achieve some output expansion at the cost of inflation may find it optimal initially to build an anti-inflation reputation.

This behaviour by a central bank raises the issue of the public's uncertainty in relation to the 'type' of central bank (see, for example, Backus and Driffill, 1985; Barro, 1986; Ball, 1995; Muscatelli, 1998). More concretely, there is uncertainty as to whether the central bank prefers to stabilize inflation variability (i.e., the 'dry' type of central bank) or to stabilise output-gap variability (i.e., the 'wet' type of central bank).

Recent theoretical research on monetary policy rules has demonstrated the possibility of a trade-off between output-gap variability and inflation variability. In particular, Taylor (1980, 1994) shows that a short-run trade-off between the level of inflation and output-gap implies a long-run trade-off between their respective variances. The link between inflation and output-gap variabilities may be shown analytically. We follow Cecchetti (1998) and derive the trade-off between inflation and output-gap variability by assuming that a quadratic loss function is additionally subject to the dynamics of output and prices; it can, thus, be made a function of the policy control variable (i.e., the interest rate) and the stochastic processes driving the economy. In particular, we may begin by minimizing the following loss function as described in (6.1):[4]

$$L = E_t\left[\sum_{i=0}^{m}\beta^i\{\lambda[p_{t+i} - p_{t+i}^*]^2 + (1-\lambda)[y_{t+i} - y_{t+i}^*]^2\}\right] \qquad (6.1)$$

subject to (6.2) and (6.3):

$$y_t = \gamma(i_t - d_t) + s_t \qquad (6.2)$$

$$p_t = -(i_t + d_t) - \theta d_t \qquad (6.3)$$

where λ is the weight that the central bank attaches to inflation, relative to output stabilization, γ is the inverse slope of the supply curve and θ is the slope of the aggregate demand; d_t and s_t are the demand and the supply shocks respectively.[3] In this linear model the optimal policy will be linear, that is:

$$i_t = \alpha d_t + \beta s_t \qquad (6.4)$$

Substituting this optimal policy into y_t and p_t we obtain the respective variances σ_y^2 and σ_π^2.[5] Cecchetti (1998) shows that the ratio σ_y^2/σ_π^2 is a function of policy preferences α and of the inverse of the slope of the supply curve γ:[6]

$$\sigma_y^2/\sigma_\pi^2 = [\lambda/\gamma(\lambda - 1)]^2 \qquad (6.5)$$

Equations (6.2) and (6.3) show that a trade-off can arise from supply shocks. Ball (1995) assumes that the supply shocks and central bank behaviour follow a Markov process. We adopt this assumption in what follows, along with another assumption: namely, that supply shocks are state dependent. In particular, Cukierman (1999) and Olmedo (2002) show that central bank preferences are asymmetric and depend on the state that the economy is in. If the economy is in expansion, central banks react more to inflationary pressures than in recession. Alternatively, a central bank is more reactive to the deviation of output gap from its target level when the economy is in recession than in expansion.

We assume that supply shocks occur only in a high volatility regime, which is associated with recession.[7] In the high volatility regime, inflation expectations and the nominal interest rate are high, which have negative effects on economic growth. This implies that in this regime economic growth is low. Alternatively, a period with no supply shocks being present (i.e., a low volatility regime) is associated with high economic growth. On the basis of these assumptions we can extend the linear model described by Cecchetti (1998) in a non-linear framework. In particular, the central bank is hypothesized as having an asymmetric loss function, which can be minimized subject to the standard constraints of aggregate supply and demand curves.[8] The solution to this minimization will lead to a two-state Taylor-type rule. Following Cecchetti (1998) the solution leads to equation (6.5), which is state dependent.

In what follows, however, we do not estimate equation (6.5) in each state. Instead, we measure the uncertainty regarding the type of central bank as a deviation of the interest rate policy from a target level, where this target is the interest rate of a country with low inflation reputation (Ball, 1995). This is based on the assumption that supply shocks in Ball (1995) occur in recession and are absent in expansion. Giavazzi and Pagano (1988) argue that during the 1980s, the EMS countries designated the Bundesbank as their 'dry central bank' by pegging their exchange rate to the German mark, themselves becoming the 'wet central banks'. In our case the domestic interest rate is the interest rate of each of the eight individual countries and the target interest rate is the German interest rate. We thus use Germany to represent the dry type of central bank and the eight countries to represent the wet type of central bank. We concentrate on the variability of the interest rate differential between the rate of interest of the eight individual countries and that of Germany, which reflects the risk premium for the wet central bank to deviate from the policy pursued by the dry central bank.

Preferences of the central bank regarding the objective of price stability could be estimated in a time-varying transition probability model, where the probability to switch between regimes is a function of inflation variability and output-gap variability. However, in a time-varying transition probability model, feedback effects between the transition probabilities and the information variables might exist (Filardo, 1998). Although in such a case one might use the dynamic transition probability model suggested by Chourdakis and Tzavalis (2001), we deal with this econometric problem by modelling the dependent variable and the information variables jointly, utilizing an MRS-BVAR model. We prefer this solution since, in the Chourdakis and Tzavalis (2001) specification of the dynamic transition probability model, no information variable can be included in the transition probability other than its lagged value and the lagged error term. It thus makes it impossible to evaluate whether any macroeconomic variables affect the transition probability. The MRS-BVAR model, by contrast, does not suffer from this weakness.

Empirical methodology of modelling credibility: a Markov regime-switching bivariate autoregressive model

We utilize MRS-BVAR models where the information variables and the interest rate differential are jointly estimated. Under such specification we avoid any econometric problems due to endogeneity between the information variables and the unobserved state variable. Moreover, we can still evaluate the effects of inflation variability and output-gap variability on the interest rate differential. We use two MRS-BVAR models: the first draws on the relationship between the interest rate differential and inflation variability; and the second draws on the relationship between the interest rate differential and output-gap variability.

A trivariate VAR could be used to measure monetary policy preferences based on (6.5). This has been applied by Cecchetti and Ehrmann (1999) in a linear framework using structural VAR. In particular, Cecchetti and Ehrmann (1999) estimate the inverse slope of a supply curve (γ) using an impulse response function, where γ is measured as the ratio of the inflation/output, gap response to the interest rate shock. The same analysis could be applied here following Ehrmann, Ellison and Valla (2001). However, there are two reasons why using this analysis here could be a bad idea. First, Cecchetti and Ehrmann (1999) use the levels of inflation and output gap in their analysis to estimate (γ). This point can be taken here by using also the levels of the series instead of their volatilities. However, the second reason is more serious. Computation of equation (6.5) is based on the unconditional volatilities of inflation and output gap. In our study we are concerned with the effects of conditional volatilities on interest rate policy. In particular, we concentrate on the real time preferences of the central bank. Naturally, we do not take into account data revisions for the simple reason that real time data are not available. Consequently, we cannot use equation (6.5) to estimate a short-run trade off between inflation variability and output-gap variability.[9] This implies that if we use a trivariate MRS-VAR model, calculation of γ is not feasible since this requires the levels of inflation and output gap and not the volatilities that we employ here to estimate the short-run preferences of the central bank.[10]

The estimation procedure of the MRS-VAR model is an extension of the basic VAR model. More precisely, consider a pth order vector autoregression for y_t:

$$y_t = c_0 + A_1 y_{t-1} + \cdots A_p y_{t-p} + U_t \tag{6.6}$$

where $u_t \sim IID(0, \Sigma)$, Σ is the variance-covariance matrix and $y_0, \ldots y_{-p}$ are fixed. The most general specification of an M-state MRS(M)-VAR model can be presented as follows:

$$y_t = \begin{cases} c_{01} + A_{11} y_{t-1} + \cdots A_{p1} y_{t-p} + \sum_{T}^{1/2} u_t \\ \vdots \\ \vdots \\ c_{0m} + A_{1m} y_{t-1} + \cdots A_{pm} y_{t-p} + \sum_{m}^{1/2} u_t \end{cases}_t \tag{6.7}$$

where $u \sim NID(0, I_n)$, I_n is the n-dimensional identity matrix, $\Sigma_{it}^{1/2}$ is the square root of the variance-covariance matrix in regime $i = 1, 2 \ldots m$ and A_{ji} is the $(n \times n)$ matrix of the autoregressive coefficients at the jth lag (for $j = 1 \ldots p$) in regime i (for $i = 1 \ldots m$).[11] In our case A is a 2×2 matrix, and the order of VAR is one. Therefore, we can write a two-state bivariate first order MRS model as follows:

$$y_t = c_{01.i} + A_{11.i} y_{t-1} + \sum_{i}^{1/2} u_t \tag{6.8}$$

where $y_t = \begin{bmatrix} i^D - i^G \\ x_t \end{bmatrix}$ and x_t denotes either inflation variability or output-gap variability of the domestic country. Therefore (6.3) can be written as:

$$\begin{bmatrix} (i^D - i^G)t \\ x_t \end{bmatrix} = \begin{bmatrix} \alpha_{11.i} & \alpha_{12.i} \\ \alpha_{21.i} & \alpha_{22.i} \end{bmatrix} \begin{bmatrix} (i^D - i^G)_{t-1} \\ x_{t-1} \end{bmatrix}$$
$$+ \begin{bmatrix} \sum_{11.i}^{1/2} & \sum_{12.i}^{1/2} \\ \sum_{21.i}^{1/2} & \sum_{22.i}^{1/2} \end{bmatrix} u_t \tag{6.9}$$

where $i = 1,2$ indicates the current regime. In the case of regime dependent variance-covariance matrix (i.e., $\Sigma_1^{1/2} \neq \Sigma_2^{1/2}$), Krolzig (1997) gives a comprehensive description of the Maximum Likelihood Estimation (MLE) of (6.9) for an m number of states.

In the literature (see, e.g., Hamilton, 1993) it has been assumed that the standard asymptotic theory also holds for the maximum likelihood estimators of the MRS models, that is:

$$\sqrt{T}\,(\hat{\gamma}-\gamma) \xrightarrow{\quad d \quad} N(0, I^{-1})$$

where $\xrightarrow{\quad d \quad}$ stands for 'symptotic convergence in distribution', $\hat{\gamma}$ is the estimator of the true value of γ and I^{-1} is the Fisher information matrix. γ includes all the model parameters, including $\alpha_{ij.i}$ (for $i, j = 1, 2$), p and $\Sigma_{ij.i}^{1/2}$ where $\alpha_{ij.i}$ and $\Sigma_{ij.i}^{1/2}$ are the co-factors of $A_{11.i}$ and of the variance-covariance matrix in (6.8) respectively, and p is the (2×2) transition probability matrix.[12] The asymptotic normality of maximum likelihood estimators ensures that most model specification tests known from the time-invariant VAR models (Lutkephol, 1991, ch. 4), are applicable with only a slight modification in the case of MRS-VAR models (i.e., the number of regimes is unchanged under the null and alternative hypotheses; see Krolzig, 1997). Dynamic specification tests (i.e., autocorrelation, ARCH effects, varying transition probabilities, etc.) have only applied in univariate models (i.e., MRS-AR(p) models; see, e.g., Hamilton, 1996).

The MRS-VAR are reduced-form models, and therefore no structural interpretation can be given to the coefficients of output-gap variability and inflation variability on the interest rate differential. However, the significance of these variables in the equations of interest rate differential is based on some theoretical models regarding the effects of inflation expectations on economic growth, and the uncertainty surrounding the type of central bank behaviour. This leads to certain conclusions about the preferences of the central bank. In particular, high inflation expectations increase the *ex-ante* nominal interest rate which affects economic growth negatively. Under such circumstances, the incentives for the monetary authorities to inflate become stronger. In the framework of Ball (1995) concerning the uncertainty in terms of the type of central bank, this means that in the high volatility regime the risk premium for the wet type of central bank to deviate from the policy pursued by the dry type is so intense that it prefers to reveal its identity as a wet type.[13] Under such circumstances where inflation expectations affect the policy makers' preferences and, therefore, the risk premium to deviate from a low inflation country, we interpret evidence of the significance of inflation variability and output-gap variability in the equation of interest rate differential in the following way.

In the low credibility regime (i.e., high volatility regime), the wet type of central bank has an incentive to inflate. Therefore, in this regime we expect the central bank under consideration to deviate from German monetary policy, emphasizing domestic issues such as growth and unemployment rather than credibility gains. Output-gap variability, then, is expected to be significant in the low credibility regime. This is also consistent with the asymmetric behaviour of the central bank. In particular, within this framework the central bank reacts more strongly to the deviation of output-gap from its target in recession than in expansion. Assuming, as we mentioned in the last section, that the high volatility regime is associated with recession, we expect the effect of output-gap variability on the interest rate differential to be stronger in the high volatility regime than in the low volatility regime. Alternatively, if in the high volatility regime output-gap variability is not significant, but inflation variability is significant, then monetary authorities place more weight on the stabilization of inflation variability than on the stabilization of output-gap variability. When both inflation and output-gap variability are significant in the high volatility regime, then the credibility of monetary policy regarding the objective of price stability depends on whether the coefficient of inflation variability is higher than the coefficient of output-gap variability. If the coefficient of inflation variability is higher than the coefficient of output-gap variability, then monetary policy is considered credible regarding the stabilization of inflation variability.

In the high credibility state (i.e., low volatility regime), output-gap variability is expected to be insignificant. This is so because in a free-shock environment the wet type of central bank has no incentive to deviate from the low inflation policy pursued by the dry type of central bank, and therefore monetary authorities will react to the deviation of inflation from its target level. This is also in line with the asymmetric behaviour of the central bank, which prefers to be more reactive to deviation of inflation from its target in expansion than in recession. Using the assumption that expansion is associated with the low volatility regime, we expect inflation variability to have stronger effects on the interest rate differential in the low volatility regime than in the high volatility regime. However, if output-gap variability is significant in the high credibility regime, while inflation variability is not, then the monetary authority prefers to stabilize the output-gap variability. Finally, if inflation variability and output-gap variability are significant at the same time in the high credibility state, then we compare the size of their coefficient to reach a conclusion regarding policy preferences.[14]

Database and data sources

We employ monthly data for interest rates, inflation and industrial production for the eight Economic and Monetary Union countries included in our sample. The interest rate data were taken from line 60b of the *International Financial Statistics* (IFS) data base (Datastream). They are monthly averages of day-to-day money rates defined by the IFS as the rate at which short-term borrowing is effected by financial institutions. The Consumer Price Index (CPI) is taken from line 64 and industrial production from line 66 of the same publication. Data are used over the whole period of the EMS (i.e., from March 1979 to December 1998). Exceptions are the cases of Luxembourg and Portugal where data are available from January 1986 and January 1983 respectively.

The annualized inflation and output-gap are measured by $(CPI - CPI_{12})/CPI_{12}$ and $(IP - IP_{12})/IP_{12}$ respectively, where CPI is the consumer price index, and IP stands for industrial production; the subscript denotes the lag order. We use the twelve order difference mainly because central banks concentrate on the annual inflation rate. The output-gap series have been measured by assuming that the trend follows a random walk process. We also experimented with the following additional assumptions relating to the trend: (1) a smooth stochastic process uncorrelated with the cyclical component (Hodrick–Prescott detrending method); (2) a log-linear trend; and (3) a linear deterministic trend uncorrelated with the cyclical part. The empirical results under different measures of output gap were qualitatively similar.

Modelling strategy

In the estimation of the output-gap variability and of the inflation variability, we have employed a stochastic volatility model. This model is used for series that, although uncorrelated, might not be independent because of serial dependence in the second moment. In particular, if the squares of the logarithms of inflation and of output-gap are serially correlated, then there is evidence of non-linearity. This can be modelled as follows:

$$\log y_t^2 = \kappa + h_t + \xi_t \tag{6.10}$$

$$\xi_t = \log \varepsilon_t^2 - E(\log \varepsilon_t^2) \tag{6.11}$$

$$\kappa = \log \sigma_t^2 + E(\log \varepsilon_t^2) \tag{6.12}$$

where y_t is the log either of inflation or of output-gap, $E(\varepsilon_t) = 0$, $\mathrm{var}(\varepsilon_t) = 1$ and the conditional variance of y_t is equal to σ_t^2 and $h_t = \log(\sigma_t^2)$. Working with logarithms ensures that σ_t^2 is always positive.[15] A practical problem arises when some of the observations are zero, in which case the following transformation, based on Taylor series, is undertaken (Breit and Carriquiry, 1996):

$$\log y_t^2 \cong \log(y_t^2 + cs_y^2) - cs_y^2/(x_t^2 + cs_y^2) \tag{6.13}$$

where s_y^2 is the sample variance of y_t and c is a small number (a value of 0.02 is suggested by Koopmans *et al.*, 2000). Our estimates of the stochastic volatility model are based on (6.13).[16] We thus avoid the problem of a two-step estimation that would arise if we based our estimate of h_t, (i.e., the systematic part of $\log y_t^2$) on (6.10). The computation of stochastic volatilities, both for the inflation variability and for the output-gap variability, was undertaken on STAMP 6.0 computer software (Koopmans *et al.*, 2000).[17] RATS 4.2 computer software was employed for the estimation of the MRS-BVAR models. The estimates thus derived are reported in Tables 6.1–4.

The MRS(2)-BVAR(1) model

We specify a model where the autoregressive coefficients and the variance-covariance matrix are state dependent, while the state vector follows a Markov process. In this general MRS-BVAR model, an increase in the number of states leads to a statistical model with an excessively large number of coefficients. This makes the estimation difficult and problems of convergence of the MLE arise.[18] Moreover, a number of lags higher than one does not increase the value of the likelihood function. We therefore retain only one lag. It is for these reasons that we retain eventually a first order Bivariate model with two regimes, MRS(2)-BVAR(1).

We allow the autoregressive coefficient to be state dependent because under such specification we can test for asymmetric effects of inflation variability and output-gap variability in the high and low credible states. More concretely, we can account for the fact that the impact of inflation variability and output-gap variability on monetary policy preferences is regime dependent.[19] We also allow the variance-covariance matrix to be regime dependent for two reasons. First, we can distinguish between a high volatility and a low volatility regime. Second, if the variance is regime dependent then a regime generating process affects the contemporaneous relationship of the error term u_t and, therefore, the orthogonilized impulse response function. In this sense, regime switching affects the relationship between the interest rate differential and inflation variability as well as the output-gap variability. In general, in our specification we incorporate the effects that unobserved state variables have on the autoregressive dynamics.

General observations

We begin this section by clarifying the coefficients in Tables 6.1–4. In Tables 6.1 and 6.2, the estimated equations describe the relationship between the interest rate differential and the inflation variability. In Tables 6.3 and 6.4, the estimated equations refer to the relationship between the interest rate differential and the output-gap variability. The subscripts of each coefficient have the following meanings. The first subscript before the dot indicates the equation and the second the regressor under consideration. The subscript after the dot indicates the regime. The coefficient $c_{i0.1}$ denotes the constant coefficient in the $i = 1, 2$ equation in the first regime (i.e., high credible regime); the coefficient $\alpha_{ij.1}$ is the coefficient of the $j = 1, 2$ regressor in the $i = 1, 2$ equation in the first regime. Similarly, $c_{i0.2}$ is the constant coefficient in equation $i = 1, 2$ in the second regime (i.e., low credible regime); and $\alpha_{ij.2}$ the coefficient of $j = 1, 2$ regressor in the second regime. The variance-covariance matrix $\Sigma_{ij.1}$ denotes the covariance between $i = 1, 2$ and $j = 1, 2$ in the first regime, and the variance-covariance matrix $\Sigma_{ij.2}$ is the covariance matrix in the second regime. The transition probability, p_{12}, denotes the transition from the high credible regime to the low credible regime. The transition probability p_{21} is the transition from the low credible regime to the high credible regime.

The model is a reduced form and we concentrate only on the significance of the information variables in the equations of interest rate differential. In all the cases reported in Tables 6.1–4 there are four main characteristics that separate the two regimes.[20] First, the variance of the interest rate differentials in the low credible regime (i.e., $\Sigma_{11.2}$) is many times greater than that in the high credible regime (i.e., $\Sigma_{11.1}$). However, this is not always true for the equations of inflation variability and output-gap variability. In particular, in the cases of Italy, Spain, and Portugal the variance of inflation variability in the high credible state is higher than the variance in the low credible state (i.e., $\Sigma_{22.1} > \Sigma_{22.2}$). Moreover, in the cases of France, the Netherlands and Finland the variance of output-gap variability in the high credible state is also higher than the variance in the low credible state. An important implication is that in these cases the regime generating process of inflation variability and output-gap variability might be independent from the regime generating the process

Table 6.1 Parameters estimates and related statistics for MS(2)-BVAR regime-switching model: the case of inflation variability

	France	Italy	The Netherlands	Belgium	Austria
$c_{10.1}$	−0.382 (0.137)	0.910 (0.003)	0.375 (0.015)	–	−0.046 (0.858)
$\alpha_{11.1}$	0.9666 (0.000)	0.969 (0.000)	0.887 (0.000)	0.777 (0.000)	0.908 (0.000)
$\alpha_{12.1}$	−0.049 (0.112)	0.130(0.001)	0.049 (0.018)	−0.144 (0.000)	−0.013 (0.727)
$c_{10.2}$	−5.509 (0.001)	2.163(0.398)	0.634 (0.263)	–	0.465 (0.564)
$\alpha_{11.2}$	0.393 (0.024)	0.867 (0.000)	0.569 (0.007)	0.512 (0.015)	0.197 (0.203)
$\alpha_{12.2}$	−0.571 (0.002)	0.241 (0.547)	0.101 (0.189)	−0.318 (0.151)	0.028 (0.778)
$c_{20.1}$	−0.456 (0.000)	−0.047 (0.598)	−0.400 (0.004)	–	−0.129 (0.170)
$\alpha_{21.1}$	−0.023 (0.000)	0.0007 (0.869)	−0.021 (0.444)	−0.002 (0.877)	0.011 (0.605)
$\alpha_{22.1}$	0.945 (0.000)	0.995 (0.000)	0.948 (0.000)	0.990 (0.000)	0.982 (0.000)
$c_{20.2}$	0.100 (0.539)	0.222 (0.175)	−1.675 (0.060)	–	−1.175 (0.137)
$\alpha_{21.2}$	−0.0003 (0.98)	−0.015 (0.007)	0.407 (0.212)	0.064 (0.501)	−0.048 (0.865)
$\alpha_{22.2}$	1.025 (0.000)	1.030 (0.000)	0.789 (0.000)	0.906 (0.000)	0.859 (0.000)
$\Sigma_{11.1}$	0.056 (0.000)	0.104 (0.000)	0.049 (0.000)	0.499 (0.000)	0.115 (0.000)
$\Sigma_{12.1}$	−0.0005 (0.830)	0.004 (0.170)	0.005 (0.124)	−0.007 (0.625)	0.007 (0.190)
$\Sigma_{22.1}$	0.017 (0.001)	0.010 (0.000)	0.037 (0.000)	0.049 (0.000)	0.022 (0.000)
$\Sigma_{11.2}$	3.212 (0.043)	1.390 (0.192)	0.353 (0.000)	3.684 (0.000)	0.192 (0.000)
$\Sigma_{12.2}$	−0.139 (0.086)	−0.027 (0.076)	−0.021 (0.888)	0.039 (0.919)	−0.037 (0.588)
$\Sigma_{22.2}$	0.134 (0.000)	0.003 (0.007)	0.717 (0.000)	0.463 (0.000)	0.549 (0.000)
p_{12}	0.135 (0.000)	0.052 (0.089)	0.043 (0.0266)	0.021 (0.158)	0.124 (0.001)
p_{21}	0.459 (0.000)	0.283 (0.019)	0.156 (0.001)	0.134 (0.052)	0.434 (0.000)

Note: *p*-values are in brackets (i.e., the null hypothesis that the given coefficient is equal to zero).

Table 6.2   Parameters estimates and related statistics for MS(2)-BVAR regime-switching model: the case of inflation variability

	Finland	Portugal	Spain
$c_{10.1}$	0.033 (0.738)	0.172 (0.664)	0.161 (0.641)
$\alpha_{11.1}$	1.001(0.000)	0.982 (0.000)	0.955 (0.000)
$\alpha_{12.1}$	0.005 (0.630)	0.031 (0.497)	0.005 (0.904)
$c_{10.2}$	−0.057 (0.889)	7.095 (0.001)	3.048 (0.250)
$\alpha_{11.2}$	0.933 (0.000)	0.666 (0.000)	0.806 (0.000)
$\alpha_{12.2}$	−0.017 (0.713)	0.949 (0.009)	0.265 (0.635)
$c_{20.1}$	−0.258 (0.001)	0.058 (0.755)	−0.210 (0.162)
$\alpha_{21.1}$	0.011 (0.053)	−0.001 (0.886)	0.003 (0.709)
$\alpha_{22.1}$	0.963 (0.000)	1.007 (0.000)	0.971 (0.000)
$c_{20.2}$	−0.094 (0.733)	0.031 (0.768)	−0.112 (0.441)
$\alpha_{21.2}$	0.022 (0.588)	−0.004 (0.210)	0.002 (0.468)
$\alpha_{22.2}$	1.001 (0.000)	1.009 (0.000)	0.986 (0.000)
$\Sigma_{11.1}$	0.023 (0.109)	0.055 (0.004)	0.151 (0.000)
$\Sigma_{12.1}$	−0.002 (0.188)	−0.004 (0.290)	−0.003 (0.641)
$\Sigma_{22.1}$	0.018 (0.000)	0.041 (0.000)	0.025 (0.000)
$\Sigma_{11.2}$	0.302 (0.003)	5.490 (0.000)	5.956 (0.000)
$\Sigma_{12.2}$	0.005 (0.774)	−0.008 (0.732)	−0.027 (0.499)
$\Sigma_{22.2}$	0.308 (0.098)	0.011 (0.000)	0.016 (0.000)
p_{12}	0.250 (0.000)	0.078 (0.015)	0.025 (0.066)
p_{21}	0.539 (0.005)	0.084 (0.162)	0.016 (0.227)

Note: *p*-values are in brackets (i.e., the null hypothesis that the given coefficient is equal to zero).

of the interest rate differential.[21] Second, the coefficient of the lagged value of the interest rate differential is greater in the high credibility regime (i.e., $\alpha_{11.1}$) than in the low credibility regime (i.e., $\alpha_{11.2}$). Also, the transition probability from the low credibility regime to the high credibility regime (i.e., p_{21}) is higher than the transition probability from the high credibility regime to the low credibility regime (i.e., p_{12}).[22] This implies that high credible regimes are more persistent than low credibility regimes. This is consistent with the Friedman and Laibson (1989) findings that small to moderate shocks (i.e., regime of low volatility) were more persistent than very large shocks (i.e., regime of high volatility). They explain this result by referring to the regime of high inflation expectation, where monetary authorities show their intentions to reduce these expectations by exercising a strong pressure on short-term interest rates. This action leads to a large but not persistent (i.e., not gradual) change in interest rates, thereby relieving the pressure arising from the uncertainty surrounding inflation expectations.

Table 6.3   Parameters estimates and related statistics for MS(2)-BVAR regime-switching model: the case of output-gap variability

	France	Italy	The Netherlands	Belgium	Austria
$c_{10.1}$	−0.007 (0.956)	0.641 (0.015)	0.004 (0.980)	–	1.175 (0.003)
$\alpha_{11.1}$	0.986 (0.000)	1.007 (0.000)	0.914 (0.000)	0.670 (0.000)	0.716 (0.000)
$\alpha_{12.1}$	−0.004 (0.823)	0.102 (0.002)	0.002 (0.925)	0.004 (0.159)	0.238 (0.004)
$c_{10.2}$	0.728 (0.721)	10.837 (0.103)	0.295 (0.917)	–	−2.330 (0.710)
$\alpha_{11.2}$	0.521 (0.011)	0.744 (0.000)	0.677 (0.007)	0.641 (0.000)	0.240 (0.851)
$\alpha_{12.2}$	0.277 (0.447)	1.224 (0.130)	0.040 (0.912)	0.089 (0.000)	−0.591 (0.653)
$c_{20.1}$	−0.159 (0.000)	−0.172 (0.312)	−0.058 (0.706)	–	0.070 (0.041)
$\alpha_{21.1}$	0.006 (0.329)	−0.002 (0.569)	0.002 (0.913)	0.097 (0.104)	−0.010 (0.004)
$\alpha_{22.1}$	0.976 (0.000)	0.973 (0.000)	0.996 (0.000)	0.994 (0.000)	1.014 (0.000)
$c_{20.2}$	−0.210 (0.526)	−1.613 (0.078)	−0.637 (0.283)	–	−5.738 (0.050)
$\alpha_{21.2}$	−0.010 (0.546)	0.010 (0.647)	−0.075 (0.121)	−0.015 (0.136)	−0.067 (0.906)
$\alpha_{22.2}$	0.983 (0.000)	0.799 (0.000)	0.899 (0.000)	1.004 (0.000)	−0.232 (0.680)
$\Sigma_{11.1}$	0.059 (0.001)	0.103 (0.000)	0.049 (0.000)	0.023 (0.000)	0.135 (0.000)
$\Sigma_{12.1}$	0.004 (0.299)	−0.002 (0.664)	−0.002 (0.492)	0.0001 (0.961)	0.0002 (0.800)
$\Sigma_{22.1}$	0.041 (0.000)	0.044 (0.000)	0.411 (0.000)	0.031 (0.000)	0.0007 (0.000)
$\Sigma_{11.2}$	4.812 (0.045)	1.118 (0.020)	0.507 (0.002)	1.548 (0.000)	0.448 (0.288)
$\Sigma_{12.2}$	0.002 (0.964)	−0.007 (0.882)	−0.029 (0.601)	−0.030 (0.202)	−0.085 (0.271)
$\Sigma_{22.2}$	0.039 (0.000)	0.043 (0.007)	0.049 (0.051)	0.043 (0.000)	0.037 (0.152)
p_{12}	0.064 (0.005)	0.052 (0.993)	0.016 (0.341)	0.042 (0.076)	0.042 (0.042)
p_{21}	0.337 (0.006)	0.285 (0.442)	0.104 (0.124)	0.032 (0.064)	0.655 (0.011)

Note: *p*-values are in brackets (i.e., the null hypothesis that the given coefficient is equal to zero).

Table 6.4   Parameters estimates and related statistics for MS(2)-BVAR regime-switching model: the case of output-gap variability

	Finland	Portugal	Spain
$c_{10.1}$	−0.076 (0.301)	−0.034 (0.866)	0.095 (0.512)
$\alpha_{11.1}$	1.006 (0.000)	0.988 (0.000)	0.959 (0.000)
$\alpha_{12.1}$	−0.009 (0.430)	0.007 (0.789)	−0.005 (0.811)
$c_{10.2}$	−0.137 (0.500)	2.871 (0.009)	3.162 (0.011)
$\alpha_{11.2}$	0.959 (0.000)	0.762 (0.000)	0.811 (0.000)
$\alpha_{12.2}$	−0.028 (0.389)	0.171 (0.217)	0.199 (0.113)
$c_{20.1}$	−0.202 (0.095)	−0.140 (0.525)	−0.580 (0.001)
$\alpha_{21.1}$	−0.007 (0.502)	−0.040 (0.005)	−0.020 (0.000)
$\alpha_{22.1}$	0.967 (0.000)	0.968 (0.000)	0.886 (0.000)
$c_{20.2}$	−0.020 (0.876)	0.257 (0.024)	−0.998 (0.008)
$\alpha_{21.2}$	0.017 (0.151)	−0.016 (0.025)	0.013 (0.308)
$\alpha_{22.2}$	0.997 (0.000)	1.011 (0.000)	0.905 (0.000)
$\Sigma_{11.1}$	0.008 (0.000)	0.040 (0.000)	0.187 (0.000)
$\Sigma_{12.1}$	−0.005 (0.018)	−0.006 (0.380)	−0.009 (0.203)
$\Sigma_{22.1}$	0.055 (0.000)	0.046 (0.000)	0.047 (0.004)
$\Sigma_{11.2}$	0.244 (0.000)	5.020 (0.000)	4.883 (0.000)
$\Sigma_{12.2}$	0.013 (0.198)	−0.086 (0.167)	0.049 (0.687)
$\Sigma_{22.2}$	0.040 (0.000)	0.070 (0.000)	0.532 (0.000)
p_{12}	0.155 (0.001)	0.052 (0.048)	0.091 (0.006)
p_{21}	0.195 (0.001)	0.044 (0.085)	0.118 (0.015)

Note: p-values are in brackets (i.e., the null hypothesis that the given coefficient is equal to zero).

Third, in the equation of interest rate differential and in the majority of cases, the autoregressive coefficient of inflation variability and of output-gap variability in the low credible state is higher than the coefficient in the high credible state (i.e., $\alpha_{22.2} > \alpha_{22.1}$). This is in line with the view that the higher the variance of inflation variability and of output-gap variability, the longer the economy is expected to stay in the low credible regime. Fourth, in the majority of cases, the covariances $\Sigma_{12.i}$ and $\Sigma_{21.i}$ (with $i = 1, 2$) are both equal to zero. This result does not indicate that there is no relationship between the two variables, since $\alpha_{12.i} \neq 0$. However, it implies that the unobserved state variables for each equation in the BVAR-MRS model are not perfectly correlated.[23]

These results also show that credibility in the EMS went through different phases. This is demonstrated in Figures 6.1–8, which present filtered probabilities. They indicate the extent to which a country is in the high credible state. Each figure presents on the left-hand side the filtered probability of being in the high credible state of inflation variability, and on the right-hand side the filtered probability of being in the high

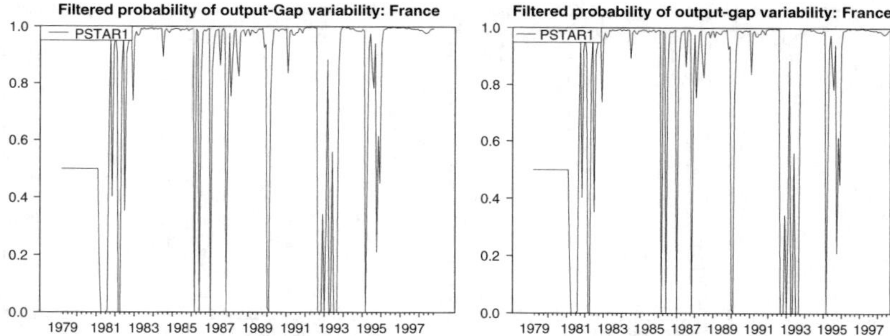

Figure 6.1 Filtered probabilities of the high credible state of French inflation variability and output-gap variability

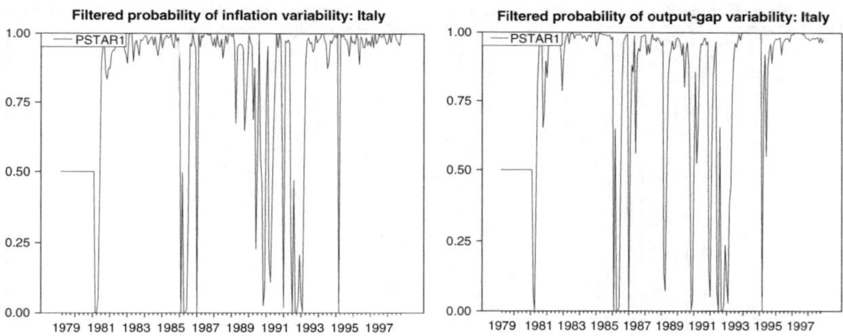

Figure 6.2 Filtered probabilities of the high credible state of the Italian inflation variability and output-gap variability

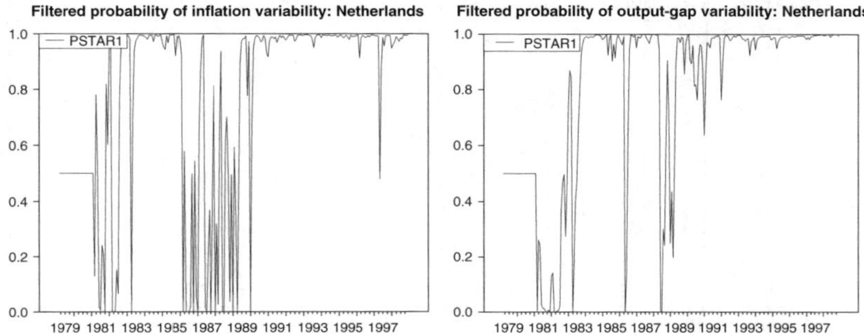

Figure 6.3 Filtered probability of the high credible state of the Dutch inflation variability and output-gap variability

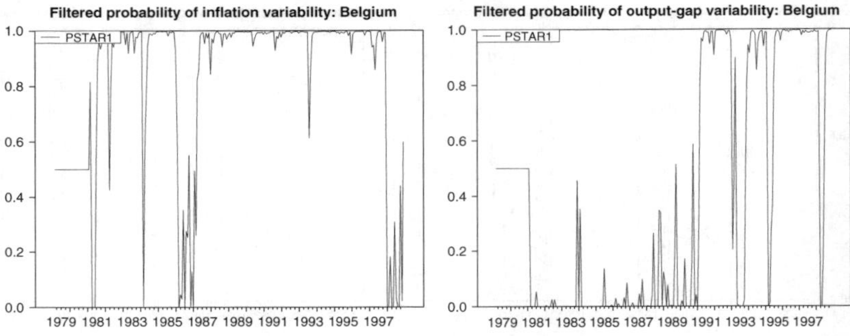

Figure 6.4 Filtered probabilities of the high credible state of Belgian inflation variability and output-gap variability

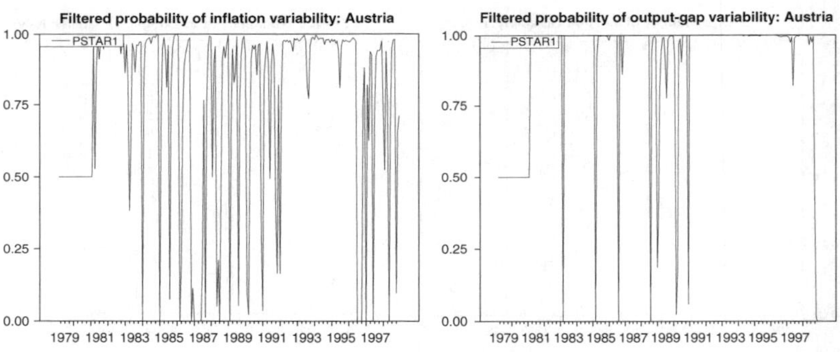

Figure 6.5 Filtered probabilities of the high credible state of Austrian inflation variability and output-gap variability

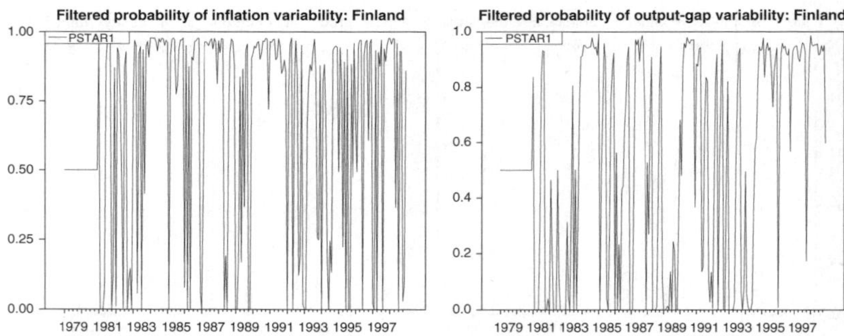

Figure 6.6 Filtered probabilities of the high credible state of Finnish inflation variability and output-gap variability

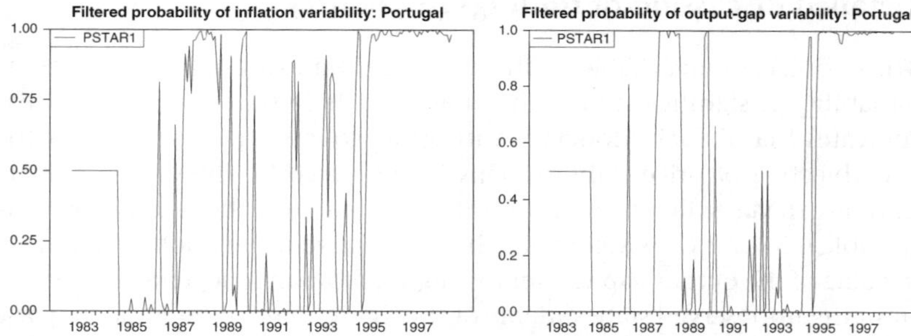

Figure 6.7   Filtered probabilities of the high credible state of Portuguese inflation variability and output-gap variability

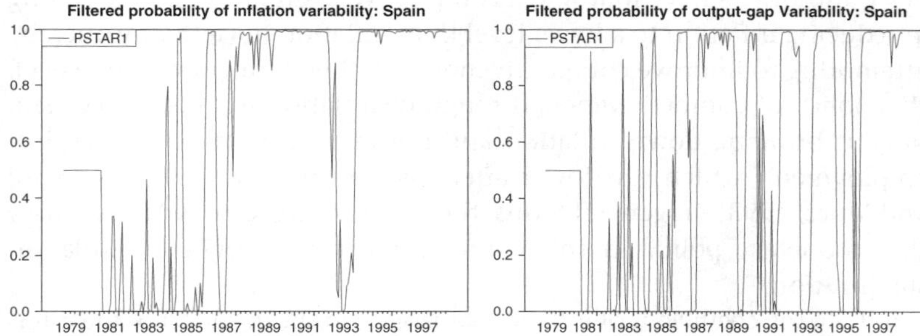

Figure 6.8   Filtered probabilities of the high credible state of the Spanish inflation variability and output-gap variability

credible state of output-gap variability. The filtered probability of the high credible regime is the probability that at a given point in time, the regime process is in the high credible state, given the observations obtained at that point in time and the knowledge of population parameters (see Hamilton, 1994). These figures show that the EMS countries experienced periods of low credibility succeeded by periods of high credibility. In particular, 1979–86 represents a period where the filtered probability of being in a high credible state was reduced on many occasions. This is consistent with the fact that during that period eleven realignments took place in the EMS. During the period 1986–91, the probability of a country being in a credible state is high because most of the convergence of interest rates had taken place without any realignment. Moreover, these figures also show that the probability of being in the high credible state declined at exactly the time when the currency crises took place (i.e., 1992, 1993 and 1995).

Detailed discussion of findings by country

The second column of Table 6.1 indicates that in the case of France inflation variability is significant only in the low credible state (i.e., $\alpha_{12.2}$). This indicates that French monetary authorities follow a policy in line with the objective of price stability. This is reinforced by the evidence that output-gap variability is insignificant in all states (see the second column of Table 6.3). It is consistent with the evidence that the unobserved state variable of the output-gap variability might follow an independent process from the unobserved state variable of the interest rate differential. In particular, as mentioned above, the variance of the output-gap variability in the high credibility regime is higher than the variance in the low credibility regime. This might be due to the fact that since 1983 French monetary authorities have followed a competitive disinflation policy aiming at reducing inflation to a lower level than inflation in Germany, thereby attempting to improve competitiveness and therefore growth. However, this policy of competitiveness through disinflation has been successful only at bringing down inflation and not at creating a higher level of employment, which was lower after than before 1983 (see Blanchard and Muet, 1993). In general terms, the results in the case of France show that monetary policy in this country put more weight on inflation stabilization.

In Italy the coefficient of inflation variability in the equation of the interest rate differential is significant in the high credibility state (i.e, $\alpha_{12.1}$ in the third column of Table 6.1). Moreover, the output-gap variability is significant in the high credible state in the equation of the interest rate differential (see coefficient $\alpha_{12.1}$ in the second column of Table 6.3). This implies that it is not clear whether monetary authorities in Italy put more weight on inflation-variability stabilization than on output-gap-variability stabilization. Although the inflation-variability significance in the high credibility state is consistent with our theoretical priors, significance of output-gap variability in the high credibility regime indicates a policy driven by the objective of output-gap stabilization.[24] However, the results from the equation of inflation variability show that the coefficient of the interest rate differential is significant in the low credibility regime (i.e., $\alpha_{21.2}$ in the third column of Table 6.1). This implies that in a state of high inflation expectations (i.e., low credibility regime), the interest rate instrument is used to stabilize inflation. This is consistent with the evidence that the variance of inflation variability in the low credibility state is lower than the variance in the high credibility state. This indicates that the priority of Italian monetary authorities was to keep inflation low and stable.

The coefficient of inflation variability is slightly higher than the coefficient of output-gap variability, indicating that the Italian monetary authorities emphasize low and stable inflation.

In the case of the Netherlands, inflation variability is significant in the high credibility state (i.e., coefficient $\alpha_{12.1}$ in the fourth column of Table 6.1) and insignificant in the low credibility state (i.e., coefficient $\alpha_{12.2}$ in the fourth column of Table 6.1). The significance of inflation variability only in the high credibility state, and the small interest rate differential between the Dutch interest rate and the German interest rate, implies a close relationship between monetary policies in the two countries.[25] The fourth column of Table 6.3 indicates that output-gap variability is not significant in any state. This is not surprising since the variance of output-gap variability in the high credibility state is higher than the variance in the low credibility state, indicating that the unobserved state variables of output-gap variability and interest rate differential might be independent of each other. In general, the significance of inflation variability and insignificance of the output-gap variability in the equation of the interest rate differential indicate that Dutch monetary authorities prefer to stabilize inflation variability rather than output-gap variability. Therefore, the credibility of monetary policy in the Netherlands regarding the objective of price stability was high.

The fifth column of Table 6.1 shows that in Belgium inflation variability is significant in the high credibility state (i.e., coefficient $\alpha_{12.1}$). Output-gap variability is significant in the low credible state (see the coefficient $\alpha_{12.2}$ in the fifth column in Table 6.3). These results are consistent with our theoretical priors and indicate that the preferences of Belgian monetary authorities regarding the stabilization of output-gap variability and inflation variability are regime dependent. Therefore, in the low credibility regime monetary authorities concentrate on the stabilization of output-gap variability, and in the high credibility regime on the stabilization of inflation variability.

In Austria the results show that inflation variability is not significant in any state (i.e., $\alpha_{12.1}$ and $\alpha_{12.2}$ in the sixth column of Table 6.1), while the output-gap variability is significant only in the high credible state (see the coefficient $\alpha_{12.1}$ in the sixth column of Table 6.3). These results show that Austrian monetary authorities place more weight on the stabilization of output-gap variability. This might be due to the high credibility of Austrian monetary policy in view of their success in shadowing German monetary policy.[26] This can be seen in Figure 6.5 (right-hand side) where the filtered probability of a high credible regime, with the exception of some cases, is close to unity during the whole period.

In Finland inflation variability is not significant in any state (i.e., coefficients $\alpha_{12.1}$ and $\alpha_{12.2}$ in the second column of Table 6.2). This result is strange since Finland was an inflation-targeting country. The insignificance of the inflation variability variable might be due to the high credibility of low inflationary policy, thereby reducing inflationary expectations and therefore the persistence of the low credible state. This is consistent with the fact that the high credible state shows higher persistence than the low credible state (i.e., $p_{12} < p_{21}$ and $\alpha_{11.1} > \alpha_{11.2}$). This implies that the economy remained in the high credible regime for longer than in the low credible regime. Therefore, the incentive of Finnish monetary authorities to inflate was relatively small. This leads to a weak impact of inflation variability in the high credible state. Additionally, output-gap variability is also insignificant in both states (i.e., coefficients $\alpha_{12.1}$ and $\alpha_{12.2}$ in the second column of Table 6.4). This shows that the insignificant effects of inflation variability on the interest rate differential were not due to the priority that the Finnish central bank put on output-gap stabilization, but to the high credibility that these authorities enjoyed over the period, with respect to their low inflation target. The insignificance of output-gap variability in the equation of interest rate differential might be due to the fact that the regime-generating variables of interest rate differential and of output-gap variability might be independent from each other. This is strengthened by the finding that the variance of output-gap variability is higher in the regime of high credibility than the variance in the regime of low credibility.

In Portugal only inflation variability and in the low credibility state is significant (i.e., coefficient $\alpha_{12.2}$ in the third column of Table 6.2). The fact that output-gap variability is not significant in any state shows the determination of the central bank to stabilize inflation irrespective of the cost that this policy implies for the output-gap variability. There is also evidence that in the equation of output-gap variability, the interest rate differential is significant in both states (see coefficients $\alpha_{21.1}$ and $\alpha_{21.2}$ in the fourth column of Table 6.4). Moreover, the variance of inflation variability in the high credibility regime is higher than the variance in the low credibility regime. This indicates that the unobserved state variable of inflation variability is independent of the unobserved state variable of interest rate differential. The implication is that the interest rate responds to inflation variability in the low credibility regime and this response increases the variance of output-gap variability. Under such circumstances the interest rate differential and the output-gap variability are always in the same regime and inflation variability is in the opposite regime. This implies that the main objective of Portuguese central bank was to keep inflation low and stable according to the Maastricht criteria.

In Spain, as in the case of Finland, none of the inflation variability or output-gap variability coefficients is significant in any regime (see column 5, Tables 6.2 and 6.4 respectively). Moreover, the variance of inflation variability, in the low credible state, is lower than the variance in the high credible state. This implies that the regime-generating process of inflation variability might be independent of the regime-generating process of interest rate differential. This might be due to the fact that interest rate differentials reflect changes in the exchange rate with respect to the German mark plus a risk premium (see Froot and Rogoff, 1991). Spain moved gradually from an exchange-rate-targeting regime to an inflation-targeting regime.[27] In particular, Spain experienced a trade-off between retaining an exchange rate peg and concentrating on the domestic inflation target. Spain did not choose to respond to exchange rate changes that partly reflected international macroeconomic movements, and to keep both inflation expectations and interest rate stable (see Bernanke *et al.*, 1999). Therefore, the response of the Spanish interest rate to domestic inflation rather than to changes in the German interest rates might be the reason that the regimes of inflation variability and interest rate differential moved independently. This transition from an exchange-rate-targeting regime to an inflation-targeting regime was accompanied by a substantial increase in transparency and accountability. This helped the central bank to make clear to the public the consequences of fiscal consolidation that took place. In general, Spanish monetary authorities adopted a flexible inflation target accompanied by better communication to the public. They thus managed to increase flexibility and transparency, without experiencing any cost in terms of credibility, higher inflation and even exchange rate instability.

Summary and conclusions

We have used two different MRS(2)-BVAR(1) models to analyse the credibility of monetary policy in a sub-set of EMS countries. In the first specification we used an MRS(2)-BVAR(1) model between the interest rate differential of individual EMS countries and the German interest rate and inflation variability. In the second model we used an MRS(2)-BVAR(1) model between the same interest rate differential and the output-gap variability. We have employed an MRS(2)-BVAR(1) model to avoid the problem of endogeneity from which time varying transition probability models might suffer. We have covered the entire EMS period in the case of eight EMU countries.

The evidence adduced indicates the existence of asymmetric effects, with the output-gap variability and inflation variability having different effects in each state. The impact of inflation variability and output-gap variability for most countries is significant in the high credible state and insignificant in the low credible state. This might be due to the high credibility of central bank monetary policy concerning future disinflationary policies. An exception to this result is the case of inflation variability in France and Portugal, where it is significant in the low credible state. This can be explained by the negative effects on economic growth that high inflation expectations exert in the low credible state, forcing the monetary authorities to respond to these expectations. Moreover, in the case of Belgium output-gap variability is significant in the low credible state. This implies that when the Belgian authorities are faced with a high volatile environment with a potentially negative impact on economic activity, they prefer to stabilize output-gap variability rather than inflation variability.

An important result is that in the cases where both inflation variability and output-gap variability are significant, the former has greater effects than the latter on the interest rate differential. Only in Italy and Belgium are both output-gap variability and inflation variability significant, and only in Italy are both of these variables significant in the same regime. The overall conclusion of this chapter is that most of the countries under consideration followed a monetary policy that was more sensitive to inflation variability. However, the effects of output-gap variability and inflation variability are not the same across the EMS countries under consideration.

Notes

1   Ideally all twelve Economic and Monetary Union (EMU) countries should be included in our sample of countries. Unfortunately, for Greece and Ireland consistent data simply do not exist for the period 1979–98.
2   The difference between this study and Arestis and Mouratidis (2004a) is that we estimate the preferences of monetary authorities in a system specification (in the current contribution), whereas Arestis and Mouratidis estimate these preferences in a single equation framework. Consequently, the current contribution contains work further to that of Arestis and Mouratidis (2004a).
3   The loss function (6.1) includes only inflation and output and not exchange rate. The argument for this formulation is that policy makers are not concerned with the behaviour of intermediate targets, such as exchange rate, but with the optimal path of output and inflation.
4   An interest rate smoothing can be introduced in (6.4) in line with Clarida *et al.* (1998) and with our empirical model as per below.

5   Equation (6.4) can be presented in the form used by Taylor (1993). This can be accomplished by using equations 6.2 and 6.3 to express the supply shocks in terms of output y_t and inflation π_t.

6   Equation (6.5) indicates that when $\lambda = 0$ (i.e. monetary authorities care only about output variability), $\sigma_y^2/\sigma_\pi^2 = 0$ and when $\lambda = 1$ (i.e., monetary authorities care only about inflation variability), $\sigma_y^2/\sigma_\pi^2 = \infty$. Different values of λ between zero and one give the entire output-inflation variability frontier, which depends on the slope of the aggregate supply curve and is independent of the aggregate demand curve and the variance of supply shocks.

7   This is a rather strong assumption but it is consistent with the theoretical argument of Ball (1995) where, as long as supply shocks are absent, the wet type of central bank sets inflation equal to zero and inflates at the discretionary level when supply shocks occur. Therefore, the high volatility regime where the risk premium of the wet type of central bank to deviate from the low inflation policy pursued by the dry type is high can be associated with the presence of supply shocks which raise a trade-off between inflation variability and output-gap variability.

8   A formulation of such a loss function can be presented as follows:

$$L(\pi(y)) = \begin{cases} \lambda_1(\pi - \pi^*)^2 + (1 - \lambda_1)(y - y^*)^2 & \text{if } s_t = \text{expansion} \\ \lambda_2(\pi - \pi^*)^2 + (1 - \lambda_2)(y - y^*)^2 & \text{if } s_t = \text{recession} \end{cases}$$

where $\lambda_1 > \lambda_2$, $(1 - \lambda_1) < (1 - \lambda_2)$ and s_t denotes an unobserved state variable which follows a Markov process.

9   High values of γ (i.e., a flat supply curve) imply that any move by the central bank to put more weight on inflation will increase output gap variability.

10   Arestis and Mouratidis (2004b) show that explicit modelling that takes into account short-run dynamics can yield useful information on the long-run relationship between output-gap and inflation variability. Arestis and Mouratidis measure the efficiency of monetary policy taking into account the short-run trade-off inflation and output-gap variability. In particular, using a bivariate stochastic volatility model of inflation and output gap variability, Arestis and Mouratidis (2004b) identify as supply shocks those that move the coefficient of inflation variability and output-gap variability in the factor loading matrix in different directions. The model has been identified using a rotation matrix in line with Harvey, Ruiz and Shephard (1994). Arestis and Mouratidis (2004b) measure the efficiency of monetary policy based on a perceived indifference curve for two sub-periods. The construction of these indifference curves is based on the estimated coefficient of factor loading matrix that corresponds to supply shocks. The sub-periods were selected based on structural stability tests.

11   Krolzig (1997) describes MRS-BVAR model specifications, where the autoregressive parameters and the mean, or the intercept, are state dependent and the error term is homoscedastic or heteroscedastic.

12   In particular, the elements p_{ij} of p give the transition probability that state i will be followed by state j. Moreover, every column of p sum to unity $\left(\sum_{j=1}^{2} p_{ij} = 1, \text{ for } i = 1,2\right)$ This implies that $p'\mathbf{1} = \mathbf{1}$, where $\mathbf{1}$ is a (2×1) vector with unity elements.

13   Ball (1995) shows that the wet type of central bank sets inflation equal to zero so long as supply shocks are absent, and inflates at the discretionary level (see text for its meaning) when supply shocks occur.

14   Significance of output-gap variability in the high credibility state might be due to an increase in the correlation between the business cycle in an individual EMS member country and in that of Germany. The effect of business-cycle correlation on interest rate policy can be implemented in a multivariate MRS model, if a proxy of business-cycle correlation is available. This would be an interesting exercise for future research.

15   One attractive feature of stochastic volatility models is that they can be extended to a multivariate framework (see Harvey, Ruiz and Shephard, 1994). Stochastic volatility models, based on the log of variabilities, can capture the presence of a variability trade-off between inflation and output-gap in a way that no other multivariate model of variabilities can capture (see Arestis, Caporale and Cipollini, 2002).

16   An alternative way to compute stochastic volatilities is as follows:

$$SV - p = \log \left\{ \left[\log p_t - \left(\sum_{t-1}^{T} \log p_t \right) / T \right]^2 \right\}$$

$$SV - y = \log \left\{ \left[\log y_t - \left(\sum_{t-1}^{T} \log y_t \right) / T \right]^2 \right\}$$

where SV is stochastic volatility, p is inflation, and y is output-gap.

17   In the case of industrial production the series of stochastic volatility was so erratic that convergence did not take place in the estimation of the MRS-BVAR models. We were thus forced to smooth the series by using a twelve-order moving average.

18   Moreover, Mouratidis and Spagnolo (2003) show that the interest rate differentials in a number of EMS countries is characterized by the presence of only two states. In particular, they examine the number of states for the interest rate differential, and, they also employ Hansen's (1992 and 1996) standardized likelihood ratio to test the hypotheses of one state against two states, and two against three states. Moreover, they consider selection procedures based on the ARMA representation of Markov regime-switching models. Evidence both from Hansen tests and from the ARMA representation selection procedures strongly supports the hypothesis of two states.

19   In an alternative specification, suggested by Krolzig (1997), where autoregressive coefficients are state-invariant and only the mean, or the intercept, is regime dependent, it is not possible to measure the effect of inflation variability and output-gap variability on interest rate differential in different regimes. In this case implications about the preferences of the central bank are ignored.

20   Krolzig (1997, ch. 6), generalizing the arguments of Leroux (1992), shows that identifiability of a MRS-VAR model requires that the VAR parameter vectors in each regime are distinct, and the Markov chain associated with the transition probability matrix is irreducible and aperiodic.

21 See Proposition 1 of Warne (2000), for conditions under which each regime-generating process of MRS-BVAR follows an independent process.
22 The exception to these results is the case of Belgian output-gap variability where the autoregressive coefficient of interest rate differential in the high credible state (i.e., $\alpha_{11.1}$) is slightly higher than the autoregressive coefficient in the low credible regime (i.e., $\alpha_{11.2}$). However, the transition probability from the low credible regime to the high credible regime is higher than the transition probability from the high credible regime to the low credible regime (i.e., $p_{21} < p_{12}$).
23 An interesting question that arises is whether the unobserved state variables are intertemporally perfectly correlated (Philips, 1991; Ravn and Sola, 1995; and Sola, Spagnolo and Spagnolo, 2002). Under such a framework, there would be four states (i.e., $P_1 \otimes P_2$) where P_i, with $i = 1,2$, is the transition probability matrix of each variable in the system. It would be sensible to estimate them. However, in our specification where the autoregressive matrix and the variance-covariance matrix are regime dependent, it would be computationally demanding, if not impossible, to estimate them.
24 Significance of the output-gap variability in the high credibility regime might reflect an increase in the business cycles correlation between Italy and Germany. However, as we mentioned in the section on empirical methodology, the issue of the effects of business cycles correlation on monetary policy is better left for future research.
25 In the 1980s there was the view that the EMS included two block currency areas: a hard-currency block which included up to 1987 only the Deutschmark and the Dutch Guilder, and a soft-currency block which included the other currencies that were shadowed by the French franc.
26 The Austrian interest rate differential in relation to the German interest rate was almost close to zero during the period under investigation.
27 The central bank of Spain announced an inflation target on 28 November 1994. The announcement was made in line with the law of the Autonomy Banco de Espana, introduced on January 1995, and it was effectively applied in June of the same year.

References

Arestis, P., Caporale, M.G. and Cipollini, A. (2002) 'Is There a Trade-off Between Inflation and Output Gap?', *Manchester School*, 70(4), 528–45.

Arestis, P. and Mouratidis, K. (2004a) 'Credibility of EMS Interest Rate Policies: A Markov Regime-Switching Approach', *Manchester School*, 72(1), 1–23.

Arestis, P. and Mouratidis, K. (2004b) 'Is there a Trade-off Between Inflation Volatility and Output-Gap Volatility in the EMU Countries?', *Scottish Journal of Political Economy*, 51(5), 691–706.

Backus, D.K. and Driffill, J. (1985) 'Inflation and Reputation', *American Economic Review*, 75(3), 530–8.

Ball, L. (1995) 'Time-consistence and Persistence Changes in Inflation', *Journal of Monetary Economics*, 36, 329–50.

Barro, R.J. (1986) 'Reputation in a Model of Monetary Policy with Incomplete Information', *Journal of Monetary Economics*, 17, 3–20.

Barro, R.J. and Gordon, D.B. (1983a) 'A Positive Theory of Monetary Policy in a Natural Rate Model', *Journal of Political Economy*, 91(4), 589–610.

Barro, R.J. and Gordon, D.B. (1983b) 'Rules Discretion, and Reputation in a Model of Monetary Policy', *Journal of Monetary Economics*, 12(1), 101–21.

Bernanke, B.S., Laubach, T., Mishikin, F.S. and Posen, A.S. (1999) *Inflation Targeting* (Princeton, NJ: Princeton University Press).

Blanchard, O. and Muet, A.P. (1993) 'Competitiveness through Disinflation: An Assessment of French Macroeconomic Policy', *Economic Policy*, 16, 11–56.

Breit, F.J. and Carriquiry, A.L. (1996) 'Improved Quasi-Maximum Likelihood Estimation for Stochastic Volatility Models', in J.C. Lee, W.O. Johnson and A. Zellner (eds), *Modelling and Prediction: Honoring Seymour Geisser* (New York: Springer-Verlag), 228–47.

Cecchetti, S. (1998) 'Policy Rules and Targets: Framing the Central Banker's Problem', *Economic Policy Review*, Federal Reserve Bank (New York), June, 1–41.

Cecchetti, S.C. and Ehrmann, M. (1999) 'Does Inflation Targeting Increase Output Volatility? An International Comparison of Policymakers' Preferences and Outcomes', *NBER Working Paper Series*, No. 7426 (Cambridge, MA: NBER).

Clarida, R., Gali, J. and Gertler, M. (1998) 'Monetary Policy Rules in Practice: Some International Evidence', *European Economic Review*, 42(2), 1033–68.

Chourdakis, K.M., and Tzavalis, E. (2001) 'Option Pricing under Discrete Shifts in Stock Returns', *Working Paper Series*, No. 426, Department of Economics, Queen Mary University London.

Cukierman, A. (1999) 'The Inflation Bias Result Revisited', mimeo, Tel Aviv University.

Dahlquist, M. and Gray, S.F. (2000) 'Regime Switching and Interest Rates in the European Monetary System', *Journal of International Economics*, 50, 399–419.

Ehrmann, M., Ellison, M. and Valla, N. (2001) 'Regime dependent impulse response functions in a Markov Vector Autoregression Model', *Economics Letters*, 98, 295–9.

Engels, C. and Hakkio, C.S. (1996) 'The Distribution of the Exchange Rate in the EMS', *International Journal of Economics and Finance*, 55, 55–67.

Filardo, A.G. (1998) 'Choosing Information Variables for Transition Probabilities in a Time-Variance Transition Probability Markov-Switching Model', *Working Paper Series*, No. RWP98-09, Federal Bank of Kansas City.

Friedman, B.M. and Laibson, D.L. (1989) 'Economic Implications of Extraordinary Movements in Stock Prices', *Brooking Papers on Economic Activity*, 2, 137–89.

Froot, K.A. and Rogoff, K. (1991) 'The EMS, the EMU and the Transition to a Common Currency', in National Bureau of Economic Research, *Macroeconomics Annual* (Cambridge, MA: NBER), 269–327.

Giavazzi, F. and Pagano, M. (1988) 'The Advantage of Tying One's Hand, EMS Discipline and Central Bank Credibility', *European Economic Review*, 32, 1,055–82.

Gray, S.F. (1996) 'Modelling the Conditional Distribution of Interest Rate as Regime-Switching Process', *Journal of Financial Economics*, 42, 27–62.

Hamilton, J.D. (1993) 'Estimation, Inference and Forecasting of Time Series Subject to Changes in Regime', in G.S. Maddala, C.R. Rao and H.D. Vinod (eds), *Handbook of Econometrics*, Vol. 4 (Amsterdam: North-Holland).

Hamilton, J.D. (1994) *Time Series Analysis* (Princeton, NJ: Princeton University Press).

Hamilton, J.D. (1996) 'Specification Testing in Markov-Switching Time-Series Models', *Journal of Econometrics*, 70, 127–57.

Hansen, B.E. (1992) 'The Likelihood Ratio Test Under Nonstandard Conditions: Testing the Markov Switching Model of GNP', *Journal of Applied Econometrics*, 7, 61–82.

Hansen, B.E. (1996) 'Erratum: 'The Likelihood Ratio Test Under Nonstandard Conditions: Testing the Markov Switching Model of GNP', *Journal of Applied Econometrics*, 11, 195–8.

Harvey, A.C., Ruiz, E. and Shephard, N. (1994) 'Multivariate Stochastic Variance Models', *Review of Economic Studies*, 61, 247–64.

Koopmans, S.J., Harvey, A.C., Doornik, J.A. and Shephard, N. (2000) *Stamp 6.2: Structural Time Series Analysis, Modeller and Predictor* (London: Timberlake Consultants).

Krolzig, H. M. (1997) *Markov-Switching Vector Autoregressions: Modelling, Statistical Inference, and Application to Business Cycle Analysis* (Berlin: Springer).

Leroux, B.G. (1992) 'Maximum-likelihood for Hidden Markov Models', *Stochastic Processes and their Application*, 40, 127–43.

Lutkephol, H. (1991) *Introduction to Multiple Time Series Analysis* (Berlin: Springer).

Mouratidis, K. and Spagnolo, N. (2003) 'Evaluating Currency Crises: The Case of European Monetary System', *Working Paper*, No. 207 (London: National Institute of Economic and Social Research).

Muscatelli, A. (1998) 'Optimal Inflation Contracts and Inflation Targets with Uncertain Central Bank Preferences: Accountability through Independence?', *Economic Journal*, 108, 529–42.

Olmedo, A. (2002) 'Asymmetries in the Central Bank Behaviour', *Working Paper*, Université de Cergy Pontoise I, http://thema.u-paris10.fr/papers/DT/2002-06Olmedo.pdf.

Phillips, K.L. (1991) 'A Two-Country Model of Stochastic Output with Changes in Regime', *Journal of International Economics*, 31, 121–42.

Ravn, M.O. and Sola, M. (1995) 'Stylized Facts and Regime Changes: Are Prices Procyclical?', *Journal of Monetary Economics*, 36, 497–526.

Sarantis, N. and Piard, S. (2000) 'Credibility Macroeconomic Fundamentals, and Markov Regime Switches in the EMS', *Discussion Paper*, No. 00–05, Department of Economics, London Guildhall University.

Sola, M., Spagnolo, F. and Spagnolo, N. (2002) 'A Test for Volatility Spillovers', *Economic Letters*, 76, 77–84.

Taylor, J.B. (1980) 'Aggregate Dynamics and Staggered Contracts', *Journal of Political Economy*, 88, 1–23.

Taylor, J.B. (1993) 'Discretion Versus Policy Rules in Practice', *Carnegie-Rochester Conference Series on Public Policy*, 39, 95–214.

Taylor, J.B. (1994) 'The Inflation-Output Variability Trade-off', in *Goals Guidelines and Constraints Facing Monetary Policymakers*, Federal Reserve Bank of Boston, Conference Series, No. 38, 21–38.

Warne, A. (2000) 'Causality and Regime Inference in a Markov Switching VAR', *Working Paper*, No. 118 (Stockholm: Sveriges Riskbank).

7
Why Do Firms Hedge? A Review of the Evidence

Amrit Judge

Introduction

The academic debate on the merits of hedging has identified five main theoretical rationales for corporate hedging:

(a) to minimize corporate tax liability;
(b) to reduce the expected costs of financial distress;
(c) to ameliorate conflicts of interest between shareholders and bondholders;
(d) to improve co-ordination between financing and investment policy;
(e) to maximize the value of the manager's wealth portfolio.

These theories provide useful insights and predictions on the firm's hedging decision. In particular, the hedging theories imply that the benefits of hedging to shareholders or managers are likely to differ across firms in ways that depend on various firm-level financial and operating characteristics. The empirical literature has confronted this theoretical debate on the merits of hedging by investigating the relative importance of the corporate hedging theories. This has been achieved by operationalizing the various theoretical predictions into empirically testable implications. Table 7.1 shows that this literature has grown considerably in the last ten years with over twenty-five empirical studies since 1995. The majority of these studies source data from the United States. This growth in the empirical literature is largely due to the mandatory disclosure of information on hedging practices and, in particular, the use of derivatives in annual reports and other financial statements. In the United States the catalyst responsible for this has been the Financial Accounting Standards Board (FASB). The FASB has issued several 'Statements of Financial Accounting

Table 7.1 Empirical studies examining non-financial firms' hedging policy and the use of derivatives (in chronological order)

Author(s)	Date of study	Area of study	Source of data	Type of firm	Sample size	Dependent variable	Methodology	Country
Francis and Stephan	1993	All hedgers	Annual Reports (1983–87)	Financial and non-financial	434	Binary	Logit	USA
Nance, Smith and Smithson	1993	All hedgers	Survey (1986)	Non-financial	169 respondents = 31.6%	Binary	Logit	USA
Dolde	1995	All hedgers	Survey (1992)	Non-financial	244 respondents = 51.3%	Binary	Logit/OLS	USA
Wysocki	1996	All hedgers and foreign exchange hedgers	Annual Reports (1993 and 1994)	Non-financial	403 (215 derivative users) and 807 (234 currency derivative users)	Binary	Logit/OLS	USA/Canada
Mian	1996	All hedgers and foreign exchange and interest rate hedgers	Annual Reports (1992)	Non-financial	771 hedgers and 2251 non-hedgers	Binary	Logit	USA
Berkman and Bradbury	1996	All hedgers	Annual Reports (1994)	Non-financial	116 firms on NZ stock exchange	Continuous	Tobit	New Zealand
Tufano	1996	Commodity price hedging: gold price hedging	Survey (1991–93)	Gold mining	48	Continuous	Tobit	USA
Fok, Carroll and Chiou	1997	All hedgers	Annual Reports (1990–92)	Non-financial	331	Binary	Logit	USA
Géczy, Minton and Schrand	1997	Foreign exchange hedgers	Annual Reports (1991)	Non-financial	372 Fortune 500	Binary	Logit//Simultaneous equation	USA

(*Continued*)

Table 7.1 (Continued)

Author(s) of study	Date	Area of study	Source of data	Type of firm	Sample size	Dependent variable	Methodology	Country
Gay and Nam	1998	All hedgers and interest rate hedgers	Proxy statement (1995)	Non-financial	486	Continuous	Tobit	USA
Howton and Perfect	1998	All hedgers and foreign exchange and interest rate hedgers	Annual Report (1994)	Non-financial	451 Fortune 500/ S&P 500 and 461 random firms	Continuous	Tobit	USA
Goldberg, Godwin, Kim and Tritschler	1998	All hedgers and foreign exchange and interest rate hedgers	10-K forms (1993)	Non-financial	410	Binary/ Continuous	Probit/Tobit/ OLS/Cragg	USA
Fehle	1999	All hedgers	10-K forms and 10-K 405 (1993–1997)	Non-financial	2,528 (7336 firm years)	Binary	Probit	USA
Jalilvand	1999	All hedgers	Survey	Non-financial	77	Binary	Logit	Canada
Haushalter	2000	Commodity price hedging: oil and gas price hedging	Annual Report (1992–94) and Survey (1995)	Oil and gas producers	100	Continuous	Tobit/Cragg	USA
Graham and Rogers	2000	Foreign exchange interest rate hedgers	10-K forms (1994–95)	Financial and non-financial	531 (derived from a random sample of 10-K filings)	Continuous	Tobit/Cragg	USA
Allayannis and Ofek	2001	Foreign exchange hedgers	Annual Reports (1992–93)	Non-financial	724 firm years (S&P 500)	Binary/ Continuous	Probit/Tobit/ OLS/Cragg	USA
Graham and Rogers	2002	All hedgers	10-K forms (1994–95)	Financial and non-financial	442 (derived from a random sample of 10-K filings)	Continuous equation	Tobit/Simultaneous equation	USA
Knopf, Nam and Thornton	2002	All hedgers	Annual reports (1996)	Non-financial	260 (S&P 500)	Continuous	Tobit	USA

Study	Year	Area of Study	Data source	Sample type	Sample size	Dependent variable	Method	Country
Rogers	2002	All hedgers	10-K forms (1994–95)	Financial and non-financial	524 (derived from a random sample of 10-K filings)	Continuous	Tobit/ Simultaneous equation	USA
Hagelin	2003	Foreign exchange hedgers	Survey (1997)	Non-financial	101 respondents = 63%	Binary/ Continuous	Logit/Cragg	Sweden
Bartram, Brown and Fehle	2004	All hedgers and foreign exchange, interest rate and commodity price hedgers	Annual reports (1999–2000)	Non-financial	7,309	Binary	Logit	48 countries
Pramborg	2005	Foreign exchange hedgers	Survey (2000)	Non-financial	60 Korean respondents = 16% 103 Swedish respondents = 41%	Binary	Logit	Sweden/ South Korea
Judge a	2005	Foreign exchange hedgers	Annual reports (1995)	Non-financial	366	Binary	Logit	UK
Faulkender	2005	Interest rate hedgers	10-K forms (1994–1999)	Chemical industry	133 (275 debt issuances over 6-year period)	Binary	Probit	USA
Judge b	2005	All hedgers	Annual reports (1995)	Non-financial	412	Binary	Logit	UK

OLS = Ordinary Least Squares

Note(s): Under the 'Area of Study' column, 'All hedgers' indicates that firms hedging any category of exposure were defined as hedgers.

Standards (SFASs)' requiring firms to disclose in their annual reports both qualitative and quantitative information on hedging and derivatives use.

This chapter examines the literature that has focused on testing the various theories of hedging. It begins by looking at how the empirical literature has defined hedging and measured hedging. It then examines whether the definitions of hedging employed are appropriate indicators of hedging or are potential proxies for speculation. This is followed by a look at some inherent problems of single exposure hedging studies and a conclusion.

Hedging defined and measured

The ability to identify which firms hedge and don't hedge and, for those that do, the extent to which they hedge is vital if reliable tests of hedging theories are to be undertaken. The empirical examination of hedging theories has been hindered by the general unavailability of data on hedging activities. Until recently, a firm's exact position in hedging and its methods of hedging (for example, use of derivatives) was information closely guarded by the firm because it was deemed to be of strategic importance. It is only in the last few years that firms have been encouraged to disclose in their annual reports information on their hedging policies and their methods of hedging. In the absence of this information, most of the earlier empirical studies used survey data to examine the determinants of corporate hedging (Nance, Smith and Smithson, 1993; Dolde, 1995). In these studies, authors surveyed firms, asking respondents whether their firm used derivative instruments. As disclosure of hedging practices in financial reports improved, several studies searched these reports for qualitative disclosures and defined hedgers as firms whose reports included references to terms such as 'hedging' or 'risk management' or 'derivatives', or to particular derivative instruments such as 'interest rate swaps' or 'foreign currency derivatives' (Francis and Stephan (1993), Mian (1996), Wysocki (1996), Fok, Carroll and Chiou (1997), Géczy, Minton and Schrand (1997)).[1] Further improvements in the quality of annual report disclosures have made it possible for recent studies to employ quantitative data on derivative usage to measure the 'extent of hedging'.[2]

How is hedging defined?

The question of how hedging is defined is critical to any empirical examination of the determinants of corporate hedging. In their seminal paper formulating the economic rationale for hedging, Smith and Stulz (1985) point out that a 'firm can hedge by trading in a particular futures, forward, swap or option market' (p. 392). They also suggest that a firm can hedge via its operating strategies: for example, a merger can generate similar effects to those of hedging through derivatives. Other operating strategies, also referred to as on-balance sheet strategies, include relocating production facilities abroad or funding in a foreign currency. Given the different methods a firm can employ to reduce its risks, how hedging is defined is crucial for the purposes of precisely classifying firms as 'hedgers' and 'non-hedgers'. Several studies take firms' investment and on-balance-sheet financing strategies as predetermined and define hedging as the use of financial derivatives (Nance, Smith and Smithson, 1993; Dolde, 1995; Berkman and Bradbury, 1996; Mian, 1996; Wysocki, 1996; Gay and Nam, 1998; Howton and Perfect, 1998; Graham and Rogers, 2002). Two studies (Francis and Stephan, 1993; Mian, 1996) employ key word searches. Key words, such as 'hedging' or 'derivatives' or references to specific types of derivatives, are used to identify hedging firms. Firms not disclosing the use of derivatives are classified as non-hedgers.

The failure to allow for the fact that firms can and do use other techniques to manage risk is a major weakness in these studies.[3] This is because the methodologies employed in these studies do not directly distinguish between derivatives use and risk reduction. Hedging can be pursued through changes in the firm's operating characteristics or other financial policies. Recently studies have demonstrated that foreign currency debt is used in hedging firms' foreign currency exposure (Allayannis and Ofek, 2001; Elliott, Huffman and Makar 2003; Kedia and Mozumdar, 2003). Kedia and Mozumdar (2003) suggest that an implication of this result is that studies of foreign currency hedging 'need to go beyond the firms' derivative positions and look at other financial and operational hedges to fully comprehend the firms' exposures and risk management activities' (p. 545). Guay and Kothari (2003) also stress the importance of considering a multifaceted approach to hedging in empirical studies of corporate risk management. They find that derivatives usage by many US non-financial firms is too small relative to their risk exposures. They suggest that this result is potentially consistent with firms 'using derivatives to "fine tune" their overall risk-management program that likely includes other means of hedging' (p. 425). They go on to suggest that this implies that derivatives use is a noisy proxy for firms' risk management activities, which might explain the mixed results reported in the literature such as those pertaining to financial distress and underinvestment costs.

Some studies, however, do include foreign currency debt use, but this is as an exogenous variable in models explaining currency derivatives hedging (Géczy, Minton and Schrand 1997; Hagelin, 2003; Bartram,

Brown and Fehle, 2004). These studies report a positive coefficient for the foreign debt variable which is consistent with foreign debt acting as a complement to derivatives or creating a foreign currency exposure on average. This approach, and that of excluding alternative risk management methods (such as choosing to finance in the currency of the firm's assets), fails to distinguish between foreign currency derivative use and foreign currency risk management. For example, two firms may manage their foreign currency exposure arising from foreign assets, one firm using a currency swap to create a liability in the required currency, and the other using foreign denominated debt to act as a natural hedge of foreign revenues. Therefore, by equating 'foreign currency hedger' with 'foreign currency derivative user', the former would be characterized as a 'hedger' and the latter, while functionally equivalent, a 'non-hedger'.[4] This approach would make it far more difficult to identify differences between foreign currency hedgers and foreign currency non-hedgers.

Similarly, in the context of interest rate risk management, Faulkender (2005) points out that a firm that raises fixed rate debt possesses the same final interest rate exposure as one that issues floating rate debt and swaps into fixed. However, most empirical studies have equated 'interest rate hedger' with 'interest rate derivative user' and therefore the former would be characterized as a 'non-hedger' and the latter as a 'hedger'. As noted above, this approach fails to recognize that firms may be hedging their financial price risks by methods other than financial derivatives. Faulkender goes on to say: 'an empirical examination of whether firms are hedging, and what the benefits are of smooth cash flows, should examine the final interest rate exposure of the debt, not the intermediate step of how many derivatives the firm uses' (p. 932).

Faulkender is effectively suggesting that some firms may be naturally hedged if they issue a debt contract that is correctly aligned with their desired interest rate exposure. A firm may have highly variable operating cash flows, but if its supply of cash flow is matched to its demand for cash flow, it is naturally hedged. Thus, a firm is naturally hedged when, for example, its ability to generate operating cashflow is positively correlated with its investment opportunities. However, precisely classifying firms as hedgers and non-hedgers may not be possible empirically. One way of alleviating this problem is to examine the use of derivatives rather than hedging in general, and introduce variables that indicate the existence of other hedging methods. Therefore, firms that are naturally hedged will not be expected to use derivatives.[5] Some studies attempt to take account of hedging achieved through operational or alternative financial policies (Tufano, 1996; Fok, Carroll and Chiou, 1997; Géczy, Minton and Schrand,

1997; Haushalter, 2000; Allayannis and Ofek, 2001; Faulkender, 2005; Judge, 2005b; Pramborg, 2005).

Tufano's (1996) investigation of risk management practices in the North American gold mining industry attempts to address this problem by recognizing that risk management strategies can be implemented using explicit derivative transactions, such as the forward sale of gold, or they can be combined with financing activities. For example, in borrowing via a gold or bullion loan, a mining firm combines dollar-based financing with a forward sale of gold. Therefore, he attempts to identify both on- and off-balance sheet risk management activity so as to avoid what he refers to as 'the inaccurate categorisation of functionally-equivalent financial positions' (p. 1,103).

Fok, Carroll and Chiou (1997) use a measure for unrelated business line diversification and a dummy variable identifying multinational firms which proxies for production or operational hedging. Only the multinational dummy variable was significant, although the sign was opposite to that predicted. If this variable is a good proxy for operational hedging, then the Fok, Carroll and Chiou (1997) results imply that operational hedging and derivatives hedging are more likely to be complements rather than substitutes.

How is hedging measured?

In some studies researchers measure 'risk management' by using a dichotomous variable that equals one if the firm indicates that it hedges or uses derivatives and zero otherwise. Thus hedging in is seen as a binary decision, the decision to hedge or not to hedge. However, it could be argued that the theories of hedging predict relationships between the extent of risk management and various firm level financial and operating characteristics. For example, *ceteris paribus*, a firm with a high proportion of export sales might be expected to hedge a greater proportion of its exposure than, say, a firm with a lower proportion of export sales.[6] The aforementioned approach is clearly a crude way to measure hedging since it does not discriminate between firms that fully hedge and those that part hedge. Consequently, firms that hedge 1 per cent of their exposure will make up the population of hedging firms just the same as those that hedge 100 per cent of their exposure. These types of hedging firms might differ significantly in terms of their exposure characteristics and other financial and operating traits. Therefore, it may not be possible to detect differences between hedgers and non-hedgers since a firm that hedges a small portion of its exposure might be closer to a non-hedging firm than to one that hedges most of its risk.[7] Dolde (1995) attempts to allow for the variation in the extent of hedging by asking firms to indicate what proportion of their exposures are hedged, first, when a firm holds no view on future financial price changes, and second, when a firm holds a view on future financial price changes. He then uses a dichotomous variable to distinguish between firms lying above or below the median of all responses.

Due to the limitations of the data on hedging the above studies examine the determinants of the decision to hedge and cannot examine the determinants of the decision of how much to hedge. The former is concerned with the likelihood of hedging and the latter is concerned with the extent of hedging. However, as the disclosure of quantitative data on derivatives use has improved, several recent studies have attempted to derive a continuous measure of hedging in order to provide more reliable tests of the determinants of hedging (Berkman and Bradbury, 1996; Tufano, 1996; Gay and Nam, 1998; Howton and Perfect, 1998; Haushalter, 2000; Allayannis and Ofek, 2001; Graham and Rogers, 2002; Knopf, Nam and Thornton, 2002; Rogers, 2002). Several of these studies employ total notional values of derivatives scaled by firm size to measure the level (or extent) of derivatives use (or hedging: see Berkman and Bradbury, 1996; Gay and Nam, 1998; Howton and Perfect, 1998; Allayannis and Ofek, 2001; Knopf, Nam and Thornton, 2002).

A problem with the use of total notional values is that they are an aggregate of long and short positions and therefore are an over-estimation of the level of derivative use, and so a biased measure of the extent of hedging. For example, in the case of swaps, the notional amount can be quite large, whereas the 'net' position may be small. Where hedging is undertaken at a decentralized level, the reported notional value of derivatives may be larger than if hedging is undertaken at a group level, yet the same net position may result. Graham and Rogers (2002) attempt to correct for this by restricting their sample of derivative users to those for which they can determine the net notional amount of derivatives. However, this factor will only be important if many firms enter into offsetting long and short positions.

Two studies also use fair values of derivatives scaled by firm size as an indicator of the extent of hedging (Berkman and Bradbury, 1996; Howton and Prefect, 1998), although it is not clear what this variable is measuring. The fair value is the amount at which an instrument could be exchanged in a current transaction between willing parties other than in a forced or liquidation sale. Fair values are estimated by discounting the future cash flows to net present value using appropriate market rates prevailing at the year-end. The fair value of a derivative contract at origination is zero even though the firm might be fully hedged. Clearly this variable provides no indication of the extent of risk management undertaken, and therefore its value in testing the theories of hedging is questionable.

Another problem is that the notional values employed in these studies do not take into account the risk characteristics of the derivative instrument such as the term, denomination and settlement price of the outstanding contracts. For example, suppose a swap's principal is £250 million and the debt with which it is associated is £500 million. Either the swap is covering only half the debt issue and its consequent interest expense, or the entire interest expense is being hedged in some other way: for example, through an amplified interest rate.[8] Also, different firms can hold the same notional value of derivatives and still have very different hedging practices (Smith, 1995): for example, two firms may hold swaps with a notional principal of £200 million, but for one the term is one year and for the other the term is five years. What is important is which firm is hedging more extensively. It might seem that the latter is more extensively hedged; however, if the first firm is hedging debt that matures in one year and the other firm is hedging debt that matures in five years, then their hedging practices are similar. Therefore, no conclusions can be drawn from examining notional principal amounts, but relating them back to their underlying exposures prompts closer investigation into companies' risk management activities and philosophies. Existing financial reporting regimes do not require firms to disclose the underlying asset or liability that is associated with a derivative contract, so researchers are not able to determine the precise relationship between the item hedged and the hedging instrument.

A weakness in using gross or net notional amounts of derivatives scaled by firm size as the dependent variable is that it is not clear what this is actually measuring: for example, Allayannis and Ofek (2001) expect a relation between the value of foreign currency derivatives and factors that expose the firm to foreign currency risks (overseas operations, imports and exports). However, unless firm size is correlated with these exposure characteristics, the exact relationship between their dependent variable, the ratio of notional value of currency derivatives to total assets, and the size of the exposures is unclear.

If the dependent variable in these studies is attempting to measure the degree of hedging then the fundamental problem with this measure is that it does not scale by the firm's underlying financial price exposure. All studies use firm size as their scaling variable. Unless this is a good proxy for the level of a firm's exposure it is not clear whether this is actually a measure of the extent of risk management undertaken. These studies fail to recognize that it is necessary to scale the firm's financial risk management activity against its natural exposure to understand its economic import-ance. Therefore, it is not clear from these studies what additional insights they provide relative to the studies employing a binary dependent variable to the question of the empirical determinants of hedging.

Two industry-specific studies attempt to address this criticism (Tufano, 1996; Haushalter, 2000). Tufano calculates a measure of the degree of risk management undertaken by firms in the US gold mining industry, by using the delta of a firm's risk management portfolio divided by the amount of gold expected to be produced over a three-year period as a measure of the extent of risk management activity. Tufano refers to this as the delta per-centage: the percentage of production accounted for by portfolio delta.[9] Haushalter (2000) examines the hedging policies of US oil and gas pro-ducers for the period 1992–4. Using both survey and financial statement data he measures the extent of hedging as the fraction of the firm's pro-duction for the year that is hedged against price fluctuations. The implicit assumption made by both of these studies is that the size of a firm's expo-sure is equal to its level of production rather than the level of its sales. Ultimately it is the amount sold in a given period that is exposed to price risk. The Tufano and Haushalter dependent variables are appropriate if production levels in a given period are similar to sales for that period, otherwise these measures may over- or under-estimate the level of hedging.

A potential weakness in these industry-specific studies is that although variability in the commodity price is the exposure that dominates for firms in the oil, gas and gold mining industries, these studies take no account of firms' other hedging activities, such as interest rate and foreign currency hedging. This point is pertinent since shareholders in a commodity com-pany might prefer a company to keep its commodity price exposure unhedged to preserve all of its upside to commodity price appreciation. Hedging commodity price exposure may limit the ability of the com-pany to benefit fully from increases in the price of the commodity (some-thing shareholders would have expected when buying the shares).

Speculation

The previous section shows that all empirical studies incorporate the use of derivatives into their hedging definition. However, derivatives can be used for speculation as well as hedging. Ljungqvist (1994) and Campbell and Kracaw (1999) identify several incentives for non-financial firms to speculate. Given these incentives it is possible that derivative users are speculating rather than hedging. Recently the debate on derivatives use has focused on whether firms use these instruments for hedging or for speculation (Géczy, Minton and Schrand, 2004; Faulkender, 2005), so an important issue is whether risk management studies are measuring hedging or speculation. If the motives for optimal hedging and speculation are correlated, empirical results might not distinguish between these two activities. For example, Campbell and Kracaw (1999) propose a model which implies that some speculative behaviour may be optimal and that such optimal behaviour should be observed with firms that have significant growth opportunities but modest internal resources and high asymmetric information costs. Conversely, Froot, Scharfstein and Stein (1993) present analysis which suggests that firms faced with a similar set of circumstances possess an incentive to hedge. Several studies find that firms with higher levels of research and development (R&D) expenditure, which is considered to be indicative of high growth opportunities, are more likely to use derivatives. They interpret this as evidence of more hedging by these companies. However, this set of results is also consistent with Campbell and Kracaw's analysis that firms might be speculating with derivatives rather than hedging.

It follows from the above discussion that it may not be possible empirically to distinguish between hedgers and speculators. Notwithstanding this, five empirical studies ignore the possibility that firms may use derivatives to enhance rather than reduce their exposures (Nance, Smith and Smithson, 1993; Wysocki, 1996; Fok, Carroll and Chiou, 1997; Gay and Nam, 1998; Howton and Perfect, 1998), although, Nance, Smith and Smithson (1993) find, using contemporaneous and lagged data, no significant difference in the volatility of pretax income between hedgers (derivative users) and non-hedgers (non-users) *ex post*. Nance, Smith and Smithson point out that since hedging reduces cash flow volatility, there might not be significant differences in volatility *ex post*. This evidence would seem to imply that derivative users in the Nance, Smith and Smithson sample are hedging rather than speculating.

Two studies use key word searches to identify hedging firms (Francis and Stephan, 1993; Mian, 1996). A potential weakness with using key word searches to make inferences about hedging is that this method has the potential of misclassifying hedgers as non-hedgers (e.g., hedging firms with no disclosure in their annual report) and speculators as hedgers. In an attempt to correct for this Mian (1996) draws the distinction between firms who explicitly disclose that they hedge their exposures and firms that disclose the use of derivatives but make no reference to hedging. Mian argues that this latter group could potentially be using derivative instruments for speculation and not hedging. Mian classifies firms into hedgers and non-hedgers using annual financial statements for 1992 available on the LEXIS/NEXIS database. Out of 3,022 firms, 543 firms explicitly state that they hedge and 228 firms disclose the use of derivatives but do not mention hedging. Mian's empirical tests are conducted using hedging firm samples that include and exclude the 228 firms using derivatives while not mentioning hedging in their annual reports. His results show that potential misclassifications resulting from inclusion of derivative users as hedgers do not materially affect his results.

Three studies (Francis and Stephan, 1993; Berkman and Bradbury, 1996; Graham and Rogers, 2000) find no firms disclosing in their annual reports that they speculate with derivatives. On the contrary, they find that many firms provide statements such as 'derivatives are used for risk management purposes only' or 'derivatives are not used for speculative purposes'. However, Géczy, Minton and Schrand (2004) question the validity of such disclosures in annual reports. They find that 13 firms that admit to speculating in an anonymous survey do not report these activities in their published financial statements. Six of these firms disclose that they do not use derivatives for trading purposes. Only two of the 13 firms provide disclosures which suggest that trading with derivatives might take place. This analysis demonstrates that speculating firms are unlikely to disclose this activity in their annual reports and, in some instances, might make statements to the contrary.

Firms can incorporate their views of future price movements into determining the degree of hedging. Three surveys of corporate treasurers (Dolde, 1995; Edelshain, 1995; Bodnar *et al.*, 1996) find evidence of this kind of selective hedging. Dolde's (1995) survey of large US firms indicates that most firms hedge only a portion of their interest rate or foreign currency exposures. Edelshain's (1995) investigation into the currency risk management practices of 189 UK companies shows that 46 per cent of firms selectively hedge their foreign currency exposure. Bodnar *et al.* (1996) find that US treasurers sometimes allow their view of financial price movements to influence their hedging decisions. Some might argue this type of activity is tantamount to speculation; however, this kind of derivatives use appears more to be the conscious bearing of the firm's underlying exposures rather than speculative use of derivatives. A weakness in the aforementioned approaches to assessing whether firms are using derivatives for hedging or speculation is the reliance on qualitative data provided by firms regarding their reasons for using derivatives.

Géczy, Minton and Schrand (1997) consider firms' motives in using currency derivatives to speculate and the implications of speculation for their results. Some of their proxy variables, such as firm size, are important determinants of both optimal speculation and optimal hedging, while other firm characteristics, such as those associated with under-investment costs, are unrelated to optimal speculative motives. They argue that while currency derivative use is not a direct measure of hedging, their results suggest that, on average, their sample of firms are not speculating with currency derivative instruments.

Two studies have detailed data on the extent of risk management undertaken (Tufano, 1996; Haushalter, 2000). Tufano (1996) finds that there are no gold mining firms in any period with negative delta percentages. This, he suggests, indicates that firms are not using financial contracts to increase gold price exposure. This assumes that any speculative activity with derivatives can be observed. However, Haushalter (2000) argues that if managers anticipate that the price of oil and gas will increase and thus increase the exposure of the firm's cash flow to oil and gas prices, the fraction of production hedged will be censored at zero. Therefore negative observations for his dependent variable, constructed in a manner similar to that of Tufano, cannot be observed although, since Tufano has access to very detailed information on firms' risk management activities, derivatives usage is far more transparent making it easier to detect speculative activity.

A far better approach to determining whether firms hedge or speculate is to measure a firm's risk exposure and then examine the effect risk management has on this exposure. Nine studies attempt this by measuring the impact hedging has on firms' risk characteristics. Tufano (1998) shows that as US gold producers increase their hedging the sensitivity of equity value to gold price falls. Petersen and Thiagarajan (2000) report that a gold price hedger possesses gold exposure that is only slightly smaller than a gold price non-hedger. Guay (1999) finds that initiation of corporate derivatives use is associated with declines in various measurements of firm risk such as market risk. Hentschel and Kothari (2001) show that derivative users and non-users exhibit few measurable differences in risk characteristics. Several studies find that foreign currency derivatives use lowers firms' exchange rate exposure (Allayannis, Ihrig and Weston, 2001; Allayannis and Ofek, 2001; Carter, Pantzalis, and Simkins, 2004; Kim, Mathur and Nam, 2004). Jin and Jorion (2005) demonstrate that the risk management activities of oil and gas producers decreases sensitivity of equity returns to oil and gas prices. These results suggest that the use of derivatives is associated with lower levels of risk which is consistent with firms using derivatives to hedge rather than speculate.

Despite these findings, recent empirical evidence provides some support for the notion that non-financial firms use derivatives for speculation rather than for hedging. Faulkender (2005) demonstrates that interest rate risk management practices are motivated by speculative rather than hedging considerations. Faulkender's analysis builds on the belief that the final interest rate exposure of a new debt issue best reflects the implementation of the firm's interest rate risk management programme. The results show that the strongest determinant in explaining final interest rate exposure is the yield spread, which is the difference in yields between long-term and short-term bonds. As the yield curve steepens, firms are more likely to take on floating rate debt. According to Faulkender, this suggests that firms are trying to lower their short-term cost of capital; but, as the yield curve flattens, firms are more likely to raise debt funds that have a fixed final interest rate exposure. These findings are consistent with both short-term earnings management and speculation. Firms might swap the interest rate profile of their debt into floating when there is a large difference between fixed and floating rates in order to reduce their short-term debt service payments, which generates higher quarterly earnings. Alternatively, managers may be speculating by incorporating their views of anticipated interest rate movements into their interest rate profile decision, which leads to significant sensitivity to the yield spread, given that such views are correlated with the shape of the yield curve.

Géczy, Minton and Schrand (2004) utilize survey data collected by Bodnar *et al.* (1998) to investigate why firms speculate with derivatives. Bodnar *et al.* (1998) ask non-financial firms if their market views of interest rates and exchange rates cause them to actively take positions. Thirteen firms indicated that they frequently actively took positions, 66 firms indicated that they sometimes took active positions and for 290 firms the response was they never speculated. Géczy, Minton and Schrand find that speculators are larger than firms that do not take views. Firms that frequently speculate on exchange rates have more foreign currency revenue and costs relative to firms that do not, which is consistent with theories that firms speculate to profit on what they believe is superior information.

Sample composition

Most studies impose restrictions on the types of firms included in their sample. The majority of studies focus their work on the hedging practices of large firms. This is because these firms are more likely to face the types and size of exposures that require hedging and also because information about their hedging practices is generally more readily available. Most of these studies restrict their analysis to the hedging practices of non-financial firms because financial firms are both users and providers of risk management products.[10]

A potential weakness in the sample selection process of these studies is that they fail to exclude firms that may have an incentive to reduce risk but do not have *ex ante* exposure. For example, a firm may have a high R&D ratio and a low liquidity ratio but no cash flow variability arising from exposure to financial price volatility and hence will have no requirement to hedge. Restricting the sample to firms that face *ex ante* financial price risk reduces noise in the empirical tests by focusing on the major cross-sectional differences that affect the incentives for hedging. For samples constructed in this manner a non-hedger can be interpreted as having taken a decision not to hedge its risks. This position is different from that of a non-hedger because of no exposure to financial risks.[11] Géczy, Minton and Schrand (1997), Graham and Rogers (2002), Rogers (2002) and Judge (2005a) and Judge (2005b) employ this sample selection criteria. The last three studies test the effectiveness of this selection process and find that their results are invariant to changes in the composition of their sample.

Types of exposures hedged

The ways in which hedging theoretically increases firm value are not limited to a particular type of exposure hedged or type of hedging method, but relate to hedging activities for which the primary focus is to reduce income volatility. Consequently, there is no need to arbitrarily restrict hedging activities to a particular category of exposure hedged or derivative instruments.

Table 7.1 shows that several studies follow this approach and examine firms hedging any type of financial price exposure (Francis and Stephan (1993), Nance, Smith and Smithson (1993), Dolde (1995), Berkman and Bradbury (1996), Wysocki (1996), Fok, Carroll and Chiou (1997), Gay and Nam (1998), Graham and Rogers (2002), Knopf, Nam and Thornton (2002), Rogers (2002), Judge (2005a) and (2005b)). The sample of hedgers in these studies includes firms who use any type of derivative instrument (i.e., foreign currency, interest rate, commodity price or equity price derivative). The non-hedgers do not use any type of derivative.

Capital market imperfections create an environment in which exposure to financial prices adversely affects shareholder wealth. The theories of hedging explain how these imperfections provide an incentive to hedge. However, they do not specify the source of the volatility, or which type of derivative should be used to hedge. Notwithstanding this, some studies focus on the type of exposure hedged, recognizing that different factors may be important for each type of hedging. Four studies focus on the use of foreign currency hedging instruments (Géczy, Minton and Schrand (1997), Allayannis and Ofek (2001), Hagelin (2003), Pramborg (2005), Judge (2005a)). Four studies examine separately the determinants of interest rate and foreign currency hedging (Mian (1996), Goldberg *et al.* (1998), Howton and Perfect (1998), Graham and Rogers (2000)). A further two investigate commodity price hedging in the gold mining, and the oil and gas industries, respectively (Tufano (1996), Haushalter (2000)). Although, by construction, these industry-specific studies diminish cross-sectional variation in firms' risk exposures, they do so at the expense of cross-sectional variation in the potential incentives to hedge.

Recently there has been a trend towards the examination of the determinants of hedging specific types of exposure, such as foreign currency exposure. A hitherto unrecognized problem for these types of empirical studies is the inclusion of firms hedging other exposures in the sample of non-hedgers. This is a major weakness in these studies because the inclusion of hedging firms in the non-hedging sample might blur the distinction between the two groups and hence bias any empirical tests against the a priori expectations.

Table 7.2 shows that of the nine studies that have investigated the determinants of interest rate hedging, seven included firms hedging other exposures in their sample of non-hedgers. For example, Mian's (1996) full sample includes 735 hedgers and 2,064 non-hedgers, and his interest rate sample includes 417 interest rate hedgers (318 fewer than the full sample) and 2,382 non-hedgers (318 more than the full sample). These 318 are firms hedging exposures other than interest rate exposure and join the non-hedgers in the interest rate hedging tests. Samant (1996) studies the use of interest rate swaps and obtains control samples of firms that do not use interest rate swaps but might use other interest rate derivatives and/or other derivatives. Visvanathan (1998) also studies the use of interest rate swaps for interest rate hedging and other reasons and partitions his sample into firms that report the use of interest rate swaps and those that do not report interest rate swaps. The latter includes firms that use non-interest rate derivatives, such as foreign currency options. Graham and Rogers (2000) investigate the determinants of interest rate derivative use and foreign currency derivative use. In their interest rate sample 180 out of 404 firms use some type of derivative, and 142 use interest rate derivatives. In multivariate tests, interest rate derivative non-users are sampled from the 262 firms which do not disclose the use of interest rate derivatives, of which 38 firms use other types of derivatives.

Table 7.2 Composition of non-hedging samples in previous empirical studies of interest rate hedging and/or the use of interest rate swaps

Author(s) of Study	Date	Area of study	Non-hedger sample includes hedgers	Proportion of other hedgers in non-hedger sample (%)
Mian	1996	All hedgers and foreign exchange and interest rate hedgers	Yes	13.35
Samant	1996	Interest rate swaps	Yes	Not available
Li	1996	Interest rate swaps and interest rate hedging	No	Not available
Visvanathan	1998	Interest rate swaps and interest rate hedging	Yes	Not available
Gay and Nam	1998	Interest rate hedgers	No	Not available
Goldberg, Godwin, Kim and Tritschler	1998	All hedgers, foreign exchange and interest rate hedgers	Yes	28.34
Howton and Perfect	1998	All hedgers and foreign exchange and interest rate hedgers	Yes	Not available
Graham and Rogers	2000	Foreign exchange and interest rate hedgers	Yes	14.50
Bartram, Brown and Fehle	2004	All hedgers and foreign exchange, interest rate and commodity price hedgers	Yes	Not available

The two exceptions to these studies are the Gay and Nam (1998) study which looked at the differences in characteristics between a sample of interest-rate derivatives only users and a matching sample of firms that did not use any derivatives, and the Li (1996) study of the use of interest rate swaps, comparing users of interest rate swaps, versus non-users of any derivative.

Table 7.3 shows that ten previous studies investigating foreign currency hedging include in their sample of non-hedgers firms hedging

Table 7.3   Composition of non-hedging samples in previous empirical studies investigating foreign currency hedging

Author(s) of study	Date	Area of study	Non-hedger sample includes hedgers	Proportion of other hedgers in non-hedger sample (%)
Wysocki	1996	Foreign exchange hedgers	Yes	Not available
Mian	1996	All hedgers, foreign exchange and interest rate hedgers	Yes	13.02
Géczy, Minton and Schrand	1997	Foreign exchange hedgers	Yes	30.30
Goldberg, Godwin, Kim and Tritschler	1998	All hedgers, foreign exchange and interest rate hedgers	Yes	29.20
Howton and Perfect	1998	All hedgers, foreign exchange and interest rate hedgers	Yes	Not available
Graham and Rogers	2000	Foreign exchange and interest rate hedgers	Yes	24.10
Allayannis and Ofek	2001	Foreign exchange hedgers	Yes	Not available
Hagelin	2003	Foreign exchange hedgers	Yes	Not available
Bartram, Brown and Fehle	2004	All hedgers, foreign exchange and interest rate hedgers	Yes	Not available
Pramborg	2005	Foreign exchange hedgers	Yes	Not available

other exposures. In some instances other derivative users can make up around a quarter of non-foreign currency derivative using firms (i.e., non-foreign currency hedging firms). For example, Table 7.3 shows that in Géczy, Minton and Schrand (1997), 30.1 per cent of the non-user sample are other derivative users, while in Goldberg *et al.* (1998) the figure is 29 per cent and in Graham and Rogers (2000) they make up 24 per cent.

Most surveys of derivative use tend to show that foreign currency and interest rate derivatives are the most popular categories of derivatives used, whereas the use of commodity price derivatives lags behind in third place. This is usually because only a small proportion of the sample surveyed face commodity price exposure.[12] This suggests that the majority of 'other' hedgers in the non-foreign currency hedging samples of the foreign currency studies cited in Table 7.3 are likely to be interest rate hedgers. The existence of interest rate hedgers in both the hedging and non-hedging samples might impair the ability of these studies to find statistically significant links between foreign currency hedging and indicators of debt levels and debt servicing ability. Since these variables usually act as proxies for the expected costs of financial distress, this might also explain why in probit/logit tests nine out of the ten foreign currency studies in Table 7.3 find no evidence in support of this hypothesis.[13] In the one study that does find support (Bartram, Brown and Fehle (2004)) the evidence is rather weak since leverage is significant in only two out of six individual country specifications and interest coverage is significant in only one. Judge (2005a) excludes 'other' hedgers from the non-foreign currency hedging sample and finds a significant improvement in results and in particular for those variables proxying for the expected costs of financial distress. Judge suggests that if previous studies had controlled for interest rate hedgers in the non-foreign currency hedging sample, then they might also have found evidence supporting the financial distress hypothesis.

Another weakness in these studies is that they fail to recognize that a sample of foreign currency hedgers which includes firms also hedging interest rate exposure engenders bias. This is because tests that investigate links between foreign currency hedging and factors that are potentially more relevant to interest rate hedgers, such as leverage, might be driven by the sample of foreign currency hedgers that also hedge interest rate exposure. This bias could be avoided by excluding these firms as well as those that also hedge commodity price exposure, leaving a sample of foreign currency only hedgers. Judge (2005a) argues that employing a sample of foreign currency only hedgers is the only unambiguous method for determining which factors are important in the foreign currency hedging decision.

Conclusions

This chapter has evaluated the extant empirical research on the determinants of corporate hedging. It argues that studies should attempt to adopt a more inclusive definition of hedging by incorporating other financial and operational hedging techniques into their analysis. The importance of considering a range of risk management activities has been stressed in recent research by Guay and Kothari (2003). They find that derivatives usage by many US non-financial firms is too small relative to their risk exposures, which might be consistent with firms having a preference for using other hedging methods and only utilizing derivatives to manage residual financial price exposure. Furthermore, if the hedging motives for firms using only non-derivative techniques are similar to those using derivatives, then the classification of non-derivative hedgers as non-hedgers will bias results against a priori expectations. Therefore, this might explain the mixed results in previous studies.

The chapter identifies a potential bias in several studies that have examined the hedging of specific types of financial price exposure, such as foreign currency exposure hedging studies. This bias results from the inclusion of firms hedging other financial price exposures in the sample of non-hedgers. The existence of other hedgers in the non-hedging sample might eliminate any differences between hedgers and non-hedgers and consequently bias the empirical tests.

The chapter also argued that tests examining the relationship between foreign currency hedging and factors such as leverage and interest cover, which are generally considered more relevant to interest rate hedging firms, might be biased. This is because results showing a significant relationship might be due to a sample of foreign currency hedging firms that also hedge interest rate exposure. Employing a sample of hedgers that only hedge foreign currency exposure could eliminate this problem.

Notes

1 Other studies: see, for example, Wall and Pringle (1989) and Samant (1996).
2 See, for example, Tufano (1996), Allayannis and Ofek (2001), Berkman and Bradbury (1996), Haushalter (2000), Gay and Nam (1998), Howton and Perfect (1998), Graham and Rogers (2002).
3 Firms can manage risk through diversification, hedging, and insurance (see Merton, 1993).
4 Tufano (1996) makes a similar point when investigating risk management activities in the US gold mining industry.
5 For example, Rio Tinto says: 'Rio Tinto's exposure to commodity prices is naturally diversified by virtue of its broad commodity spread, and the Group does not believe a commodity price hedging programme would provide long term benefit to shareholders.' The firm also does not believe that currency hedging provides long term benefits: 'Rio Tinto's assets, earnings and cash flows are influenced by a wide variety of currencies, which provides a substantial degree of protection against changes in currency parities'; and goes on to say:

> Rio Tinto's operating costs are influenced not only by the US dollar but by currencies of other countries where its mines and processing plants are located, in particular the Australian dollar. In any particular year, currency fluctuations may have a significant impact on Rio Tinto's financial results.

> However, in the case of the Australian dollar there is a significant degree of natural protection against cyclical fluctuations, in that the currency tends to be weak (reducing costs in US dollar terms) when commodity prices are low.
>
> (Rio Tinto 1997 *Annual Report,* on Form 20-F, pp. 84–5)

6 Allayannis and Ofek (2001) attempt to examine non-linearities in foreign currency hedging by examining the hypothesis of whether a firm with a larger proportion of foreign sales hedges a larger proportion of its foreign sales than a firm with a smaller proportion of foreign sales. In this regression, the dependent variable is the ratio of foreign currency derivatives to foreign sales, and the ratio of foreign sales to total sales is used to indicate the existence of non-linearities. They find a negative coefficient which indicates that, as the percentage of foreign sales in total sales increases, firms increase the percentage of foreign sales that is covered by foreign currency derivatives, but at a decreasing rate.

7 This problem biases the results of these studies against their a priori expectations.

8 For firms using only interest rate derivatives, Gay and Nam (1998) calculate the ratio of the firm's notional amount of interest-rate derivatives to its total debt, and zero for non-users. They use total debt to proxy for a firm's total interest rate exposure.

9 The delta percentage ignores operating risk management activities, including the real options to change the rate of production, exploration, and acquisition.

10 The exceptions are Francis and Stephan (1993) and Graham and Rogers (2000).

11 This approach implies that there are two types of non-hedgers, those that do not hedge because they have no exposure and those that do not hedge despite having some level of exposure. By focusing on firms that face *ex ante* risk (have some exposure), the absence of derivatives (or hedging) can be interpreted as a choice not to use derivatives (or hedge), rather than possibly indicating a lack of exposure to financial price risks.

12 Phillips (1995) reports that of those firms with less than $250 million in sales, 86 per cent face interest rate risk, 73 per cent face foreign exchange risk, and 30 per cent face commodity price risk. Among large firms, he reports that 97 per cent face interest rate risk, 91 per cent face foreign exchange rate risk and 63 per cent face commodity price risk.

13 For example, Géczy, Minton and Schrand (1997) use the long-term debt ratio, an industry adjusted debt ratio and S&P credit ratings and find no evidence in support of the financial distress cost hypothesis. Furthermore, they present mixed evidence for proxies measuring under-investment costs, which can be used to measure expected distress costs (Graham and Rogers, 2002). Goldberg *et al.* (1998) find that leverage is not significantly related to the foreign currency hedging decision in both univariate and multivariate probit tests. Graham and Rogers (2000) find, using a probit model, no significant relation between foreign currency hedging and measures for financial distress costs, such as debt ratio, debt ratio times market-to-book ratio, firm profitability, tax losses and credit ratings. Allayannis and Ofek (2001) use debt ratio, return on assets, Altman's z-score and liquidity in a probit model

and find that the debt ratio is significantly negatively related to foreign currency hedging (which is the opposite of the theory's prediction) and the other measures are not significantly related to foreign currency hedging. In both univariate and multivariate tests Hagelin (2003) finds no support for the financial distress hypothesis. He says this lack of evidence 'is in accordance with earlier studies on use of currency derivatives' (p. 65).

References

Allayannis, G., Ihrig, J. and Weston, J. (2001) 'Exchange rate hedging: financial vs operational strategies', *American Economic Review Papers and Proceedings*, 91, 391–5.

Allayannis, G. and Ofek, E. (2001) 'Exchange-rate exposure, hedging and the use of foreign currency derivatives', *Journal of International Money and Finance*, 20, 273–96.

Bartram, S.M., Brown, G.W. and Fehle, F.R. (2004) 'International evidence on financial derivatives use', Working paper (University of Lancaster).

Berkman, H. and Bradbury, M.E. (1996) 'Empirical evidence on the corporate use of derivatives', *Financial Management*, 25, 5–13.

Bodnar, Gordon M., Hayt G.S. and Marston, R.C. (1996) '1995 Wharton survey of derivatives usage by US non-financial firms', *Financial Management*, 25, 113–33.

Bodnar, Gordon M., Hayt G.S. and Marston, R.C. (1998) '1998 Wharton survey of financial risk management by us non-financial firms', *Financial Management*, 27, 70–91.

Campbell, T. and Kracaw W.A. (1999) 'Optimal speculation in the presence of costly external financing', in G. Brown and D. Chew (eds), *Corporate Risk Management: Strategies and Management* (London: Risk).

Carter, D.A, Pantzalis, C. and Simkins, B.J. (2004) 'Asymmetric exposure to foreign exchange risk: financial and real option hedges implemented by U.S. multinational corporations', Working paper (Oklahoma State University).

Dolde, W. (1995) 'Hedging, leverage, and primitive risk', *The Journal of Financial Engineering*, 4, 187–216.

Edelshain, D.J. (1995) 'British Corporate Currency Exposure and Foreign Exchange Risk Management', unpublished PhD Thesis, London Business School.

Elliott, W.B., Huffman, S.P. and Makar, S.D. (2003) 'Foreign denominated debt and foreign currency derivatives: complements or substitutes in hedging foreign currency risk', *Journal of Multinational Financial Management*, 13, 123–39.

Faulkender, M. (2005) 'Hedging or market timing? Selecting the interest rate exposure of corporate debt', *Journal of Finance*, 60, 931–62.

Fehle, F. (1999) 'Panel evidence on corporate hedging', *Canadian Journal of Administrative Sciences*, 16, 229–42.

Fok, R.C.W., Carroll, C. and Chiou, M.C. (1997) 'Determinants of corporate hedging and derivatives: a revisit', *Journal of Economics and Business*, 49, 569–85.

Francis, J. and Stephan, J. (1993) 'Characteristics of hedging firms: an empirical investigation', in R. J. Schwartz and C.W. Smith, Jr (eds) *Advanced Strategies in Financial Risk Management* (New York: Institute of Finance), 615–35.

Froot, K. A., Scharfstein, D.S. and Stein, J.C. (1993) 'Risk management: coordinating corporate investment and financing policies', *Journal of Finance*, 48, 1,629–58.

Gay, G.D. and Nam, J. (1998) 'The underinvestment problem and corporate derivatives use', *Financial Management*, 27, 53–69.

Géczy, C., Minton, B.A. and Schrand, C. (1997) 'Why firms use currency derivatives', *Journal of Finance*, 52, 1,323–54.

Géczy, C., Minton, B.A. and Schrand, C. (2004) 'Taking a view: corporate speculation, governance and compensation', Working paper (Wharton School).

Goldberg, S.R., Godwin, J.H., Kim, M. and Tritschler, C.A. (1998) 'On the determinants of corporate usage of financial derivatives', *Journal of International Financial Management and Accounting*, 9, 132–66.

Graham, J.R. and Rogers, D.A. (2000) 'Is corporate hedging consistent with value-maximization? An empirical analysis', Working paper (Fuqua School of Business, Duke University).

Graham, J.R. and Rogers, D.A. (2002) 'Do firms hedge in response to tax incentives?', *Journal of Finance*, 57, 815–39.

Guay, W. (1999) 'The impact of derivatives on firm risk: an empirical examination of new derivative users?', *Journal of Accounting and Economics*, 26, 319–51.

Guay, W. and Kothari, S.P. (2003) 'How much do firms hedge with derivatives?', *Journal of Financial Economics*, 70, 423–61.

Hagelin, N. (2003) 'Why Firms Hedge With Currency Derivatives: An Examination of Transaction and Translation Exposure', *Applied Financial Economics*, 13, 55–69.

Haushalter, D.G. (2000) 'Financing policy, basis risk, and corporate hedging: evidence from oil and gas producers', *Journal of Finance*, 55, 107–52.

Hentschel, L. and Kothari, S.P. (2001) 'Are corporations reducing or taking risks with derivatives?', *Journal of Financial and Quantitative Analysis*, 36, 65–85.

Howton, S.D. and Perfect, S.B. (1998) 'Currency and interest-rate derivatives use in U.S. firms', *Financial Management*, 27, 111–21.

Jalilvand, A. (1999) 'Why firms use derivatives: evidence from Canada', *Canadian Journal of Administrative Sciences*, 16, 213–28.

Jin, Y. and Jorion, P. (2005) 'Firm value and hedging: evidence from U.S. oil and gas producers', forthcoming, *Journal of Finance*.

Judge, A.P. (2005a) 'The determinants of foreign currency hedging by U.K. non-financial firms', forthcoming *Multinational Finance Journal*.

Judge, A.P. (2005b) 'Why UK firms Hedge', forthcoming, *European Financial Management Journal*.

Kedia, S. and Mozumdar, A. (2003) 'Foreign currency denominated debt: an empirical investigation', *Journal of Business*, 76, 521–46.

Kim, Y., Mathur, I. and Nam, J. (2004) 'Is operational hedging a substitute for or a complement to financial hedging?', Working paper (Northern Kentucky University).

Knopf, J.D., Nam, J. and Thornton, Jr, J.H. (2002) 'The volatility and price sensitivities of managerial stock option portfolios and corporate hedging', *Journal of Finance*, 57, 801–13.

Li, H. (1996) 'Corporate use of interest rate swaps: empirical evidence', Working paper (Yale School of Management).

Ljungqvist, L. (1994) 'Asymmetric information: a rationale for corporate speculation', *Journal of Financial Intermediation*, 3, 188–203.

Merton, Robert C. (1993) 'Operations and regulation in financial intermediation: a functional perspective', in P. Englund (ed.), *Operation and Regulation of Financial Markets* (Stockholm: The Economic Council).

Mian, S.L. (1996) 'Evidence on corporate hedging policy', *Journal of Financial and Quantitative Analysis*, 31, 419–39.

Nance, D.R., Smith, Jr, C.W. and Smithson, C.W. (1993) 'On the determinants of corporate hedging', *Journal of Finance*, 48, 267–84.

Petersen, M.A. and Thiagarajan, S.R. (2000) 'Risk management and hedging: with and without derivatives', *Financial Management*, 29, 5–30.

Phillips, A.L. (1995) '1995 Derivatives practices and instruments survey', *Financial Management*, 24, 115–25.

Pramborg, B. (2005) 'Foreign exchange risk management by Swedish and Korean non-financial firms: a comparative survey', forthcoming, *Pacific-Basin Finance Journal*, vol. 13, 343–66.

Rogers, D.A. (2002) 'Does executive portfolio structure affect risk management? CEO risk-taking incentives and corporate derivatives usage', *Journal of Banking and Finance*, 26, 271–95.

Samant, A. (1996) 'An empirical study of interest rate swap usage by nonfinancial corporate business', *Journal of Financial Services Research*, 10, 43–57.

Smith, Jr, C.W. (1995) 'Corporate risk management: theory and practice', *Journal of Derivatives*, 2, 21–30.

Smith, Jr, C.W. and Stulz, R.M. (1985) 'The determinants of firms' hedging policies', *Journal of Financial and Quantitative Analysis*, 20, 391–405.

Tufano, P. (1996) 'Who manages risk? An empirical examination of risk management practices in the gold mining industry', *Journal of Finance*, 51, 1,097–137.

Tufano, P. (1998) 'The determinants of stock price exposure: financial engineering and the gold mining industry', *Journal of Finance*, 53, 1,015–52.

Visvanathan, G. (1998) 'Who uses interest rate swaps? A cross-sectional analysis', *Journal of Accounting, Auditing and Finance*, 13, 173–200.

Wall, L. and Pringle, J. (1989) 'Alternative explanations of interest rate swaps: a theoretical and empirical analysis', *Financial Management*, 18, 59–73.

Wysocki, P. (1996) 'Managerial motives and corporate use of derivatives: some evidence', Working paper (Simon School of Business, University of Rochester).

8
Concentration versus Efficiency and Financial Liberalization in Latin American Banking

Georgios Chortareas, Jesús Gustavo Garza García and Claudia Girardone

Introduction

The processes of financial liberalization and international integration have contributed to significant changes in the banking sectors of many developing countries. In Latin America, banking sectors have experienced an accelerated process of consolidation. Enhanced consolidation has been accompanied by a significant increase in the degree of market concentration in the banking industry. A direct effect of such measures has been the inflow of foreign capital which, although necessary for recapitalizing the financial system, increases the market concentration of the sector. A number of current concerns about the implications of market concentration on competitiveness in the banking industry and its possible impact in the economy exist. The banking sector seems to be highly concentrated in many countries in Latin America and therefore studying the sector and identifying the impact of the enhanced degree of concentration and its potential collusion effects seems an appropriate task. For example, some of the collusion effects that may have been driven by a highly concentrated banking sector may include high commercial lending rates, credit rationing and low deposit rates.

The financial systems of most Latin American countries have shared a number of key characteristics over recent decades. Recurrent economic crises and a sudden financial liberalization has been a common feature for many of them. Recurrent high levels of inflation throughout several decades gave rise to intense dollarization and a high degree of concentration of public debt in the assets structure of banks. The vulnerability of the banking system in Latin America is considered by many analysts a direct outcome of these conditions. The so-called 'tequila' crisis in Mexico was an example of how economic crises can manifest themselves in Latin

America. In the aftermath of this crisis the market structure of the banking industry in Mexico changed dramatically, with the total number of commercial banks declining from 40 to 23 in a couple of years (Yeyati and Micco, 2003).

According to the Inter-American Development Bank (IDB), Latin America's ranking is the highest in terms of recurrent banking crises. In the region, 35 per cent of countries have experienced recurrent crises, almost three times higher than other regions in the world. These figures underline the importance of financial stability-oriented policies in this area and the need for further institutional reforms to prevent such crises in the future.

It is worth mentioning two main examples that are indicative of the region's problems which resulted in financial instability and economic crises; the Mexican crisis of 1995 and the Argentinian crisis of 2001. The banking sectors of those two countries shared similar characteristics before the sudden collapse of their banking systems. The main problems identified were macroeconomic, such as the loss of monetary policy autonomy resulting from attempts at dollarization or, more generally, the pegging of their currencies. Another set of problems was informational, giving rise to specific forms of moral hazard and adverse selection. As Calvo and Mishkin (2003) emphasize, during financial crises, which constitute a disruption of financial markets, adverse selection and moral hazard become much more intense. A direct consequence is that the financial sector becomes inefficient in performing its main function of funds allocation. A third set of problems was related to liquidity factors. Liquidity factors may relate to sudden stops in capital flows, which generate a major vulnerability to financial stability. In Mexico, for example, large amounts of short-term government bonds triggered a shortage in cash, which provoked illiquidity in the economy (see Yacaman, 2001).

The experience of severe financial crises in Latin America's financial and banking systems was followed by a process of bank consolidation and entry of foreign banks during the 1990s. These developments, however, are not free from potential complications and many analysts have expressed serious concerns about the level of concentration in the banking sector and the potential spillovers to the rest of the economy.

In this chapter we focus on whether the behaviour of the banking system can be better explained by the SCP (Structure–Conduct–Performance) paradigm or the ES (Efficiency–Structure) model and the implications for the competitive structure of the banking industry. We review the literature and then present and interpret the results obtained for various countries and groups of countries. This discussion emphasizes the policy implications; if bank profitability has been driven by market concentration then antitrust policies should be taken into consideration to reduce further market concentration, otherwise the profitability can be explained by higher managerial efficiency or low cost of production. The ES model can measure the relationship between efficiency and profitability.

In the following two sections we provide an overview of the banking sector in Latin America and then we review the existing literature focusing on the Structure–Conduct–Performance and the Efficiency–Structure models. We compare different outcomes from the estimation of these models in different groups of countries. It is worth noting that while various relevant studies exist for the EU countries and the US, the research dedicated to Latin American countries is very limited.

Bank liberalization and its effects on the structure of the banking sector

The banking structure of the majority of Latin American countries in recent times shares similar characteristics, and financial liberalization is a major one of them. Financial liberalization permitted large amounts of the FDI (foreign direct investment) necessary to recapitalize the financial system, and one important element of this process is allowing foreign banks to participate in the domestic market. Nevertheless, there are serious concerns about the degree of concentration in the banking sector in many countries in Latin America. Foreign banks have purchased and taken over domestic banks, consolidating their market share and in general decreasing the number of banks. The underlying idea behind financial liberalization was to allow foreign banks to participate actively in the domestic market. Under this scenario, policy makers expected more competition and, as a result, more attractive rates for consumers such as more credit and lower interest rates. The academic literature provides a set of arguments for such policies. Beck, Loayza and Levine (2000) find that foreign banks tend to spur competition and contribute to a more efficient banking system. Claessens, Demirguc-Kunt and Huizinga (2001) also find that foreign bank entry leads to greater efficiency in the domestic banking system. One of the main characteristics of financial liberalization in Latin America, however, was the acquisition of domestic banks by foreign ones, resulting in the same market concentration problems as before but with the ownership of capital changed.

Table 8.1 shows the general decline in the number of banks of eight Latin American countries from the late 1980s to the early millennium.

Table 8.1   Decline in the number of banks

	1996	2002	Change	% Change
Argentina	117	80	−37	−32
Brazil	253	177	−76	−30
Chile	31	25	−6	−19
Colombia	39	27	−12	−31
Costa Rica	30	21	−9	−30
Mexico	40	32	−8	−20
Peru	22	15	−7	−32
El Salvador	18	13	−5	−28

Source: National Superintendencies of Banks, 1996–2002 (from Singh *et al.*, 2005).

The magnitude of the reduction of the number of banks in the countries considered is impressive. The percentage change averages −28 per cent for the selected countries. The reduction in the number of banks in most Latin American countries during the last decade implies an increment in the degree of market concentration and there are serious concerns about possible effects on bank competition, borrowing costs, bank efficiency and financial stability. One of these concerns is that large international banks could exploit their market power by paying lower deposits, charging higher interest rates, and downgrading their services. Under this assumption, there is evidence suggesting that lower deposit rates and higher lending rates characterize highly concentrated markets, as explained by the SCP paradigm, which acknowledges a causality relationship between market performance and market structure.

To help assess the degree of market concentration Table 8.2 shows some relevant variables and their percentage share for the top 10 banks of the countries analysed. It emerges that the share of total assets and deposits of the top 10 banks is greater than 60 per cent, in some cases up to 95 per cent of the total market share. On the other hand, the shares of total deposits and total credit are also very high when analysing the top 10 banks of each country. These figures clearly indicate the high degree of market concentration which the region's banking system is currently experiencing. Moreover, foreign banks have an important share of total assets and deposits as well. In the case of Mexico, for example, this figure is up to 77 per cent of the total share, and the trend is rising.

From 1994 to 1999 foreign bank participation in Latin American countries was observed, from 13.1 per cent to 44.8 per cent in the region.[1] Levy and Micco (2003) argue that while foreign bank participation more than doubled in many cases, banking concentration increased mainly due to

Table 8.2 Selected Latin American countries: structure of banking systems (percentage)

	Argentina	Brazil	Chile	Colombia	Ecuador	Mexico	Paraguay	Peru	Uruguay	Venezuela
Institutions										
Number of Banks	71	135	28	32	40	35	22	15	23	39
Concentration[a]										
Share of total assets	62	70	76	67	82	95	79	95	87	81
Share of total deposits	71	77	78	68	79	90	79	96	85	36
Share of total credit	66	70	80	65	78	93	59	94	88	64
Foreign bank participation[b]										
Number of banks	28	27	18	11	. . .	20	17	12	16	21
Share of total assets	54	28	60	21	. . .	82	81	64	35	68
Share of total deposits	48	21	47	20	. . .	82	86	62	34	67
Share of total credit	46	25	45	21	. . .	77	74	62	35	72

Notes: This table considers only deposit-taking universal banks. Data are for 2000, except for Uruguay and Mexico, for which 2002 data are used.
[a] Top 10 banks of each country.
[b] Domestic banks with foreign participation or control. Offshore banks are not included.
Sources: IMF, excerpt from *Stabilisation and Reform in Latin America: A Macroeconomic Perspective on the Experience since the Early 1990s*; elaborated with data from National central banks, and bank supervisory agencies.

consolidation processes led generally by mergers that were triggered in many circumstances by financial crises and regulatory tightening. Of course these 'twin developments' may raise concerns about their impact on competition, and in particular about the implications for borrowing costs and banking efficiency (see Levy and Micco, 2003). Moreover, wider implications for financial stability may exist. The high degree of concentration and the lack of competition within banks can be a legitimate concern. Such lack of competition may result in high prices and credit rationing, which will in turn impede the efficient working of the economy.

One of the appealing implications from liberalizing financial markets is that it will produce a higher volume of more competitive credit, at least in theory. Nevertheless, credit seems to be a recurrent problem in the region, including high interest rates and credit rationing. This problem can be directly related to the concentration of the market. A high degree of concentration has serious implications for competitiveness and direct effects on credit rationing, either through high interest rate spreads or through adverse selection.

Bank credit in Latin America and the Caribbean is very scarce compared to other regions of the world. During the 1990s the average level of credit to the private sector in the region was only 28 per cent of GDP. This rate is significantly lower than that found in other groups of developing countries, such as East Asia and the Pacific (72 per cent), and the Middle East and North Africa (43 per cent). It falls far behind the developed countries which have a credit share of 84 per cent of GDP. The same trend is observed when analysing the financial sector broadly, including capital markets. Although the level of credit available to the private sector has grown in the region since the 1960s (from 15 per cent of GDP to 28 per cent), it does not compare to the level of growth of financially intermediated credit as, for example, in East Asia (where it increased from 15 per cent of GDP to 70 per cent).[2]

The under-development of the banking system is not only related to lower amounts of credit, but also to higher interest rate spreads (the difference between the interest rate charged to borrowers and the rate paid to depositors), and thus higher lending rates and lower net returns to savings. This large spread may reflect various aspects of the financial system, such as (1) the efficiency and market power of the banking sector; (2) the default risk on loans; (3) risk pertaining to liquidity, currency, and other issues; (4) underlying regulations; and (5) explicit and implicit bank taxation. In general, there is a close relationship between small banking systems and high interest rate spreads. According to the World Bank, Venezuela currently has the third-highest margin in the world (18.3 per cent), while Panama has the lowest (3.8 per cent), which is close to the mean spread observed in developed countries (3.5 per cent). Claessens, Demirguc-Kunt and Huizinga (2001) find that, in developing nations, the presence of foreign banks is typically associated with higher net interest margins and higher profitability than domestic banks. Moreover, they find that foreign banks experience high overhead costs, thus contradicting the hypothesis that foreign banks' profits are driven by efficiency.

Table 8.3 shows the interest rate spreads and efficiency in various regions. Table 8.3 reveals that there seems to be a positive relationship between high spreads in interest rates and efficiency, measured as overhead costs as a percentage of assets. As seen above, the greater the interest rate margin, the greater the value of the overhead cost which measures efficiency in this case. Moreover, there also seems to be a positive relationship between lower interest rate margins and greater credit to the private sector. This may be due to low lending rates that may be more accessible to private companies or individuals. The interest rate spreads in Latin America and the Caribbean are 8.5 points, compared to only 5.1 in East Asia and the Pacific.

In terms of bank performance, the region has improved substantially during the last two decades following important financial reforms. Nevertheless, in terms of return on assets and returns on equity, the region still trails behind major economies (see Table 8.4). This situation has persisted despite high interest rate margins in private lending, considering

Table 8.3   Interest spread and efficiency by region, 1995–2003

Region	Number of countries	Interest margin (%)	Overhead costs (percentage of assets)	Credit to private sector (percentage of GDP)
Sub-Saharan Africa	32	10.6	5.1	15
Eastern Europe and Central Asia	23	8.8	5.0	26
Latin America and the Caribbean	26	8.5	4.8	37
East Asia and the Pacific	16	5.1	2.3	57
South Asia	5	4.6	2.7	23
Middle East and North Africa	13	4.0	1.8	38
Developed Countries	30	2.9	1.8	89

Sources: IMF and Bankscope data.

Table 8.4 International comparisons: bank performance indicators, 2000[a]

	Argentina	Brazil	Chile	Colombia	Mexico	Paraguay	Peru	Venezuela	USA	Japan	Europe[b]
Source of revenue[c]											
Net interest margin	110	87	92	97	90	...	100	97	82	86	67
Other net income[d]	−10	13	8	3	2	...	0	3	18	14	33
Efficiency											
Operating costs	74	76	53	78	92	89	94	99	61	61	67
Personnel costs	68	42	32	36	43	44	42	42	24	7	33
Provisions	26	23	29	43	27	63	66	9	...	...	...
Asset quality											
Non-performing loans		9.5	7.8	11.9	5.8	16.2	7.6	2.8	0.9	6.1	1.2
Profitability											
Return on assets	0.4	0.0	0.5	−1.4	0.3	1.4	0.4	1.4	1.8	0.1	0.7
Return on equity	3.2	−0.4	...	...	...	12.4	2.8	...	22	−30.4	16.8

[a] Performance indicators may differ from traditional definitions to improve cross-country comparability. Operating income usually includes extraordinary income, but the latter is not included here to provide a more accurate assessment of bank performance. Operating costs exclude provisions, which are year- and bank-specific.
[b] The 11 European Union countries included are: Austria, Belgium, Finland, France, Germany, Ireland, Italy, Luxembourg, the Netherlands, Portugal and Spain. Aggregate data are for 1998.
[c] Operating income is defined as the sum of net commission income and net fee.
[d] Sum of net commission income (from asset management and other services) and net fee income (from foreign exchange trading and underwriting).
Sources: IMF, excerpt from *Stabilization and Reform in Latin America: A Macroeconomic Perspective on the Experience since the Early 1990s*; elaborated with data from national central banks, and bank supervisory agencies for Latin American countries; Belaisch *et al.* (2001) for industrial countries; and IMF staff calculations. Data are for 2000.

that higher spreads are normally related to higher profits to banks. In countries such as Uruguay, Brazil and Peru the interest rate spread averaged more than 50 percentage points (see Singh *et al.*, 2005). The weak profitability may be explained by the reliance on interest earnings from lending and the holding of government bonds as the main source of revenue.

The banking sector in Latin America: concentration and its effects

The background of the Latin American banking sector suggests that the region may be experiencing a highly concentrated market and thus some effects from this concentration may be taking place. The implications of a highly concentrated market in the banking sector are the collusion effects that may be expressed by higher lending rates, lower deposit rates or credit rationing. Higher lending rates imply that less credit is distributed to the private sector and thus there is less credit in the economy. The natural beneficiaries of high lending rates are the banks and financial institutions. The scarcity of credit generates a chain problem in the sense that less money is injected in the economy and wealth transfer is not fully accomplished. Lower deposit rates imply that banks may be taking advantage of their market position to offer low rates; and if every bank acts in a similar fashion, investors receive low interest rates for their investment, thus generating higher profits for banks. Credit rationing is a classic example of adverse selection, in which banks decide whom to lend to and the amount of credit is reduced due to tighter regulations governing money lending. All these effects have adverse implications for consumers and may boost banking profitability above competition levels. Under this scenario, it is important to analyse data for Latin America to see if there is a concentrated banking sector. In other words, one needs to focus on the relationship between commercial banks and their profitability, as well as examine whether they are driven by higher market concentration or higher efficiency. In this chapter we discuss the arguments in favour and against this proposition using two different theoretical frameworks, one focusing on market concentration and the other on efficiency.

Many authors, such as Molyneux and Forbes (1995), observe that a high degree of concentration produces collusion effects that drive profits above market levels. Their study on a set of European countries finds a direct relationship between concentration and profitability. On the other hand, Berger (1995) finds a strong link between bank efficiency and profitability. In his study, based on the US banking industry, the author finds that the level of profitability is influenced by better efficiency and cost reduction, thus rejecting the hypothesis that higher concentration is directly linked to higher profitability. It follows that the two hypotheses addressed above have contrasting implications for merger and antitrust policies. To the extent that the concentration (SCP) hypothesis is correct, mergers would be motivated by the desire to set less favourable prices for consumers, which would in turn decrease consumer and producer surplus. On the other hand, if the efficiency hypothesis (ES) holds, mergers may be motivated by efficiency considerations that would increase the total surplus (Berger, 1995).

The Structure–Conduct–Performance approach

The traditional SCP paradigm would interpret an observed high degree of concentration as an indication of collusion and anti-competitive practices' (see Molyneux and Forbes, 1995). There have been a wide variety of studies that have analysed the relevance of the SCP paradigm and its applications in diverse industries. In banking, the results have been contrasting, with some studies confirming the SCP paradigm and others strongly rejecting it and contemplating other factors that may drive market participants to receive profits above a competitive market level.

In general, the SCP analysis can be divided into two different groups according to Gilbert (1984). The first group relies on the measurement 'of the price of certain banking products and services in order to capture the performance of the firm, while the second group uses some kind of profitability measure, such as return on assets or return on equity' (Molyneux and Forbes, 1995, p. 156). The first approach is usually very problematic in the banking industry since the banking industry provides a variety of services, and thus the prices of the products may be misleading. Therefore, the second approach proves to be more efficient and accurate. Molyneux and Forbes (1995) measured bank performance using the return on assets (ROA: i.e., net income divided by total assets).

According to the SCP hypothesis, the degree of concentration of a market exerts a direct influence on the degree of competition among firms. This means that the more concentrated the market, the lower the degree of competition. This can be demonstrated by obtaining a positive value on the level of market concentration in regarding their degree of profitability. Therefore, according to Molyneux and Forbes (1995), 'firms operating in more concentrated markets will earn higher profits (for collusive or monopolistic reasons) than firms operating in less concentrated ones, irrespective to their efficiency' (p. 155).

Molyneux and Forbes (1995) study the European banking system over the period 1986–9. The study includes a pool of accounting data for banks from 18 European countries. Their analysis of the standard SCP profits equation supports the traditional SCP paradigm and rejects the efficiency hypothesis. The concentration ratio is positive and statistically significant, yet the market share variables yield a negative sign and are not statistically significant. The capital to assets ratio is positive and significant, which can be considered as surprising given that low levels of capital ratios are normally related to greater risk taking. The size variables turn out to be insignificant and negative and therefore do not have any effect on profits. Demirguc-Kunt, Laeven and Levine (2003) study a broader set of 70 countries for the period 1980–97. They find a positive relationship between banking concentration and interest rate margins, thus suggesting that these are collusion effects from a high degree of concentration reflected in large spreads on interest rate margins. Nevertheless, this finding does not hold when they include regulatory restrictions on banks and macroeconomic stability variables in their model. One of their main conclusions, however, is that the countries which are less likely to suffer a financial crisis are those with more concentrated banking systems, fewer regulatory restrictions on bank competition and activities, and national institutions that encourage competition. This argument relies on a traditional view which considers the possibility of government control as one of the advantages of a concentrated banking system.

Other authors who study the SCP include Rhoades (1977) and Gilbert (1984). Rhoades (1977) finds from a survey of 39 studies that 30 of them support evidence of the SCP hypothesis. Bourke (1989) finds a positive relationship between concentration and profitability for 17 French banks for the period 1972–81. Lloyd-Williams, Molyneux and Thornton (1994) also find a positive relationship for the Spanish banks during 1986–8.

Berger (1995) studies the SCP model in the US banking industry for the 1980s. He analyses four possible hypotheses for the determination of banking profits: namely, the SCP hypothesis, the relative market power hypothesis (RMP), the scale-efficiency hypothesis, and the X-efficiency hypothesis. The first two can be considered as theories of market concentration and the others as efficiency-based theories. He concludes that profitability is determined by greater administrative efficiency although he utilizes the market structure theory in which he acknowledges that large banks have the power and influence to determine the prices of well-differentiated products. Nonetheless, the findings of this study do not support the SCP hypothesis thoroughly, thus implying a greater importance for efficiency. Berger and Hannan (1998) study 5,000 banks in the US, analysing their efficiency in different local markets by comparing them to the same national frontiers, in order to identify the influence of local market power on even the most efficient firm in the local market. The methodologies used to compute the efficiency variables include the distribution-free approach and the stochastic frontier approach. The results find evidence suggesting that firms experience poorer cost efficiency in more concentrated markets.

Several other studies that followed have rejected the SCP hypothesis and considered alternative explanations for the increase in profitability. For example, Evanoff and Fortier (1988) and Smirlock (1985) conclude that the performance of firms depends on market share regardless of concentration in the market. Smirlock strongly rejects the traditional SCP hypothesis and suggests that other variables possibly included when measuring market share are the determinants of higher profitability in banking markets. He suggests that superior efficiency in leading firms is the principal factor when explaining raising profits in a more concentrated market.

More recently Rodriguez Montemayor (2002) analysed the SCP and the ES hypotheses with regard to the Mexican banking industry. His sample includes 16 banks over 1995–2000, which accounted for 85.2 per cent of the market share. The model used is the traditional SCP model, and the final conclusions were that, for the period under consideration, market concentration had a positive effect on banking profits. On the other hand, the coefficient of market share was negative, which may be explained by the current mergers and fusions in the industry that have resulted in a higher degree of capitalization. He finds that the liquidity risk measure, loans/deposits, is not significant which implies that in the period of the study the risks that the banks undertook did not have a direct effect on the profitability levels. The same conclusion is obtained by the positive effect of the capitalization ratio (equity/total assets). Notably, the results are similar to those of Molyneux and Forbes (1995). The implication is that capitalization has a direct impact on profitability. He also finds a positive relationship between total assets and the level of profits.

There is substantial evidence regarding the market concentration in the banking sector in Latin America. Berstein and Fuentes (2003) state that in the case of Chile, as well as in other countries in Latin America, market concentration in the banking industry has increased considerably over recent years. They indicate that more concentrated markets imply lower deposit rates than less concentrated markets. In the case of Chile, for example, they find strong evidence of the sluggishness of adjustment in the case of lending interest rates, but significant price rigidity for deposit interest rates when the market experiences more concentration. On the other hand, Yeyati and Micco (2003) conclude, in their study of seven Latin American countries (Argentina, Brazil, Chile, Colombia, Costa Rica and Peru), that their banking sector is concentrated but appears not to have decreased competition in the sector. They argue that foreign penetration in the Latin American banking systems has apparently led to a less competitive banking sector.

The Efficiency–Structure model

A challenge to the SCP hypothesis was first posed by Gilbert (1984), who introduced the 'efficiency hypothesis'. He argued that market concentration is not a random event, but rather the result of firms having superior efficiency. This hypothesis states that since efficient firms can generate higher profits they should grow in size and market share, and therefore one should expect this process to create a high degree of concentration in the industry. Proponents of the efficiency hypothesis, however, usually assume that the dispersion of efficiencies within markets that creates high levels of concentration also results in greater than average efficiency in these markets, yielding a positive profit–concentration relationship.

Alternative approaches towards explaining bank profitability include the two efficiency theories of positive profit–structure relationship. The two ES hypotheses are mentioned by Berger (1995) as X-efficiency (ESX), in which firms with superior management or production technologies have lower costs and thus experience higher profits, and scale-efficiency (ESS), where firms have equally good management and technologies, but some produce at more efficient scales than others, therefore having lower unit costs and higher unit profits. The predictions of those theories contrast with the SCP model. To the extent that the ES hypotheses are correct, then mergers and acquisitions have increased the efficiency of banks and are the main driving forces of greater profits. If they are not correct, the market concentration is generating collusion effects, driving positive profits to the banks. A relevant study from Peristiani (1997) analyses the effects of mergers in US banking in X-efficiency and scale efficiency. The period considered is 1980–90, and the study reveals that mergers did not improve the X-efficiency factor. Acquiring banks, however, produces moderate additional gains in terms of scale efficiency.

Although previous literature has analysed the effect of efficiency in their corresponding models, a serious problem arises when interpreting a variable that denotes efficiency. Some studies, such as Smirlock, Gilligan and Marshall (1984), assume that a positive finding in the variable of market share (MS) supported ESX, arguing that there is a positive relationship within these two variables. Other authors, such as Gale and Branch (1982), do not include any control variables for scale effects, assuming again that the market share may be correlated with any efficiency variables. Berger's (1985) work is critical towards these approaches and suggests a methodology that computes the efficiency variables. Berger and Mester (1997) measure the efficiency of financial institutions for a study of US banks between 1990 and 1995. They argue that many studies have found large inefficiencies, sometimes on the order of 20 per cent or more of the total banking industry costs, and about half of the industry's potential. They state that there is no general consensus on efficiency measurement. Their main result emphasizes the importance of the different efficiency measurements used and their independent results. In particular, they examine three concepts to evaluate efficiency: cost, standard profit, and alternative profit efficiencies. An example of their findings regarding the importance of the difference in efficiency measurement is that the measures of profit efficiency are not positively correlated with cost efficiency.

Each one of the various approaches for estimating efficiency has its own advantages and drawbacks. Berger and Humphrey (1997) classify papers according to the technical approach employed. They identify these as parametric – Stochastic Frontier Approach (SFA), Distribution Free Approach (DFA) and Thick Frontier Approach (TFA) – or non-parametric – Data Envelopment Analysis (DEA), Free Disposal Hull, Index Numbers (IN), and Mixed Optimal Strategy (MOS). Serrano, Mar and Chaparro (2002) find that DEA is by far the most popular technical approach, which was applied in 62 of the papers they surveyed. DEA is appropriate for sets of homogeneous units with similar inputs and similar outputs since it performs multiple comparisons using a linear programming-based approach. One of its advantages is that the inputs and outputs need not be measured in the same units.

Bonin, Hasan and Wachtel (2004) analyse the implications of bank ownership when talking about foreign banks, and its relationship with efficiency. They study a group of Eastern European countries using stochastic frontier estimation and compute both cost and profit efficiency. Their main results imply that privatization of banks is not sufficient to increase bank efficiency. They also suggest that foreign-owned banks are more cost-efficient than other banks and that they provide better services as well.

One way to measure efficiency is through the DEA model, which is considered as highly accurate. Yeh (1996) discusses the uses and benefits of the DEA methodology in the measurement of efficiency for a group of banks in Taiwan. He compares the common financial ratios and DEA as different approaches to measure efficiency. He argues that the utilization of the DEA technique is useful to differentiate efficient banks from inefficient ones. The study concludes that using DEA estimation improves substantially the ability to evaluate firm efficiency.

Conclusion

Since the late 1980s, many Latin American countries have liberalized their financial systems in an attempt to strengthen them. The liberalization of these markets has included the lowering of reserve requirements on bank deposits, removing interest rate controls on bank assets and liabilities, and reducing asset allocation programmes. All these reforms are intended to encourage reliance on market forces, rather than on direct bank controls, in order to allocate credit more efficiently. A main concern about the efforts to liberalize the financial system, however, has been related to the highly volatile capital flows and their (sometimes erratic) behaviour in these economies. Financial liberalization in Latin American countries had strong implications for their banking system, which sometimes intensified the effects of capital flows volatility.

Many countries in Latin America experienced financial crises soon after financial liberalization and some commentators argued against financial liberalization, suggesting that the large amounts of unrestricted inflows and outflows of capital were contributing to financial instability. It is worth noting that, in Latin America, the majority of financial inflow was in the form of short-term debt. Such concerns have led some sceptics of liberalization to argue for measures such as high reserve requirements in order to control the growth of bank credit in Latin America.

Financial liberalization aims to enhance competition in the formerly regulated and inefficient financial sector, and in many cases foreign capital and know-how were injected into the banking system. A naturally expected effect of financial liberalization measures was to create more credit, allocate it efficiently, and produce lower interest rates for consumers. A typical element in such financial liberalization programmes was the reduction of reserve requirements and the gradual elimination of interest rate controls on deposits and loans. Towards the end of the

1980s, many countries experienced much lower reserve requirements on domestic currency deposits. Another trend associated with financial liberalization was an increase in the number of banks. In addition to generating more competition, a large number of financial institutions could help to diversify the market structure of the banking sector. In many cases, however, foreign investment was directly transmitted in the purchasing of domestic banks maintaining the same market structure. Moreover, the idea of generating more competition was over-shadowed by foreign investment buying current market share and not generating more competition.

The banking sectors of many Latin America countries are currently experiencing a high degree of concentration. In addition, many banks in major economies in the region are now foreign-owned. It is has not been fully assessed yet whether these developments have had a negative or positive impact on market agents (consumers) and the macroeconomic environment, and clearly further analytical work is required to establish whether financial liberalization in the above context has been welfare-improving and has generated gains for consumers. Has, for example, liberalization resulted in more credit and more favourable interest rates for consumers? Should stronger regulatory efforts be pursued order to allow more competition in the banking system?

Liberalization of the banking and financial system has been a common experience for many Latin American countries and it was expected to lead to further market capitalization and more competition within financial institutions, especially within commercial banks. Nonetheless, this process of liberalization was followed almost immediately by economic instability and sometimes financial crises. Cuadro, Gallego and Garcia-Herrero (2002) have argued that in some cases financial liberalization is normally followed by a banking crisis. A more detailed analysis of the implications of financial liberalization for concentration effects in the region's banking industry is required.

In this chapter we have discussed some recent developments in the Latin American banking sector. Our main focus was on the extent to which profitability in banking has been generated by greater market concentration or by better efficiency and the implications of financial market liberalization for this question. We used two theoretical frameworks to address this question: the Structure–Conduct–Performance paradigm and the Efficiency–Structure model. The market structure model suggests that the markets in most Latin American countries are highly concentrated and thus the SCP could be positively related to profitability. Nevertheless, it is necessary to establish whether these banks have obtained higher profits by reducing costs and increasing managerial efficiency, and whether these were achieved by mergers. Under this scenario, even if the market structure appears to be highly concentrated, the results would suggest that the profitability of the banks is driven by better efficiency. While several authors have addressed this issue focusing on US, European and East Asian banks, limited work exists on Latin America. Focusing on the analysis of these hypotheses in a cross-sectional study for Latin American countries would constitute an interesting topic for further research.

Notes

1　Figure obtained from Demirguc-Kunt, Laeven and Levine (2003)
2　Data obtained from IDB (Inter-American Development Bank).

References

Beck, T., Loayza, N. and Levine R. (2000) 'Financial Intermediation and Growth: Causality and Causes', *Journal of Monetary Economics*, 46, 891–911.
Belaisch, A., Kodres, L., Levy, J. and Ubide, A. (2001) 'Euro-area Banking at Crossroads', *IMF Working paper*, WP/01/28.
Berger, A. (1995) 'The Profit–Structure Relationship in Banking – Tests of Market Power and Efficient-Structure Hypotheses', *Journal of Money, Credit and Banking*, 27(2), 404–31.
Berger, A. and Hannan, T. (1998) 'The Efficiency Cost of Market Power in the Banking Industry: A test of the "Quiet Life" and related Hypotheses', *The Review of Economics and Statistics*, 80(3), 454–65.
Berger, A. and Humphrey, D. (1997) 'Efficiency of Financial Institutions: International Survey and Directions for Future Research', *European Journal of Operational Research*.
Berger, A. and Mester, L. (1997) 'Efficiency and productivity change in the U.S. commercial banking industry: a comparison of the 1980s and 1990s', *Federal Reserve Bank of Philadelphia*, Working Papers 97–5.
Berstein, S. and Fuentes, R. (2003) 'Concentration and Price Rigidity: Evidence for the Deposit Market in Chile', *Central Bank of Chile*, October 2003.
Bonin, J., Hasan, I. and Wachtel, P. (2004) 'Bank Performance, Efficiency and Ownership in Transition Economies', *Journal of Banking and Finance*, 29, 31–53.
Bourke, P. (1989) 'Concentration and Other Determinants of Bank Profitability in Europe, North America and Australia', *Journal of Banking and Finance*, 13, 65–79.
Calvo, G. and Mishkin, F. (2003) 'The Mirage of Exchange Rate Regimes for Emerging Market Countries', *NBER Working paper*, No. 9808 (Cambridge, MA: National Bureau of Economic Research).
Claessens, S., Demirguc-Kunt, A. and Huizinga, H. (2001) 'How Does Foreign Entry Affect the Domestic Banking System?', *Journal of Banking and Finance*, 25, 891–911.
Cuadro, L., Gallego, H. and Garcia-Herrero, A. (2002) 'Why do Countries Develop More Financially than Others?', mimeo.

Demirguc-Kunt, A., Laeven, L. and Levine, R. (2003) 'The Impact of Bank Regulations, Concentration, and Institutions on Bank Margins', *World Bank*, WPS3030.

Evanoff, D. and Fortier, D. (1988) 'Reevaluation of the Structure–Conduct–Performance Paradigm in Banking', *Journal of Financial Services Research*, 1, 277–94.

Gale, B. and Branch, B. (1982) 'Concentration versus Market Share: Which Determines Performance and Why Does it Matter?', *Antitrust Bulletin*, 27, 83–105.

Gilbert, A. (1984) 'Bank Market Structure and Competition', *Journal of Money, Credit, and Banking*, 23, 617–45.

Levy, E. and Micco, A. (2003) 'Concentration and Foreign Penetration in Latin American Banking Sectors: Impact on Competition and Risk', Working Paper No. 499 (Washington, DC: IDB).

Lloyd-Williams, D.M., Molyneux, P. and Thornton, J. (1994) 'Market Structure and Performance in Spanish Banking', *Journal of Banking and Finance*, 18, 433–43.

Molyneux, P. and Forbes, W. (1995) 'Market Structure and Performance in European Banking', *Applied Economics*, 27, 155–9.

Peristiani, S. (1997) 'Do Mergers Improve the X-Efficiency and Scale Efficiency of US Banks? Evidence from the 1980s', *Journal of Money, Credit and Banking*, 29 (3), 326–37.

Rhoades, S. (1977) 'Structure-Performance studies in Banking: A Summary and Evaluation' Staff economic papers, 92 (Washington, DC: US Federal Reserve Board).

Rodriguez Montemayor, E. (2002) 'Concentración industrial y rentabilidad de la banca en México. Evaluación posterior a la crisis de 1995', *El Trimestre Economico*, LXX(2).

Serrano, C., Mar, C. and Chaparro, F. (2002) 'Behind DEA Efficiency in Financial Institutions', *Discussion Papers in Accounting & Finance*, AF02-7.

Singh, A., Belaisch, A., Collins, C., De Masi, P., Krieger, R., Meredith, G. and Rennhack, R. (2005) 'Stabilisation and Reform in Latin America: A Macroeconomic Perspective on the Experience since the Early 1990s', *IMF Occasional Paper*, No. 238.

Smirlock, M. (1985) 'Evidence on the Non-Relationship Between Concentration and Profitability', *Journal of Money, Credit, and Banking*, 17(1), 69–83.

Smirlock, M., Gilligan, T. and Marshall, W. (1984) 'Tobin's q and the Structure Performance Relationship', *American Economic Review*, 74, 1050–60.

Yacaman, J. M. (2001) 'Competition and Consolidation in the Mexican Banking Industry after the 1995 Crisis', *BIS Papers*, 4, 102–12.

Yeh, Q. (1996) 'The Application of Data Envelopment Analysis in Conjunction with Financial Ratios for Bank Performance Evaluation', *The Journal of the Operational Research Society*, 47(8), 980–8.

Yeyati, E. and Micco, A. (2003) 'Concentration and Foreign Penetration in Latin American Banking Sectors: Impact on Competition and Risk', *Business School Working Papers*, 5, Universidad Torcuato Di Tella.

9
The Role of Financial Institutions in the Context of Economic Development

Santonu Basu

Introduction

The financial sector plays an important role in the context of economic development. However, the role that financial institutions played in developed countries was very different from the one they play in developing countries. In developed countries financial institutions largely emerged within the process of industrialization. The process of industrialization increased the demand for finance, and many entrepreneurs recognized that there was an opportunity to make a profit from the intermediation between savers and investors or between lenders and borrowers, and this led to the growth of varieties of financial institutions. Thus there was a mutual feedback between the two, arising from mutual benefit.[1] In developing countries the process of industrialization was not a natural process of transition from a backward state to an advanced industrial state; instead it relied on the respective governments' deliberate attempts to reach such a state. Thus there is very little scope, if any, to make profit from engaging in financial intermediation. Yet the financial institutions had a very important role to play in fostering the process of industrialization via the coordination between savers and investors.

Thus the question is whether, in the presence of low profit opportunity, it is possible for the financial sector to grow by itself by taking an active role, or should assistance be required? Furthermore, will the development of the financial sector alone be sufficient or will government intervention in the operation of this sector be required to facilitate economic growth?[2] This is the subject matter of this chapter, and it will be examined with reference to South Korea and India.

The remainder of the chapter is divided into three sections. In the first we investigate the state of the economy at the initial stage, looking in particular at the opportunity to make a profit from engaging in further financial intermediation. In the second section, we investigate whether it is possible for private banks, or what is commonly referred to as the market, to take the initiative to finance the process of development with some assistance from the government, or whether direct intervention will be required. Having established that intervention will be required, in the third section we investigate what went wrong with the intervention. This will be followed by the conclusion.

The state of the financial sector

At the time when India and South Korea were undergoing the process of development, their economies were suffering from high poverty, low education and high mortality rates, and so forth and so on. The majority of the population was deriving their living from agriculture. They had neither any surplus to invest in the industrial sector nor sufficient income to generate demand for industrial products. It was recognized that there existed no internal mechanism which indicated that this state was likely to change by itself in the near future. This meant some degree of intervention would be required to transform these economies from their backward state to an advanced industrial state, which would involve changing the structure of the economy from one state to another.

Given the problem described above, the South Korean government adopted an export-led growth policy, while the Indian government adopted an import-substitution policy, in order to develop their respective nations. The export-led growth policy allowed South Korea to avoid the problems that arise from the internal demand deficiency which follows from poverty, while the import-substitution policy did not permit India to overlook the problems that arise from internal demand deficiency. The problem for the South Korean government was to provide information about export opportunities to would-be participatory firms and induce these firms to participate in these ventures. The problem for the Indian government was that it had to address the uncertainty that arises from internal demand deficiency. This meant the Indian government had to simultaneously address the issue of poverty and the issue of industrialization. This added to the complexity of the problems, which were twofold. First, the government had to directly address how to reduce the level of poverty, so that the standard of living could be raised to a level which could adequately address the problem of demand deficiency. Second, it had to plan for industrialization in a manner that could take care of the problem of externalities.[3] This meant the nation's scarce resources would be divided into two parts, one of which would be spent directly on addressing the issue of poverty and the other on industrialization. Thus the Indian growth rate was expected to be lower compared than the South Korean growth rate, at least in the early stages of development.

Given the complexities of the problem, financing development has to be carried out by banks. This is mainly because banks are the main vehicles for mobilizing savings and allocating these savings in the form of credit. However, it was not recognized that the banking sector operates in the presence of uncertainty. This uncertainty principally arises from the fact that the advancement of loans and the repayment of loans does not take place simultaneously; repayment takes place some time in the future. This means the element of a time gap enters into the loan equation, which in turn introduces the possibility that the borrower may not be able to repay the loan. This possibility emerges either due to changes in the borrower's own financial circumstances or because the borrower may be an impostor. The lender cannot ascertain either of these in advance, and consequently asks for collateral or some form of security as an alternative means to recoup the loan, should the borrower default. This alternative means of recouping the loan, should the borrower's ability or willingness to pay change, is referred to as the credit standard (Basu, 2002, 2003).

The banks' principal objective is to make a profit. Their principal task is to raise deposits by offering interest, to re-lend these deposits to borrowers in the form of credit at a higher interest rate, and to make a profit from the difference between the loan rate and the deposit rate. Any borrower who can meet a bank's credit standard requirements and who promises to pay the interest rate will receive a loan. Should the borrowers fail to meet their obligations, banks will resort to the credit standard. Banks as profit-seeking organizations are neither concerned with whether these borrowers are likely to use their loanable funds for productive or unproductive purposes, nor with whether the project for which the borrower seeks a loan produces any social return or not.

The above argument suggests that there is a need to change the banks' mode of operation in order to make them conform to the requirements of the development process. This effectively means that bankers would now be required to concentrate more on assessing the merits of the borrowers' projects, not only in terms of their expected private rates of return but also in terms of their social rates of return, and not just on investigating borrowers' creditworthiness.

Banks that were operating in the early stage of independence in developing countries mostly engaged in advancing loans for trade-oriented activities and meeting working capital requirements. In most cases, the size of their operation was small, mainly advancing short-term loans comprised of smaller-sized loans, and their survival depended upon short-term returns. However, the process of development requires large long-term loans. These bankers have neither the capital nor the skill that is required to assess the merits of projects, which involve large long-term loans. These problems are further compounded by the fact that the greater proportion of the money market was in the hands of the informal credit market.

Thus the first task of the government was to bring the informal credit market under the control of the formal credit market, so that a greater proportion of savings could be brought into the orbit of the formal market. One method is to open a number of branch facilities, not only in the metropolitan area but also outside it. But the problem is that opening branch facilities, especially outside the metropolitan area, can be costly and a private bank whose main motivation is to make a profit and whose survival also depends upon profit is unlikely to participate in such a venture. In addition to this, banks may not have sufficient capital to open additional branch facilities. Another method is to raise the interest rate on deposits, partly to induce savers to move away from the informal sector and partly to transfer that portion of the savings that was kept in the form of unproductive assets into financial assets. But this process also requires banks to raise the interest rate on loans. The problems for banks here are twofold: first, where to find borrowers who are not only willing to pay such high interest rates, but who will also be able to meet the banks' higher credit standard which will rise as a result of high interest rates; and second, even if banks find such borrowers, these borrowers may not agree to undertake projects whose expected rates of return are not known to them but which comply with the objectives of development. Thus whichever method one decides to use there remains a serious difficulty in raising the mobilization of savings without banks having to sacrifice some profit, at least in the early stage of development. But in the absence of higher levels of savings, a country cannot finance its development programme.

Thus the paramount question that needs to be investigated, given the problem described above, is how the governments of both countries will induce banks to participate in their respective development projects.

Can markets be effective or should intervention be required?

The South Korean government recognized that the private banks, whose principal objective is to make profit, are unlikely to participate in the development programme, and in 1961 they nationalized their major banks, while the Indian government initially chose to follow the path of persuasion.

South Korea used the interest rate as a vehicle for the mobilization of savings. The interest rate on time deposits was raised from 15 to 30 per cent in 1965, and although this rate gradually declined it remained above 20 per cent up to 1971.[4] As a result of this high rate on deposits, the M2/GNP ratio rose from less than 9 per cent to a little over 33 per cent between 1964 and 1971.[5] This higher rate also helped to increase the capital inflow, especially from Japan. Needless to say, this higher rate of mobilization was made at the cost of banks, as the rates on time deposits remained higher than those on non-preferential loans between 1965 and 1968, implying that the banks were running at a loss, independent of the performance of the project for which the banks advanced the loans.[6]

The Indian government, in contrast to South Korea, mainly used the extension of branch facilities as a vehicle to mobilize savings. However, it recognized that, given the smaller size of operation of these banks, individually they would not have sufficient resources to open branch facilities outside the metropolitan area. Thus banks were encouraged by the Reserve Bank of India (RBI) to merge with other banks, and as a result the total number of banks fell from 605 to 85 between 1950 and 1969. The number of bank branches increased from 4,151 to 8,262, and GDS as a percentage of GDP rose from 10.2 to 15.7 per cent during the same period (Krishnaswamy, Krisnamurty and Sharma, 1987). But the banks which open branch facilities in the rural area are mostly government-sponsored banks such as Cooperatives, Land Mortgage Banks and the State Bank of India (SBI); private banks remain reluctant to participate in the government's venture.[7] In fact, in 1969 only 22.2 per cent of the banks' total branch facilities were located in rural areas.

The banks' performance, however, improved following the nationalization of banks in 1969, both in terms of the extension of branch facilities outside the metropolitan areas as well as in terms of the mobilization of savings. Between 1969 and 1985, branch numbers increased from 8,262 to 48,930. By 1985, around 57.5 per cent of the branches were operating in the rural area and a further 19.5 per cent in the semi-urban area. GDS as a percentage of GDP rose from 15.7 to 24 per cent between 1969 and 1985. By 1980, over 92 per cent of total deposits came under the control of public sector banks. By the middle of 1985, commercial bank deposits amounted to Rs. 764 billion, which was 67 per cent more than at the end of 1981 (Krishnaswamy, Krisnamurty and Sharma, 1987), and these deposits rose to Rs. 2012 billion by 1991, which is almost three times higher than the level in 1985 (RBI, 1991). But, as most of these deposits were small in size, the result was a rise in the administrative cost per unit of deposit, thereby increasing the operating costs of banks. Thus although both countries were successful in mobilizing savings, in the process banks' profitability was adversely affected.

In South Korea, as the government nationalized private banks, no problem has been observed in the allocation of loans. It is interesting to note that, despite having control over the allocation of loans, the government neither implemented any quota nor imposed any restrictions on the allocation of loans; instead it introduced an incentive mechanism to attract market participants to join in the government development programme. For example, export and infant industries received a preferential loan rate of 6 per cent and this rate remained below 10 per cent up to 1980. The rest of the economy received loans at a non-preferential rate. This rate rose from 16.9 per cent to 26 per cent between 1964 and 1965 and remained at roughly around 24.4 per cent between 1966 and 1970. This rate came down to 17 per cent by the end of 1971, and remained on average between 17 to 18 per cent up to 1980.[8] The main aim of the differential interest rate policy is to reduce the net return of those projects that are not accepted by the government. As there was hardly any difference in the deposit rate and interest rate on non-preferential loans, this suggests that profit from loan portfolios was not the concern of the government. It appears that the government used differential interest rates to induce market participants to join the government-directed development programme, and therefore this policy could be considered as an important vehicle to change the state of the economy from a backward to an advanced industrial state. As the number of firms started to join the government-directed development programme, so too did South Korea's growth rate start to increase at a rapid rate. In fact, South Korea has enjoyed an unprecedented growth rate since the mid-1960s, reaching 8 per cent in the 1980s and continuing to grow at the same rate until the early 1990s. But in the process the banking sector became fragile, leading to a financial crisis in 1997.

India, on the other hand, from the very beginning faced problems in allocating loans the way the government wanted. It was confronted with problems both in allocating loans for socially more productive areas of the economy, and in improving smaller and marginal borrowers' access to the loan market. Initially, it attempted to channel banks' credit into socially more productive areas of the economy via the RBI's regulations and incentives. To provide long-term credit it developed financial corporations and government sponsored banks, such as the Industrial Finance Corporation (IFC), Industrial Development Bank of India (IDBI), Cooperative Banks and

Land Mortgage Banks; and to provide assistance to small-scale enterprises, similar institutions were developed. The IFC and IDBI mainly provide credit for the industrial sector's development, so their clients in general were large borrowers, and no appreciable problem was observed in relation to these borrowers' ability either to raise large long-term loans or to meet large working capital requirements from the banks. But a problem did arise in the government's effort to divert credit to rural areas and small-scale enterprises. The RBI's regulations and incentives largely remained ineffective.[9] It was observed that much of the banks' credit was still being received by private traders, especially wholesale traders and large entrepreneurs. Wholesale traders used this credit for the purchase of food grains, edible oils, oil seeds, raw cotton, sugar, and so on, with the expectation that they would make a windfall gain from future changes in the prices of these items. In the case of industry, the banks' finance was principally spent on maintaining inventories, but they remained reluctant to offer credit for fixed investments.

The RBI subsequently introduced various selective credit controls, such as regulations against loans for the purchase of food grains, edible oils, oil seeds, raw cotton, sugar, and so on, in anticipation that this might force banks to divert their credit facilities from the wholesale traders. In 1965, it imposed an upper limit on the size of the loan that otherwise might have been obtained by any individual borrower as a working capital loan, known as the Credit Authorization Scheme (CAS). This scheme stated that any private individual wishing to borrow Rs. 10 million and over required official approval from the RBI.[10] In order to improve the access of small-scale enterprises, agriculture and export-oriented activities to the banks' credit, the RBI offered various incentives, including a scheme for guaranteeing bank credit to small-scale sectors, with specific incentives to promote particular types of advances. For example, to promote engineering exports, it provided loans with an interest rate of 4.5 per cent, with the agreement that the banks' lending rates on those loans should not exceed 6 per cent per annum, which was considerably less than the commercial rate. The RBI also provided extensive lending support to the Agricultural Refinance Corporation. But these measures largely remained ineffective; credit still went to those who had larger assets, and no improvement was observed in smaller and marginal borrowers' access to the loan market. While the share of credit favouring industry rose from 34 to 67.5 per cent, bank credit to the agricultural sector merely rose from 1.1 to 2 per cent of the total credit between 1951 and 1968 (Gupta, 1988).

In the mid-1960s the Indian government adopted the High Yielding Variety Programme (HYVP), with the expectation that this programme would simultaneously solve India's two most critical problems, food and poverty. Instead, this programme caused a rapid escalation of poverty in the rural area. This was largely because this programme was expensive and, consequently, credit that was previously available to agriculture was now concentrated in areas where the farmers adopted this programme, and these happened to be relatively well-off farmers who, with increasing access to credit, opted for mechanization in agriculture.[11] Combined with the impact of these factors was the declining share of credit to small farmers and the displacement of labourers from the land as a result of mechanization, which caused poverty to escalate in the rural area. The government recognized that, in order to reduce poverty, a substantial amount of credit had to be injected not only into the rural area, but also among the poor in general. The government realized that the private banks were unlikely to participate in such a venture.

The Indian experience sheds some light on why it is not possible for private banks to assist in development programmes. Private banks operate on the condition of profit; participating in the development programme meant banks not only had to make sacrifices but they also had to carry high credit risk. In the early days of independence, the financial sector was not developed; there was neither the NBFI nor a well-developed stock market; banks were the only player in such markets. Consequently, they used to enjoy monopoly power over all borrowers irrespective of their size of operation and, as a result, they were not used to taking any known credit risk that developed countries' counterparts quite often had to take, especially when operating in the large borrowers' market (Basu, 2002). As a result, bankers were neither trained on how to offer a credit-risk adjusted interest rate nor knew how to manage it. But to cooperate with the government meant they would have to undertake a substantial amount of credit risk for the reasons already explained. Furthermore, in most cases banks knew that many entrepreneurs would be reluctant to borrow if the credit risk-adjusted interest rates were implemented. This is mainly because entrepreneurs themselves do not know the expected return from these projects. In the case of agriculture, as the loans are supposed to be allocated for the purpose of reducing poverty, the issue of a credit risk-adjusted interest rate does not arise. This means profit from these loans will be low; therefore banks will have little incentive to participate in such projects.

Furthermore banks did not have much information about the past performances of these projects, whether we speak of agriculture or industry. This meant bankers themselves did not know the approximate level of financial return at regular intervals, so being involved in such projects meant that they had to carry a high liquidity risk, arising from the short-term nature of deposits (with a smaller deposit base) and a long-term commitment to investment. In this situation, if a bank had to take a higher credit risk then it could not avoid liquidity risk, arising from the possibility of an irregular financial flow, where the return from the entrepreneurs' equity might not have been sufficient to meet any shortfall that could have arisen in meeting the regular debt repayment. This problem results particularly from the fact that banks are required to relax their credit standard requirements. Therefore, from the banks' point of view, co-operating with the government means they cannot avoid liquidity risk, while their survival depends upon liquidity. Consequently, we observe that despite various attempts by the government to encourage banks to offer long-term loans, the banks' advancement policy essentially remained short-term. In 1969 India too nationalized its major commercial banks.

Following the nationalization of banks, in 1972 the government adopted a number of poverty alleviation and employment generation schemes known as the Garibi Hatao programme. It selected certain sectors of the economy, referred to as 'priority sectors' (which included agriculture and allied activities, small-scale industry, retail trade, transport operations, professionals and craftsmen/women), and decided that commercial banks must assist these sectors by facilitating cheap loans. Accordingly, the government declared that by March 1979, 'priority sectors' as a whole must receive 33 per cent of the total bank credit. A little less than 50 per cent of this was allocated to the agricultural sector, amounting to 16 per cent of the total credit. This limit was subsequently raised to 40 per cent of the total credit, with the instruction that 1 per cent of the advances must be allocated for the extreme poor at an interest rate of 4 per cent. The remainder of the sector would receive loans at an interest rate ranging from 10.5 to 14.5 per cent, compared to the commercial rate of 19.5 per cent. Furthermore, collateral requirements for these loans were reduced.

As a result of this programme, poverty started to fall for the first time in 1979. Throughout the 1980s the rates of growth in agricultural and industrial output were much higher than in any previous era.[12] India recognized that by default it had created a sizeable middle class emerging from the asymmetrical benefit flowing from the success of the HYVP and the 'priority sectors', and the size of this class continued to increase.[13] This resulted in an enlargement of the size of its market, reaching almost one-third of the population. But in the process the banking sector became fragile, carrying the cost of a number of non-performing loans, and India also recognized that it could not continue with its current method of financing such projects.

This raises an interesting question as to why, in both countries, the process of development adversely affected the banking sector which plays such an important role.

Why vulnerability emerged in the process of intervention

It is important to note that when these countries started their development programmes, the subject of finance as an academic discipline was in its infancy.[14] The understanding was that the financial market also operates within the framework of the perfectly competitive market. Essentially this means market forces determine the interest rate, and it is the interest rate which governs the allocation of loans. When it was observed that the interest rate was unable to govern the allocation of loans, it was assumed that there must remain some imperfection in the functioning of the loan market, arising either from the existence of monopolistic elements or from the market being under-developed. No investigation has been undertaken as to how the loan market operates. The concepts of uncertainty, credit standard and credit risk were largely unknown to the economists. Even today, not only do many conservative economists still continue to ignore the importance of these concepts, but more importantly the theory of financial liberalization does not fundamentally differ from the assumption of a perfectly competitive market. Yet the fundamental problem for both countries principally emerged from the fact that South Korea overlooked the importance of the credit standard, while India under-estimated the importance of the credit risk-adjusted interest rate, and furthermore refused to close down many non-profit making firms.

The evidence of the last section suggests that neither government was much concerned about the profitability of the banks; while South Korea was mainly concerned about growth, India was more concerned about the enlargement of the market. Consequently, neither paid adequate attention to the question of whether the process of financing development projects would expose banks' loan capital to a very high level of credit risk, yet both countries' problems principally emerged from ignorance of this factor. The issue of credit risk principally arises from the fact that in the early days of independence most of the entrepreneurs from developing countries had neither adequate capital nor sufficient assets to meet the banks' credit standard in order to obtain the size of loan required to undertake the projects that their respective governments wanted. In this situation, banks had to take a very high level of credit risk, which effectively meant that the banks became the principal investors. In short, the banks' share of loan capital in the total investment often exceeded the entrepreneurs' share of investment, and this introduced the possibility that, in the event of a project failure (or if the return from the project was not sufficient to maintain the debt obligation), the return from the entrepreneurs' equity might not be sufficient to meet this shortfall. This means that from the very outset of the implementation of development programmes, banks had to carry a relatively high degree of fragility compared to banks from other developed countries, and therefore the question is how, in the process of development, would one try to reduce this fragility over time?

In order to understand this issue it is necessary to examine the composition of firms' investment funds – that is, the combination of internal (i.e., entrepreneurial equity) and external funds (i.e., loanable funds) at the initial state – which will give us some indication of whether, if the project performs adversely, the return from the internal fund will be sufficient to meet the shortfall in the debt repayment rates. This will allow us to determine the extent of the fragility of the banking sector in terms of whether it is high or low. For example, in the case of South Korea, firms' internal funds initially constituted 47.7 per cent while external funds constituted 52.3 per cent in 1963–4 (Amsden and Euh, 1993), while in the case of India this figure was 60.1 per cent and 39.9 per cent respectively (A Singh, 1995). Although both of these figures are quite high, compared to, say, the average UK corporation's long-term debt of 26.6 per cent of the total investment (Cobham and Subramanium, 1998), it is reasonable to assume that if the project performed adversely, any shortfall in the repayment could be recouped from the return on the equity finance. Furthermore, if the project failed then the bank could sell all the company's assets (including the entrepreneur's share) to recoup the principal. Thus the question is, how did the problem emerge?

South Korea's problem emerged from its very success, and as the economy grew, so did its ability to service the contractual debt commitment, all things being equal. This steady flow of return on loans in turn not only increased firms' credit ratings, but also increased the confidence of the policy makers. Consequently, when the lenders' willingness to offer larger loans to these firms increased, policy makers overlooked the fact that the process could over-expose the banks' capital. With the increasing access to credit, investors (i.e., borrowers) also did not feel the need to rely on internal funds to any great extent for growth, and as a result their share of internal funds in relation to total funds shrank. This in turn caused the debt/equity ratio to rise with the growth of the firm, thereby causing the debt service ratio to rise, which in turn (in the absence of an appropriate credit standard) exposed banks' capital to very high levels of credit risk. For example, as the share of exports rose from 5 to 7 per cent in the mid-1960s to over 20 per cent of GNP by the 1970s (Cole and Park, 1983), the firms' share of internal funds in relation to total funds shrank from 47.7 per cent during 1963–5 to 25.4 per cent during 1966–71, while the share of external funds rose from 52.3 per cent to 74.6 per cent (Amsden and Euh, 1993). During the same period (i.e., between 1963 and 1971), the debt/equity ratio rose from 92 to 328 per cent, and the debt service ratio as a percentage of merchandise exports rose from 5.20 to 28.34 per cent (Amsden, 1989). The problem is that if export earnings fall and, as a result, the rate of return from the total investment falls below the repayment rate on the debt commitment, the rate of return from the internal funds may not be sufficient to meet the shortfall. Firms then have to borrow in order to meet their debt commitments. In the case of South Korea, as the large bulk of its debt was held in foreign currency, and this debt rose from US\$206 million to US\$2.922 billion, and the ratio of foreign debt/GNP rose from 7 per cent to 30 per cent between 1965 and 1971 (Amsden, 1989), this meant these debts had to be paid in foreign currency. If South Korea's central bank was unable to organize a rescue package for the troubled firms, it would have had to seek a rescue package from a de facto central bank should it wish to avoid any major financial crisis. South Korea confronted this financial problem in 1972.

As soon as the growth in export earnings slowed down, South Korean firms had a problem in maintaining their debt commitment. Although the government rescued the troubled firms (Cho, 1989), it did not pay attention to the source of the problem. By the early 1980s, the economy faced the same problem again as it slowed down, mainly as a result of the collapse of foreign markets in construction, shipping and shipbuilding. Its GNP turned negative for the first time since the Korean War. Firms started to face difficulties in maintaining the debt commitment from their own returns, and started to borrow in order to meet the shortfall in debt commitment. As a result, their share of internal funds shrank from an average of 21.1 per cent during 1975–79 to 16.4 per cent by 1980, while their share of external funds rose from 78.9 per cent to 83.6 per cent (Choong-Hwan, 1990). By 1982, a growing number of highly indebted firms found it difficult to service their debt. The South Korean government once again had to organize assistance in restructuring industrial firms that faced financial difficulties. Thus the problem in 1972 repeated itself (i.e., the problem of over-investment).

Following the crisis, the government decided to abstain from further credit-directed programmes and abolished the preferential lending rates. In addition, the NBFI were deregulated and corporations were allowed to issue bonds with a guarantee by commercial banks. The government privatized the commercial banks but, in the presence of large non-performing loans, could not withdraw from maintaining control over the banking sector, as the restructuring of the industrial sector required government supervision of credit allocation. The government maintained its control over the interest rate and the credit allocation of the banking sector, which was lifted in 1991, along with its control over the foreign capital inflow. Although the external share (as opposed to the internal share) of the total investment improved from its early 1980s position, it still remained very high. For example, between 1987 and 1991, the share of external capital funds constituted 73.6 per cent, while the internal share constituted merely 26.4 per cent, of the total investment (Amsden and Euh, 1993). Thus the banking sector remained over-exposed. By 1994, banks had to increase their allocated funds in order to make provision for non-performing loans, but it appears that inadequate attempts were made to reduce the debt/equity ratio, especially for *chaebol*. For example, even in 1996 the average debt to equity ratio for the top 30 *chaebol* was 898.49 per cent. Fourteen of these 30 *chaebol* were making negative profits in 1996, while for those who were making a positive profit, this remained marginal compared with the total assets, including loans that were invested (Lee, 1997). Thus it was no wonder that as soon as the economy slowed down it led to a banking crisis.[15]

Although India at the initial stage had taken a more conservative approach (compared to South Korea) towards financing its large economic units, it could not maintain that position because the size of the market remained very modest for some time. This was largely because of the fact that the government was unable to make any appreciable inroad in improving a sizeable portion of the population's livelihood. As a result, not only did effective demand remain quite low even in the mid-1970s, but more importantly future growth in the pattern of domestic demand remained undetected for some time. Consequently, many firms, especially the large ones, were often either unable to capture a sufficient share of the market to achieve economies of scale or were running at a loss. The government neither allowed these loss-making firms to close down nor encouraged them to search for an export market. The government did not encourage these firms to search for an export market because it was of the opinion that they might not be able to capture a sufficient share of the export market (Chakrabarty, 1987). This opinion might have been influenced by the fact that the world was then in the middle of the Cold War, and India was not particularly an ally of the Western world, and its economic policy was not following the route of the Western world, and therefore it could not expect to receive the same treatment as that received by

South Korea. Therefore, policy makers could not see any benefit in opening up the market at that juncture. Instead, the government used its 1948 Industrial Labour Dispute Act to protect these firms. This Act states that any large economic units are not allowed to close down or to retrench workers on economic grounds without central government permission. The moral justification for this Act is to protect workers' rights. In reality, this Act has allowed loss-making firms to continue to survive with government subsidies, which effectively meant that the banks were refinancing these firms. In short, in the absence of provisions for non-performing loans, banks were carrying the cost of these losses.

The above problem was further aggravated by the way in which the government used the banks to finance the anti-poverty programme known as the Garibi Hatao programme. The government allocated 40 per cent of total credit to this programme. In order to ensure that the poor borrowers' access to the loan market was not restricted by the banks' credit standard requirements, collateral requirements were reduced. This means the government decided that the banks would have to take credit risk on smaller loans. But in order to offer cheaper loans to these borrowers, it appears that the government did not permit banks to make any adjustment in the calculation of the interest rate for the credit risk. This means no provision was made for the non-performing loans, which constituted 40 per cent of the total loans. This further added to the problems of the banks. The problem was that if a small fraction of the loans performed adversely, it would have a direct impact upon the banks, and indeed this is what happened. By 1991, 4.7 million loans were advanced to this sector, of which 233,441 were declared sick, meaning the net loss from these loans exceeded the net worth of these firms (RBI, 1991). In terms of percentages, this only constituted 4.8 per cent of the total loans that were advanced to the priority sector, and altogether the total bad to doubtful debts amounted to Rs. 125.86 billion, constituting only 10.25 per cent of the total loans that were advanced (RBI, 1991). In terms of percentages, this figure was not high enough to cause any major problem for the banks, yet it still caused a major problem. Thus it appears that the banks made no provision for the non-performing loans, meaning banks had to carry the cost of these non-performing loans. This problem was further aggravated by the presence of weak bankruptcy laws which prevented banks from recouping the principal by selling the collateral. The above experience highlights the fact that in the absence of a credit risk-adjusted interest rate, if a small fraction of the loan performs adversely, it can put a severe strain on the banks. Consequently, the government realized that it could not continue with such a method of finance; the government, too, had to undertake capital market reform.

Conclusion

It is argued in this chapter that banks play a very important role in financing the process of development. But this role cannot be initiated by private sector banks; government intervention will be required in the operation of this market. In fact, the Indian experience highlights a very important lesson, which is that in the early stage of development the risk in financing development is so high that it is not possible for the private sector to bear such a risk. India, which is known for its over-regulation, did not begin as an over-regulated economy; on the contrary, as shown in the second section, it started with a market-friendly approach. Its approach was to encourage market participants (i.e., banks) through persuasion and incentive mechanisms to participate in the government development programme. But the market did not cooperate with the government in those programmes which reduced their expected profitability and increased their risk of survival. It was the refusal of the market to cooperate with the government that brought one regulation after another over the financial system without investigating the consequences of these regulations on it, and made India one of the most over- or ill-regulated economies. But the government did not realize that the refusal to cooperate principally arose from the fact that such cooperation would only increase banks' vulnerability.

Following nationalization, both governments used their banks to finance their development agendas. While South Korea became a success story, India's performance remained very modest till the early to mid-1970s, and only started to improve following the establishment of firm control over the allocation of credit. But both countries overlooked the fact that having control over the allocation of loans does not give any control over the repayment of loans. Without the latter, banks cannot survive; hence the importance of the credit standard emerges in order to ensure that the fate of the banks' loanable funds should not be tied to the borrowers' projects. As neither government realized the importance of this issue, both continued their respective agendas by exposing banks' loan capital. In the case of South Korea the problem only emerged when the economy slowed down, so concentration was given to the growth rate, without realizing it further exposed banks' loan capital. India's problem principally came from the fact that it had not offered a credit risk-adjusted interest rate, and consequently there remained a very small margin between the deposit rate and the interest rate on loans, suggesting that if a small fraction of the loan functions adversely, banks would be in trouble, and this problem was further magnified by the presence of weak bankruptcy laws. Consequently, both countries had to undertake capital market reform. Needless to say, in both countries, banks' finance played a very important role in the context of development.

Notes

1 See Goldsmith (1969) for further details on this issue.
2 The school of liberalization argues that government intervention only distorts the operation of the financial market, and thereby will produce a lower growth rate than otherwise would be achieved. See McKinnon (1973), Fry (1997), Levine (1992), Bencivenga and Smith (1991), King and Levine (1993), Saint-Paul (1992) and Roubini and Sala-i-Martin (1992) for further discussion of this line of argument. Without going through their rhetoric and risking overlapping with other authors' contributions on this subject, it is necessary to point out that the above postulation principally emerged from the presumption that financial institutions are much better equipped than the government in relation to where to invest and where not to invest. No one will dispute that financial institutions as insiders are better equipped to estimate which investments will provide a higher and safer return; the only problem is that while the financial return is important for financing further economic growth rate and development, on its own it is a determinant of neither growth nor development.
3 See Rosenstein-Rodan (1943) and Scitovsky (1954) on the concept of externality.
4 See Amsden (1989) and Cho (1989).
5 See Cole and Park (1983). See also Cho (1989) and Kim (1991) on the above issue. Amsden (1989) pointed out that household savings as a percentage of GDP increased from 0.18 per cent in 1965 to 4.15 per cent in 1966, but declined in the following year. From there onwards no systematic relationship can be observed between interest rate and saving behaviour, suggesting that higher rates perhaps mainly helped to transfer savings that were previously held in an unproductive form.
6 See Cole and Park (1983) for more on this issue.
7 For example, in 1956 the SBI and its associates were directed to open 400 branch facilities in rural and semi-urban areas in the next five years (RBI, 1969).
8 See Cho (1989), Amsden (1989) and Amsden and Euh (1993).
9 It is important to note that India is not the only country which was confronted with this problem; in fact all countries across the globe faced similar problems, irrespective of whether they were developed or developing countries. For more on this issue see Basu (1986, 1989).
10 These schemes are similar to licensing scheme arrangements, which subsequently were claimed to have brought corruption to the Indian economic system. See Bhagwati and Desai (1970) for further details on these issues.
11 See Basu (1982) and Rudra (1969) for more on this issue.
12 For example, the growth rate in agriculture was 3.5 per cent in the 1980s compared to 1.8 per cent in the 1970s; similarly, the industrial growth rate in the 1980s was 7.15 per cent compared to 4 per cent in the 1970s. See Basu and Mallick (2004) for further details on this subject.
13 By 'lopsided' or 'asymmetrical benefit' we mean that although the central aim of this programme was to benefit the poor, in reality a greater proportion

of this credit (i.e., 95 per cent) was received by those whose assets' value ranged from Rs.100,000 to 1 million, and who constituted 34 per cent of the priority sectors' population, and were not comprised of the poor, but of the lower to the middle class population. Only 5 per cent of the credit was received by those whose assets' value was less than Rs.100,000 comprising 66 per cent of the priority sectors' population. See Basu (2002), RBI (1979, vol. 2, Tables 1–2), and RBI (1987a, 1987b) for more details on this issue.

14 It is important to note that in economics, the role of finance in general is a passive one. The state of the art of the literature was that, 'by and large, it seems to be the case that where enterprise leads finance follows' (Robinson, 1979, p. 20). The role of finance in the context of economic development is also a much neglected area in the literature on economic development (Arndt, 1987). Lucas (1988) considered the relationship between financial and economic development to be 'over stressed'. Chandavarkar (1992) provides an impressive list of authors who are pioneers in economic development, including three Nobel Laureates (e.g., Bauer, Colin Clark, Hirschman, Lewis, Myrdal, Prebisch, Rosenstein-Rodan, Rostow, Singer and Tinbergen), who did not even mention finance as a factor in economic development. Furthermore, Chandavarkar (1992) points out that the recent surveys of economic development by Stern (1989), who is currently serving as World Bank vice president, also ignore the role of the financial sector in the context of development.

15 In fact, the South Korean growth rate came down from 8 per cent to 4 per cent just prior to the crisis (Arestis and Glickman, 2002).

References

Amsden, A.H. (1989) *Asia's Next Giant: South Korea and Late Industrialisation* (New York: Oxford University Press).

Amsden, A.H. and Euh Yoon-Dae (1993) 'South Korea's Financial Reforms: Good-Bye Financial Repression (Maybe), Hello New Institutional Restraints', *World Development*, 21, 379–90.

Arestis, P. and Glickman, M. (2002) 'Financial Crisis in South East Asia: Dispelling Illusion the Minskyan Way', *Cambridge Journal of Economics*, 26, 237–60.

Arndt, H.W. (1987) *Economic Development: The History of an Idea* (Chicago and London: Chicago University Press).

Bagchi, A. (1992) 'Land Tax, Property Rights and Peasant Insecurity in Colonial India', *Journal of Peasant Studies*, 20, 1–49.

Bardhan, P. and Rudra, A. (1978) 'Interlinkage of Land, Labour and Credit Relations: An Analysis of Village Survey Data in East India', *Economic and Political Weekly*, 13, Annual No., February.

Basu, S. (1982) 'An Analysis of the High Yielding Variety Programme in India', MEc Dissertation (University of Sydney).

Basu, K. (1983) 'The Emergence of Isolation and Interlinkage in Rural Markets', *Oxford Economic Papers*, 35, 262–80.

Basu, K. (1984) *The Less Developed Economy: A Critique of Contemporary Theory* (Oxford: Basil Blackwell).

Basu, S. (1986) 'Problems of Small Business', *Economic Papers*, 5, 92–110.

Basu, S. (1989) 'Deregulation: Small Business Access to the Capital Market – Theoretical Issues with Special Reference to Australian Bank Finance', *Australian Economic Papers*, 28, 141–59.

Basu, S. (1997) 'Why Institutional Credit Agencies are Reluctant to Lend to the Rural Poor: A Theoretical Analysis of the Indian Rural Credit Market', *World Development*, 25, 267–80.

Basu, S. (2002) *Financial Liberalisation and Intervention: A New Analysis of Credit Rationing* (Cheltenham: Edward Elgar).

Basu, S. (2003) 'Why do Banks Fail?', *International Review of Applied Economics*, 17, 231–48.

Basu, S. and Mallick, S. (2004) 'Why Does Financial Liberalisation Lead to Credit Being Switched in Favour of Unproductive Assets? The Indian Experience', mimeo.

Bencivenga, V.R. and Smith, B.D. (1991) 'Financial Intermediation and Endogenous Growth', *Review of Economic Studies*, 58, 195–209.

Bhaduri, A. (1973) 'A Study in Agricultural Backwardness under Semi-feudalism', *Economic Journal*, 83, 120–37.

Bhaduri, A. (1977) 'On the Formation of Usurious Interest Rates in Backward Agriculture', *Cambridge Journal of Economics*, 1, 34–52.

Bhagwati, J.N. and Desai, P. (1970), *India: Planning for Industrialisation* (London: Oxford University Press).

Chakrabarty, S. (1987) *Development Planning: The Indian Experience* (Oxford: Oxford University Press).

Chandavarkar, A. (1965) 'The Premium for Risk as a Determinant of Interest Rates in Underdeveloped Rural Areas: A Comment', *Quarterly Journal of Economics*, 79, 322–25.

Chandavarkar, A. (1992) 'Of Finance and Development: Neglected and Unsettled Questions', *World Development*, 20, 133–42.

Chandra, B. (1977) *Rise and Growth of Economic Nationalism in India* (New Delhi: People's Publishing House).

Cho, Y. Je (1989) 'Finance and Development: The Korean Approach', *Oxford Review of Economic Policy*, vol. 5, 88–102.

Choong-Hwan, R. (1990) 'Korean Corporate Financing', *Monthly Review*, Korean Exchange Bank (April), 24, 3–13.

Cobham, D. and Subramanium, R. (1998) 'Corporate Finance in Developing Countries: New Evidence for India', *World Development*, 26, 1033–47.

Cole, D. and Park, Y.C. (1983) *Financial Development in Korea, 1945–1978* (Cambridge, MA: Harvard University Press).

Fry, M. (1997) 'In Favour of Financial Liberalisation', *Economic Journal*, 107, 754–70.

Goldsmith, R.W. (1969) *Financial Structure and Development* (New Haven, CT: Yale University Press).

Gupta, S.B. (1988) *Monetary Economics: Institutions, Theory and Policy* (New Delhi: S. Chand).

Karkal, G.L. (1967) *Unorganised Money Markets in India* (Bombay: Lalvani).

Kim, K.S. (1991) 'The Interest-rate Reform of 1965 and Domestic Savings', in Lee-Jay Cho and Kim Yoon Hyung (eds), *Economic Development in the Republic of Korea: A Policy Perspective*, An East-West Centre Book (Honolulu, HI: The University of Hawaii Press).

King, R.G. and Levine, R. (1993) 'Finance and Growth: Schumpeter Might be Right', *Quarterly Journal of Economics*, 108, 717–37.

Krishnaswamy, K.S., Krisnamurty K. and Sharma P.D. (1987) *Improving Domestic Resource Mobilisation through Financial Development: India* (Manila: Asian Development Bank).

Kuznet, S. (1955) 'Towards a Theory of Economic Growth', in R. Levachman (ed.), *National Policy for Economic Welfare at Home and Abroad* (New York: Doubleday) 12–85.

Lall, S. (1994) 'The East Asian Miracle: Does the Bell Toll for Industrial Strategy?', *World Development*, 22, 645–54.

Lee, S.J. (1997) 'Financial Crisis in Korea', mimeo (New Haven, CT: Yale University).

Levine, R. (1992) *Financial Structure and Economic Development*, Working Paper WPS. 849 (Washington, DC: World Bank).

Lucas, R.E. Jr (1988) 'On Mechanics of Economic Development', *Journal of Monetary Economics*, 22, 3–42.

McKinnon, R.I. (1973) *Money and Capital in Economic Development* (Washington, DC: Brookings Institution).

Nurkse, R. (1953) *Problems of Capital Formation in Under-developed Countries* (Oxford: Oxford University Press).

Reserve Bank of India (1969) *Reports of the All-India Rural Credit Review Committee* (Bombay: RBI).

Reserve Bank of India (1977) *Indebtedness of Rural Households and the Availability of Institutional Finance (All India Debt and Investment Survey, 1971–72)* (Bombay: RBI).

Reserve Bank of India (1979) *Report of the Working Group to Review the System of Cash Credit* (Bombay: RBI).

Reserve Bank of India (1987a) *All-India Debt and Investment Survey 1981–82 (Assets and Liabilities of Households as on 30th of June 1981)* (Bombay: RBI).

Reserve Bank of India (1987b) *All-India Debt and Investment Survey 1981–82 (Statistical Tables Relating to Capital Expenditure and Capital Formation of Households during the year ended 30th of June 1982)* (Bombay: RBI).

Reserve Bank of India (1991) *Banking Statistics*, www.rbi.org.in.

Robinson, J. (1979) 'The Generalisation of the General Theory', in *The Generalisation of the General Theory and Other Essays*, 2nd edn (London: Macmillan).

Rosenstein-Rodan, P.N. (1943) 'Problem of Industrialisation in Eastern and South-Eastern Europe', *Economic Journal*, 53, 202–11.

Roth, H.D. (1979) 'Money Lenders' Management of Loan Agreement: Report on a Case Study in Dhanbad', *Economic and Political Weekly*, 14 July.

Roubini, N. and Sala-i-Martin, X. (1992) 'Financial Repression and Economic Growth', *Journal of Development Economics*, 39, 5–30.

Rudra, A. (1969) 'Big Farmers of Punjab-Second installment of Results', *Economic and Political Weekly*, 4, (52).

Rudra, A. (1992) *Political Economy of Indian Agriculture* (Calcutta: K.P. Bagchi).

Saint-Paul, G. (1992) 'Technological Change, Financial Markets and Economic Development', *European Economic Review*, 36, 763–81.

Scitovsky, T. (1954) 'Two Concepts of External Economies', *Journal of Political Economy*, 62 143–51.

Singh, A. (1995) *Corporate Financial Patterns in Industrialising Economies: A Comparative International Study*, IFC Technical Paper No. 2 (Washington, DC: World Bank).

Singh, M.M. (1959) 'Monetary Policy and Economic Expansion', *Indian Economic Review*, 4, 45–56.

Stern, N. (1989) 'The Economics of Development: A Survey', *Economic Journal*, 99, 597–685.

Westphal, L. (1990) 'Industrial Policy in an Export-propelled Economy: Lessons from South Korea's Experience', *Journal of Economic Perspectives*, 4, 41–59.

Index

oil and gas industry   138, 141
Olmedo, A.   103
on-balance sheet strategies
    (operating strategies)   133
openness   4, 48, 59–65, 67–8,
    69–70
  and communication   60–1
  construction of a common
      understanding   61–2
  economics of   48, 62–3
  and effective democratic
      accountability   65
  and governance   64–5
  and legitimacy   64
  politics of   48, 64–5
  and the question of confidence
      62–3
  in the 3C strategy   60–2
  uncertainty, efficiency and   63
operating strategies   133
output-gap variability   5, 100–1,
    102–3, 105, 107–8, 108–9,
    110–22
outsourcing   11–12

Pagano, M.   103
Panama   158
Paraguay   157, 160
Parrish, P.   37–8
pass-through   42
Perfect, S.B.   130, 145, 146
Peristiani, S.   165
Peru   156, 157, 160
Petersen, M.A.   141
Pétursson, T.   32–3, 33–4, 35, 39
Phillips curves   36
Piger, J.   33, 34–5
politics of openness   64–5
Porter, N.   41
Portugal   110, 112, 114, 117,
    120, 122
Posen, A.   31–2, 58
Post Keynesians   73–4
poverty   172–3, 178–9
Powell, A.   39
Pramborg, B.   131, 146
Prescott, E.   48
price stability   5, 28–9, 52–3
  see also inflation targeting

priority sectors   179
production, elasticity of   14
profitability, bank   87–8, 159–61,
    161–7, 168–9
progressive taxation   24
propensity to consume   17

rating agencies, self-fulfilling
    notifications from   90
rational expectations school
    48–9
recession   103, 107
regulatory institutions   8
release of commitments, off-
    balance sheet   90–1
reputation   4, 101–2
Reserve Bank of India (RBI)   175,
    176–7
Reserve Bank of New Zealand
    30, 54
reserve requirements   167–8
responsibility   54–5
reversibility   78
Rhoades, S.   163
Rio Tinto   148–9
risk characteristics   141
risk management   133–5
  hedging   *see* hedging
Rodriguez Montemayor, E.   164
Rogers, D.A.   130, 131, 136, 144,
    145, 146
Rogoff, K.   50
rule-based policy   50

sacrifice ratio   35–6, 39, 56, 63
Samant, A.   144, 145
Samuelson, P.A.   12–13, 16
Savastano, M.A.   42
savings   14–15
  mobilization of   174, 175–6
  uncertainty and the ergodic
      axiom   15–19
scale-efficiency   165–6
Scharfstein, D.S.   139
Schmidt-Hebbel, K.   32, 35, 36,
    37, 38, 40
Schrand, C.   129, 140–1, 142,
    146
securities   79